CW00642136

A FEAST OF
VULTURES

A FEAST OF
VULTURES

THE HIDDEN BUSINESS OF
DEMOCRACY IN INDIA

Dear Aurelie,
for a better future'

JOSY JOSEPH

Aug 23, 2016

HarperCollins *Publishers* India

First published in India in 2016 by
HarperCollins *Publishers* India

P-ISBN: 978-93-5029-751-3
E-ISBN: 978-93-5029-752-0

2 4 6 8 10 9 7 5 3 1

HarperCollins *Publishers*
A-75, Sector 57, Noida, Uttar Pradesh 201301, India
1 London Bridge Street, London, SE1 9GF, United Kingdom
Hazelton Lanes, 55 Avenue Road, Suite 2900, Toronto, Ontario M5R 3L2
and 1995 Markham Road, Scarborough, Ontario M1B 5M8, Canada
25 Ryde Road, Pymble, Sydney, NSW 2073, Australia
195 Broadway, New York, NY 10007, USA

Typeset in 11/14.5 Garamond Premier Pro
By Saanvi Graphics Noida

Printed and bound at
Replika Press Pvt. Ltd.

To
My daughter Supriya and her generation
May you inherit a better India

Contents

Section Three
THE BIG LEAGUE

Introduction

The multi-lane highway, the metro that emerged from the bowels of the earth, posh residential colonies and glittering shopping malls, all of these receded in my rear-view mirror. The unauthorized village began where the road ended. I was on the northern fringes of Delhi.

A narrow pathway linked this large spread of single-room shanties to the outer world. It had rained recently, and little children in rags splashed in the puddles. Several men stood around aimlessly by small shops. I began what was to be a futile search.

Delhi was to play host to the Commonwealth Games (CWG) of 2010. According to company filings, several investors of a sports marketing company that was scooping up lucrative contracts in connection with the CWG were residents of this village of Karalla. I was looking for those lucky men.

The XIX CWG, with over 6,000 athletes from seventy-one countries competing in twenty-one disciplines and 272 events, was the biggest sporting meet India had ever hosted. The Central government, led by Prime Minister Dr Manmohan Singh, wanted to make it a grand coming-of-age show, with a total spend of almost Rs 50,000 crore by various estimates.

Multi-lane elevated roads were built over congested parts of Delhi, new metro lines snaked in fresh directions under and over the city, dedicated apartments for athletes rose up on the Yamuna river bed, shabby stadiums received impressive facelifts, and as the games inched closer, the ugly parts were covered with view blockers and thousands of beggars were carted away to government-run hostels outside the city. A sanitized India welcomed foreign visitors.

Jubilee Sports Technology Private Limited, many of whose promoters claimed to live in Karalla, played a critical role in getting the city ready for the games. I began to get curious about the company when I found out that it was floated by a man arrested in the past by government investigators for accepting a bribe on behalf of his late father, then a senior government official. After hours of searching, with active assistance from local residents, I still couldn't find the men behind Jubilee Sports, and returned to file a news story about the missing men.

This was, of course, far from exceptional. Over the years, almost every major financial transaction in India has been made by fictitious shareholders and proxy directors through shady deals, cash movements to tax havens and, often enough, outright criminal conspiracy. In fact, this modus operandi is not just limited to the financial world.

If you are able to summon the forensic skills necessary to detect the real powers behind fictitious shareholders and proxy voters, it will get you an intimate, revolting view of India's underbelly, one that will swallow the sanitized, democratic India of impressive achievements and global ambitions.

This book grew out of my anguish at the staggering size and scale of that underbelly, the dilapidated state of Indian institutions and the deep immorality at the heart of our democracy. Collectively, these factors drive the majority of India's citizens to a permanent state of helplessness, and many of them to suicide. The monotony of reading about those deaths and the insensitivity of India's elite set me out on the path to researching this book sometime in 2007.

The rules of the game in modern India are very simple, even if the structure it creates is a horribly tangled maze. In this country, it is okay to do practically anything: use fake promoters, accept bribes, commission murders, intimidate media, manipulate courts and grab power. The one big rule: don't get caught. This book is about the reality every citizen, and all visitors, experience in myriad ways. For years, I struggled to find a structure to write about that India, and even this narrative remains an incomplete rendition of a complex web.

Every individual in that web has a stake in the perpetuation of the system, and each one of them contributes to denying poor access to instruments of democracy. The courts in the world's largest democracy are crowded and expensive, the police corrupt and cruel, the powerful television and English-language media far too urban, and the political class busy plotting to grab power.

When you attempt to unmask the appalling double games of the people that run India and drive its economy, and put together evidence of their duplicity, they will deploy ingenious methods to silence you. It is not always crude intimidation.

I was meeting a former journalist in a coffee shop on the first floor of Delhi's Khan Market, one of the most expensive retail markets in the world. The winter sun poured in through the tall glass window, making it a very pleasant afternoon. That didn't help put my companion at his ease, though. Until recently an employee of a Hindi news channel, he had just taken up a well-paying new assignment as the spokesperson of a controversial Mumbai-based billionaire.

The mild February weather had no tempering influence on national politics, where things were boiling over. Yet another scandal had erupted, and the United Progressive Alliance (UPA) government led by Dr Manmohan Singh was lurching from controversy to controversy. It was 2011, and the government still had three years to go, but there was a heavy sense of hopelessness in the air. In a few months, the country would witness a huge eruption of anger against corruption through protests in various cities.

The billionaire's spokesperson had taken a two-hour flight from Mumbai, India's commercial capital, that morning to meet me. Only days earlier, his boss's lawyers had served me and my newspaper a criminal defamation notice after I reported that he was directly in contact with the criminal underworld. We responded to the legal notice, saying we were in possession of official documents to prove our claims, and would produce them in the appropriate legal forum.

Our calm reply appeared to have prompted the business magnate to change strategy. The PR manager started with a profuse apology on behalf of his boss. 'It was a mistake. The boss had in fact told his legal team not to send you the notice,' the young man said.

Both of us knew it wasn't a mistake but the standard operating procedure of India's rich and famous when an article critical of them appears. Over the years, I have received dozens of notices from some of India's biggest corporates and most powerful people. For publishing a secret audit report that accused Delhi's electricity distribution companies of massive financial irregularities, one of them served a notice demanding compensation worth almost a billion dollars. A former army chief would shoot off defamation notices every time I wrote something critical of him. Mumbai Congress leader Kripashankar Singh, whose astonishing metamorphosis from vegetable vendor to multimillionaire was part of an official probe, was equally trigger-happy when it came to defamation notices. When I reported on a member of parliament (MP) who abruptly left a parliamentary committee meeting on serious security matters, which he was chairing, he sent across a notice accusing me of breaching his parliamentary privilege.

The protection of shaky reputations is a flourishing industry. There are PR consultants whose brief is to alert the rich and famous about any possible adverse reports brewing against them in newsrooms. There are lawyers drafting defamation notices and then there are those who manage the situation if nothing else works. All of them make a killing out of the potential embarrassment of a famous client.

As we settled down after the apology, the spokesperson said, 'He wanted me to request you not to write anything more about his links because our efforts to raise FDI (foreign direct investment) have suffered a huge setback due to your article.' Their company – which had manipulated its way to procuring the licence and radio spectrum to operate second-generation mobile networks, and was facing a criminal investigation – was in the market to raise about Rs 3,000 crore from an investor in the Arab world.

The spokesperson then scanned the surrounding tables and, with sweat trickling down his forehead, whispered: 'The boss wanted me to tell you that he can take care of whatever your needs are – car, house, whatever.'

I let the silence build, then pointed to a sprawling colonial bungalow across the road. 'Do you mean one of those houses?'

Back on familiar ground, he responded: 'Don't underestimate my boss. He can take care of anything.'

I don't remember who paid for the coffee, but I called off the meeting soon enough.

Not everyone in New Delhi is uncomfortable about making such offers. On another occasion, a famous lawyer met me at Hotel Ashoka, the gym members of which include, among other notables, the Gandhi family. The lawyer had been spending a pretty penny to exercise next to New Delhi's influential lot. He was meeting me on behalf of one of his clients, a company I was investigating for allegedly misusing the police to harass its rivals. The company was backed by a political family that ruled one of the northern states, and had been accused of money laundering and other criminal activities. 'If you write the article, they will be ruined. If you drop it, only you and I will know,' he said, adding that there was a budget of Rs 3 crore available for me to drop the story. When I said I should be leaving, his parting shot was that he routinely managed the high priests of India's judiciary and politics. Why, he wondered, would I let such an opportunity pass? This time I know I didn't wait for the bill.

My mainstream media job did not always allow me the latitude to report on this aspect of the real India I met behind closed doors and in fancy hotels, and that is finally what set me off on an inquiry into the modern nation state of India. How robust is its democracy? How fair? Have its institutions been maturing over the years? Are the waves of transparency and well-fought elections improving the lot of its poor? Are the cleavages between its institutions deepening, or disappearing? Why do other institutions not challenge the duplicity of the political classes often enough? Is everyone tangled up in a grand conspiracy to subvert the republic? Is there a way to assess and report on this modern India, without self-censorship and varnishing, without betraying my childhood village by the backwaters, without omitting friends, without being seduced by the intimate glamour of the imposing capital city?

The narratives of urban India that truly decide the fate of this sovereign, socialist, secular, democratic republic remain unwritten, unreported. Constitutional lawyers manage and manipulate media coverage and public perception of almost every issue; bribes and intimidation are what you need to get your way; billion-dollar deals go through only if the right people are paid; political parties collect black money to fund their operations; coverage in the media is available for a fee and paid news is officially a business; civil servants assist the political class to subvert the system; 'facilitation' is the most successful business in its booming economy. Everything and everyone (with a few honourable exceptions) is on sale. You only need to find the right intermediary and pay the right bribe. The creaky government machinery moves only when the lubricant bribe is applied.

The cumulative result of this systemic rot is shocking. India's chaotic cities are choking on pollution. Child malnutrition is one of the highest in the world (over 42 per cent of children under five years are underweight). The country's youth population, the world's largest, has very slim access to quality education. Over 60 per cent of its people do not have bathrooms. Over 330 million Indians do not get safe drinking water. Thousands of its ordinary residents are harassed and humiliated daily by oppressive and misogynistic institutions. Violence is today a mundane reality.

For a vast majority of Indians, their country is not much of a republic and even less of a democracy. How else could a generation of entrepreneurs blatantly abuse power and still thrive? How could so many buy their way into the legislatures and parliament to manipulate public processes for their private gains? How can leaders whose immoral politics is legend continue to control the levers of power? How can 'bench hunting' be acknowledged lexicon in the Indian legal fraternity? And paid news such a thriving industry? How could a billionaire blithely build a home on a razed orphanage?

This is a crisis that privileged Indians are in denial about, because all of them – all of us – benefit from it. India has become a very rich country of too many poor people. Morality and public good have completely disappeared from the imaginations of key participants: that is the only common strand in all the news that I have reported over the years. A chief minister who allocated prohibited ridge land in Delhi to his friends; naval officers who sold secrets from the war room for a fee; politicians, generals and bureaucrats who conspired to build an apartment complex for themselves in the name of war widows – I've been working for over two decades, the list is long.

Every time a scandal breaks, there is outrage and public debates, but when the studio lights go off, the participants of the show sit down to sketch out the next conspiracy. For almost every reported scandal, there is a bigger, far worse story behind the scenes.

The unsaid and unreported, the stories that lay bare the reality of modern India, are a key reason why I set out to write this book. Intelligence agencies that manufactured a terrorist threat to the prime minister and framed innocents; a Union government that accepted forged bank guarantees at the behest of a billionaire to shower his crony with massive favours; a leader who launched high-decibel campaigns against black money on resources provided by a man accused of humongous money laundering: there are innumerable stories in every newsroom that never see the light of the day for various reasons, but those news graves chillingly capture the true face of this nation state of 1.25 billion people.

In the pages that follow, I attempt to record the realities of that unreported India drawing upon on two decades of journalistic work on how the nation works and how its institutions serve (or fail to serve) ordinary people. Everywhere I found evidence that proved my theory: everything is on sale, all you need are the resources to engage the right facilitators.

~

Ironically, the true age of the middleman dawned in the wake of India's economic reforms in the early 1990s, even if the system was perfected during the licence raj that preceded it. Before liberalization, India was a socialist state that practised import substitution and state monopoly. That old India had its own monsters, chief among which was the creation of a complex web of state controls in every walk of life. To buy a vehicle or to start a business, perhaps even to dream or breathe fresh air, you needed state permission. Bureaucrats and political leaders became immensely powerful – and extremely corrupt. Economic growth averaged just about 3.5 per cent annually, the state and a few families dominated most areas of economic and industrial activities, and the consumer had very limited choices. Middle-class Indians smuggled aerated drinks and television sets into the country.

With bankruptcy and international shame staring it in the face, India was forced to liberalize its economy in 1991. Overnight, a new vigour was palpable.

In 1991, I too was suddenly an adult, out of the safe confines of a military public school, thrown into the civilian realities of India. In many ways, India's journey as a liberal economy paralleled my own discovery of life, work, love, failures and values. Along with most of India, my generation migrated from typewriters to touch screens, from villages to metropolises, from a socialist economy to a thriving market economy – all in a matter of two decades. The one constant in our lives was the middleman, who got us what government owed us: birth certificates, driving licences, registration, appointment, name change, passports, etc.

As the wave of economic liberalization swept India, entrepreneurs began to dream big; bold investments and wild proposals were the order of the day. In a few years, India became the fastest growing major economy after China. Global investors began to celebrate India, and world leaders queued up to visit New Delhi even in the oppressive summer heat.

India was changing, and how!

The teacher who forced me to use the index finger of my right hand – I was born a leftie – on the loose silica sand of our village in the 1970s had retired. I traced the Malayalam equivalent of the vowel 'A', and the rest of the letters on the ground, seated in a temporary shed with a thatched roof that was my first school. That is what set me on my educational journey. In the kindergartens of my village, English is now the preferred language. The government elementary school where I studied up to class four is only a pale shadow of its former self. Along the tarred road in front of its small compound, private buses ferry children to private schools. Only the poorest still troop to the old school.

The government hospital that my three-year-old sister was rushed to early one Christmas morning, because she had suffered a severe seizure from high fever, is no longer the preferred health facility in our town. Private hospitals have mushroomed in recent years. The government hospital, however, continues to be in good shape – a rarity in India.

The sparkling white silica-sand mounds have but all disappeared. A broken road and a lonely telephone line snaked their ways through those mounds to reach our home by the backwaters. We ploughed through the loose sand as we walked to the local school. But many people in my village and those in neighbouring areas have been engaged in rampant and irresponsible mining of silica sand. The surreal white village I remember has been replaced by the dullness of concrete houses and shallow pits that often fill up with rain water.

The rapacious, mostly illegal, mining of natural resources is not the story of my village alone. If anything, it is one of the defining characteristics of India's liberalized economy. Across central India, where tribal communities coexisted peacefully with their environs in what are some of the most crucial biodiversity hot spots of the country, businessmen, with active support from the administration, are mining coal, iron ore and other minerals. An armed left-wing insurgency has taken root against this uninvited intrusion and the Indian state's failures. The tribal people are trapped, while the insurgents, agents of an insensitive state machinery and a new ruthless entrepreneurial class play out their games and ambitions.

These insurgencies are equally a response to the growing disparities in the country. Unrest and disaffection have been an integral part of India's evolution as an independent nation. Many of the world's oldest armed conflicts rage here, and hundreds of thousands of people – security men, insurgents, kidnappers, hooligans, informants, as well as people who were not directly involved in the conflict – have been killed. Some of the insurgencies in the country's north-east are almost as old as independent India, and Kashmir has been burning for over three decades. In central India, left-wing extremists have been fighting security forces for decades now.

Instead of dealing with the grievances that fuel these insurgencies, politicians, the mainstream media and security analysts have worked to create an ill-informed, often abusive and intolerant discourse around them. With no one to hold them accountable, the security establishment and its many arms rampantly abuse human rights. The establishment conveniently blames all the drawbacks of the Indian democracy on Pakistan, China, the US and other external forces. As this book was being completed in 2015, the government in New Delhi had just rediscovered an old ghost – NGOs – accusing them of organizing a grand international conspiracy to pull down the Indian economy and the government.

Equally worrying is the situation in the education sector. A seat in a four-year undergraduate degree in engineering or medicine – among our childhood dreams in the socialist era – is now yours for the asking. A student can walk into the many professional colleges that are proliferating across the country and secure admission, if s/he can afford the tuition fee. Politicians, banking cheats, professional scamsters, smugglers, pimps and all manner of business folk, from liquor barons to sweet sellers, have entered the lucrative business of education – a sector that is protected from slowdowns. However, even as higher education has expanded, its quality has become suspect.

The fixed-line phone that came home when I was a child still holds pride of place at my parents' home, a sepia-tinted memory made real. It rarely rings. We speak now on mobile phones operated by private companies. The state-controlled company that provided the telephone is struggling to survive in one of the most profitable and vibrant telecommunication markets in the world.

The telephone, the government primary school, the government hospital, they are all victims of the new-found ambitions of India's new masters, a loose collection of politicians, businessmen, regulators and others who managed to get a foot in. Systematic plunder has reduced many of India's public institutions and companies to mere shadows of their former selves. Expensive assets of government companies have been sold off cheap in the name of divestment.

Hotel industry veteran Ajit B. Kerkar was a member of the Air-India board, and sat on the sub-committee that decided to disinvest hotels owned by its subsidiary, Hotel Corporation of India. A day after the divestment decision was taken, Kerkar exited the board, only to return as a buyer. A company promoted by him bought it, and then re-sold it within a few years at a significant premium. That, in a nutshell, is how divestment has played out in India.

Is the India story one of all gloom? No, not really. In its urban centres and tony localities, in gated communities and high-rises, Indians are creating global success stories, resolved to doing business honestly in the face of grave temptation. In its villages, community efforts are writing new stories of empowerment. The Right to Information Act and many selfless activists are gradually, very gradually, forcing a certain transparency in government functioning. Organizations of oppressed groups, such as the Dalits, have been repeatedly mobilizing against brutal state machinery.

When I started work on this book, a new generation of oligarchs had risen in Indian politics. By the time I was midway through it, an anti-corruption movement rose up, and from it took birth a new political party, the Aam Aadmi Party led by Arvind Kejriwal, which quickly became an important component of Indian politics. The biggest beneficiary of the anti-corruption movement, however, was Narendra Modi, whose Hindutva credentials and corporate backing helped him ride the anti-establishment wave to become the prime minister in 2014. However, even that failed to settle India. The young country continues to be in ferment.

By the time this book was ready, Dalit organizations and communities had mobilized around the suicide of Hyderabad Central University (HCU) student Rohith Vemula – a volatile issue that even India's left-wing liberals have failed to engage with meaningfully. Beyond HCU, student voices are ringing through the firmament of Indian politics – voices that are refreshingly egalitarian and compassionate. The sedition charges against students in Jawaharlal Nehru University (JNU), then the violence in HCU again, resulted in an anger and mobilization that lead me to believe that India is headed towards a grand youth movement. Perhaps the next generation will win the battle against the many weaknesses of mainstream politics that I capture in the following pages.

A Feast for Vultures is intended to be a map for ordinary citizens to make sense of India and do business with it; and for its visitors to figure out the chaos that surrounds them here. Rather than a theoretical, academic framework, this is a reporter's inquiry into the state of the nation. Yet, it is not a gutter inspector's report. It is a record of the reality of India as I know it.

Prologue
WHERE EVEN THE DEAD ARE AFRAID

Shahda's cries rent the air, the boys' feet sloshed through the post-harvest field, all else was quiet. She lay on a wooden cot, heavily pregnant and miserable. A few teenagers had hoisted it up on their shoulders and were hurrying across empty fields. It was getting dark in the rain-drenched village, and kerosene lamps were flickering to life.

Only a while ago, when Mohammad Anwer Hussain returned from a round of football with his friends, he found women crowding in and around his house. He feared the worst, but it turned out that his younger sister Shahda, who had been married off at a very young age, had gone into labour. Some said she should stay back and deliver her baby with whatever facilities were available in the village, while others insisted that she be rushed to a modern hospital because it was plain that the pregnancy was complicated.

There wasn't time to debate. Anwer and his friends acted quickly. They carried her through the fields for 3 kilometres to the nearest road, where they boarded a bus to get her to a hospital. Desperate journeys like this often go badly for the residents of Hridaychak village in Bihar. Over the

1

years, so many had died and with such weary monotony that sickness and death were but brief distractions there.

'It was over twenty years ago, but my sister's screams ring in my ears even today,' Anwer told me as we sipped sugary coffee in his office near ITO (the Income Tax Office), one of New Delhi's busiest traffic junctions, flanked by media offices and several government establishments.

Fortunately for them, as they reached Kaler, the nearest road head, a bus arrived and they rode to Dawood Nagar, some 15 kilometres away, where there was a well-equipped government hospital. Shahda, whose name means witness in Arabic, was unusually lucky. Doctors were available late in the evening, and she delivered a healthy baby boy, now a young man in his twenties.

That and other incidents like it convinced Anwer his village must have two things: a road link to the national highway and a modern hospital. Sometime in 2006, when he had set himself up in Delhi, Anwer began to work towards getting sanction for a road to his village. It was a foolishly ambitious quest: pulling the levers of power in the capital, a thousand kilometres from his village. The metalled road on which a taxi took me to Hridaychak about a decade later is testimony to his perseverance.

Anwer began by seeking to meet with the MP from his area. Thus began a regular tour of government offices. In the process, he developed a uniquely Indian skill: the ability to deal with India's Kafkaesque government departments and the knack for identifying the right intermediaries everywhere.

He was a regular at the office of Raghuvansh Prasad Singh, then the Union minister for rural development, who too was from Bihar. As the weeks passed, Singh's staff got personally involved in Anwer's quest. IRCON (Indian Railways Construction Company), the government-controlled company that was tasked to build roads under the Prime Minister's Rural Road Scheme in Bihar, said it could not be built. A settlement with over a thousand people was permitted a road, they admitted, but a road to Hridaychak had already been sanctioned. Anwer was surprised.

It turned out that someone else was working towards a road in the region. The twist was that the road that had been sanctioned would link a different part of Hridaychak through several villages to the highway, taking about 18 kilometres to reach Kaler, which was only 3 kilometres on foot. 'The road was a waste, it wasn't serving any purpose,' Anwer said. By 2008, the sanctioned road had been built without any consultation with the local population. It did nothing for the people of Hridaychak. Like most public projects in India, if it did nothing at all for the village folk, it must have benefited someone else – contractors, engineers and possibly politicians.

Anwer didn't give up, and his persistence meant that Hridaychak's road link became the subject of senior-level meetings. 'I guess even if you don't have money and influence, sometimes persistence pays off in this country,' Anwer said. Those imposing buildings of New Delhi are out of the reach of ordinary folks. They are fortified with weapon-wielding sentries positioned behind sandbags and manned by poker-faced receptionists. Persistence can be a critical commodity in those spaces – and it helps if you are someone like Anwer. He already had some kind of public standing as the spokesperson of a Muslim organization, and that gave him some traction in the departments he was haunting.

At a meeting in 2008 to review the rural road programme for Bihar, minister Raghuvansh Prasad Singh had given a tongue-lashing to the IRCON engineer who said the new road to Hridaychak was not possible. If land is available, the road must be built, the minister declared.

A senior IRCON engineer who handled Bihar projects in the field got transferred to Delhi around this time. Anwer went to meet him. 'If the road is built, we will go to jail,' the engineer said, raising his hands to mimic handcuffing. He went on to explain the norms governing the rural road scheme – a frank admission that welfare could not override lifeless rules. A road to Hridaychak had already been built, at least on paper.

As Anwer became an unavoidable irritant in their lives, accompanied by an occasional prodding from the minister's office, IRCON engineers performed a neat Indian trick. Since they couldn't approve another road to Hridaychak, they signed off on a road to a different village through which it would eventually reach Hridaychak.

In 2009, when the final meeting was taking place to approve new rural roads for Bihar, it was decided that because of limited resources work would be taken up in only two districts – Aurangabad and Chhapra. Anwer's Arwal district didn't figure on the list. But one sympathetic IRCON engineer, who had been at the receiving end of Anwer's persistence, forced the members at the meeting to take up the road as an exception.

Even then, according to the original plan made by IRCON, Anwer's road was fifteenth on the list of new roads for Arwal district. Anwer's machinations and persistence ensured it took precedence over everything else, and by 2010, the road was completed. The other fourteen roads in Arwal were still in various stages of completion even at the end of 2014. 'I suppose that is how India works,' Anwer said philosophically.

In his village, Anwer became an icon, the man who got the road built. Optimistic about playing a formal leadership role in the village, Anwer filed his name as an independent candidate to fight for the post of village sarpanch in the 2011 panchayat elections. With a few thousand rupees donated by friends and relatives, he carried out a low-cost campaign. But villages have complex allegiances. Anwer lost miserably, securing just ninety-six of the 3,000 votes. Candidates spending more than he did, a splitting of the Muslim vote and, Anwer alleges, the wide distribution of alcohol as inducement to vote for a particular candidate – all these and more determine a candidate's victory even in the local elections now.

Anwer thought that becoming head of the village's elected body, which has budgetary support from the government, would be a way to tackle various issues. Sadly, local elected bodies in most villages are an extension of corrupt and inefficient governments at the state and the Centre. Elected members must align themselves with government officials who have a significant role in sanctioning contracts and expenses, and together they usurp much of the funds. In many villages, the sarpanches soon acquire SUVs and big houses and become 'professional' politicians. In a village near Hridaychak, the village chief is called 'Bolero Mukhiya' because, within months of assuming the post, he bought a Bolero SUV.

The electoral defeat has not demoralized Anwer. He is now working to get the state government to build a hospital, land for which has been identified and budget allocated a few years ago. Governments always have warm slogans for new programmes; this hospital has been allotted under a scheme called 'Aapki sarkar, aapke dwar' (Your government at your doorstep).

'Every project is a draining effort. I wish I had money to get things moving,' Anwer told me.

When the road was sanctioned in 2008, one of the officials told him: 'If you had spent Rs 10 lakh, the project would have been sanctioned a long time ago.' Bribes are the booster shot that get India's creaky government machinery moving. You just need to have the right amount and know the right middleman to pull the strings for you.

I was leaving my office one evening when I met Anwer for the first time. He was out for an after-dinner stroll along Bahadur Shah Zafar Marg. A few hundred metres from where we stood, the floodlights of the Feroz Shah Kotla Stadium, one of India's oldest cricket grounds, were glowing in the night sky. An Indian Premier League (IPL) cricket match was under way. The roads were clogged with spectators who trooped in and out, and the stadium stood like a spaceship in the evening sky.

Anwer pointed at the stadium and asked me: 'What is wrong if a poor man feels like bombing that stadium?' I had no response; it was one of those rhetorical questions activists pose. How, Anwer asked, could India waste electricity playing matches in the night when thousands of villages like Hridaychak do not yet have electricity? He just could not wrap his head around it. It was around this time that the village of Hridaychak began to occupy my mind.

Hitting his forties now, Anwer has a patchy beard a la Che Guevara. But ask him about his role model, and he promptly names his uncle

Motali Khan, who operated under the nom de plume Comrade Arjun Singh. Khan was among the many communists who took up arms in Arwal district, where poverty, government corruption and modern ideas conspired to create a fertile ground for armed rebellion. Arwal district has had a long-running history of violent communist movements and the government still considers it a district affected by left-wing-extremism.

Over the years, as I began to understand the workings of the village, it also dawned on me that Anwer was its bookkeeper. He and a few other agitated villagers were documenting their misery through petitions and meetings with politicians and civil servants. They were not unique in any way.

The majority of those living in India's 6,38,000 villages find themselves besieged. In most of these villages, agitated citizens are preparing complaints, petitions and court cases to address their corrupt and inefficient governments, and sometimes mounting violent responses in frustration and anger.

~~

Although the name Hridaychak could have been drawn from hriday, or heart, many villagers say it probably came from a man named Hardev, who owned a large plot of land in the village. Over the years, it got modified to Hridaychak. Whatever its true origin, I saw enough evidence of the warm hearts of its residents, and none at all to show that the village agitates any part of India's heart. In liberalized, market-economy India, the people's elected representatives forget Mahatma Gandhi's warning that if the villages perish, India will too.

When the hospital project did not materialize until 2014, Anwer went to meet a former journalist that he knew, who was at that time an advisor to the then Union health minister Dr Harsh Vardhan. The minister's office promptly dispatched a letter to the Bihar state government about it. But nothing has moved on the ground.

'I have petitioned and pleaded with everyone from top to bottom. I probably don't know the right person who can get it done,' Anwer tells me.

Ever since he landed in Delhi over a decade ago, this frail resident of Hridaychak has learnt to navigate the capital's machinery, but not enough to get a hospital for his village.

'Even if I get to the right person who can swing it all, I fear that someone will ask money for it,' he admits.

Anwer's frequent trips to the government offices in New Delhi and Patna are a tutorial on the modern Indian state. From the fears of a minority community to corruption, he is now an informal reference manual on India and its governance structures. He can tell you in which departments you could seek help to get a road to your village, which personal assistants have the ears of their bosses, who is likely to work if you offer a bribe, and how you can get a hospital to your village, at least on paper.

Anwer gesticulates often, a tight fist thrown in the air: 'If you fight persistently, you can get something you deserve with a lot of difficulty. If you have money, you can get it without a fight.'

The Indian democracy works only through middlemen who know how to get the moribund system moving. Ordinary Indians in their thousands wait patiently every day at the residences of local politicians, typists, professional middlemen and such intermediaries to get the system to deliver what is justifiably theirs.

Even the rich and powerful, who have mastered the art of exploiting the system, need middlemen. Every other day, corporate honchos and leaders of multinational firms are seeking out intermediaries, often gambling with their company's future. Everyone is desperate to get the system moving: for the poor, it may be to get a hospital in the village; for the rich, clearances for a government deal worth several billion dollars. When one gets to the right intermediary, though, everything changes. The process is not simple, of course: first you find the right man, then persuade him (through ample monetary and other incentives) to get the government to do your work.

Although the system of intermediaries has not been adequately studied, one can confidently assume that the business of being a middleman between the public and governments is the most flourishing industry in India. It is recession-proof and has no entry barriers; besides, it provides great social mobility to its participants. There is no licence to be obtained, no tax to report, no mandatory qualifications. A peon in a government office or the assistant to an officer, a low-level political operative or an Ivy League degree holder, all fit right in. Smooth-talking high-level operatives can swing billion-dollar deals in New Delhi if the political climate is right. Even successful businessmen may find the job of a professional intermediary sufficiently lucrative.

A significant part of India's GDP and much of its black economy is made up of the fees generated by these facilitators for getting people what is, mostly, rightfully theirs – or for getting businessmen deals that may not have gone to them otherwise. Indian political parties too are dependent on them for many crucial services, especially to divert money and, at the bottom rung, to organize crowds and even votes.

Every morning around 8.30, Mohammed Sarfaraz Khan, a tall, bearded man with a scarf around his shoulders, opens the wooden doors of a Unani medicine centre, dusts its two almirahs, a table and a chair, and sweeps the room and veranda. He then locks the centre and returns home, or stops by at the village square for a chat. This has been the middle-aged clinic attendant's routine for the past five years or so. 'There is no doctor, no compounder and no medicine. What else can I do?' he asks. Every few months, Khan travels to the nearby city of Gaya to collect his salary from the government.

Until about two decades ago, a Unani doctor from the state government used to live in Hridaychak, renting a room from Khan's family. Possibly, someone still draws a salary as the assigned doctor. One can't say for sure, there are so many uncertainties in this village.

Mohammed Saifullah Ansari, who has been practising medicine for the past fifteen years, occupies the room next to the Unani centre. He is not a fully qualified doctor, but his registered medical practitioner licence allows him to take care of primary health care. Every day, he gets around a dozen patients from the village, most of them suffering from diarrhoea, typhoid, malaria, filaria, etc., mostly waterborne diseases or the result of malnutrition. There are at least two more such physicians in the village, one of whom also doubles up as the postmaster.

Outside the row of rooms and houses, of which the Unani medicine centre and Ansari's clinic are two, runs an open drain, stagnant with dirty water, plastic and other wastes. It doesn't stink too much, but is home to a swarm of mosquitoes and other insects. Adjacent to the drain is a narrow road, recently built by the state government, which snakes its way through the congested village and connects with a road link to the national highway. This road, thanks to Anwer's efforts in New Delhi, is the village's lifeline to the outside world.

It connects Hridaychak to Kaler, the nearest town with a small hospital, a high school and the area's biggest market. It is the village's connection to NH 98, which links the state capital Patna with Aurangabad. Here, it meets the Grand Trunk Road that has run through a large part of South Asia for more than 2,000 years. The broken road from Patna to Aurangabad shows no signs of that glorious history, though.

If you cannot afford the private vehicles that run on the road, the alternative is a trek, one that most of Hridaychak's students going to the high school, and villagers to the market, must undertake even today. There is no government-run subsidized public transport yet.

The motorable link road also reinforces the traditional divisions within this society. It was laid on the existing pathways that divided the village along caste and religious lines. The village is a collection of ghettos. The Unani medicine centre is in the Muslim quarter, which lies in the middle, surrounded by Brahmin, Baniya and Bhumihar and a congested Yadav quarters. There are also a couple of Mahadalit quarters – one of them at the end of the village just before the Muslim graveyard, and the other near the middle school. This is where the poorest of the poor live, outside all caste and class hierarchies, their ghettos poorly sanitized and stinking, their homes soapboxes.

The village depends on hand pumps for its water supply and most folks bathe in the open. Relatively rich households have private hand pumps and the poor depend on a few common pumps. The rich here are only so in the context of the village. In the larger national context, not one family here would qualify as even middle-class.

There is no government-supplied piped water, nor any other source of clean drinking water. Most people pump out groundwater and drink directly; some may boil it, but even that is no guarantee that it won't carry pathogenic micro-organisms. Take the road further into the village, and there stands a 'meetha kuan' (sweet well). For years it provided drinking water to the entire village, but with no one willing to maintain the well, it fell into disuse. It is now used as a dumping ground.

'Diseases are our biggest problem,' Ansari said. 'The government doesn't care.'

We were talking about the hospital proposal. A couple of hundred metres from Ansari's clinic, close to the Brahmin quarter, we reached an open ground next to the farms and a recently opened anganwadi (kindergarten).

'This is the hospital site,' he pointed ahead, where a broken transformer rested against the barren land. The transformer was a relic of yet another futile government programme to provide electricity to the village. One day, engineers and workers of the state electricity board reached the village with power transmission lines drawn through the farms. They didn't listen to the appeal of the residents to draw them along the mud track to the village, away from the farms, insisting on working to their original plan. They damaged the season's rice, maize and vegetables, the only source of income for most families. Then the officials erected concrete poles, linked them up with transmission lines and disappeared. That was almost four years ago, yet there is no electricity to be had here.

Hridaychak is not alone in the darkness. Over 56 per cent of the rural Indian population does not have access to electricity. In absolute terms, anywhere between 300 and 400 million Indians, almost the population of the United States, live without electricity, their nights occasionally lit by kerosene lamps. Not that the rest of India has adequate power; most gated communities in its cities are sustained by private diesel generators.

By the end of 2015, electricity had reached some parts of Hridaychak after the residents made several rounds to various state government offices, finding the right intermediaries to light up their lives. Even then, it was not smooth sailing. The first contractor commissioned by the government ran away with most of the equipment when his payment was delayed. The second contractor forced the villagers to collect a few thousand rupees and buy some of the equipment, which he should have supplied. Even then, he completed only about 40 per cent of the electrification work. As this book hits the stands in July 2016, a majority of the village would still be in darkness. However, on the records of the Union government, which now has an app to track villages without electricity, Hridaychak is an electrified village, since any village with power supply to at least 10 per cent households is considered electrified in its statistics.

High above the low roofs of Hridaychak, the electricity line has added another reminder of the distant government that the villagers rarely get to see. When they do get a taste of it, the government is inefficient, corrupt and autocratic. Democracy is a regular visitor via elections; for everything else, the villagers must look for facilitators and middlemen. This is also true of most of India.

'Nobody knows when the hospital will come up. Until then, many more of us will die early,' Ansari says.

According to recent estimates, some 66 per cent of rural residents do not have access to critical medicines, while 31 per cent Indians have to travel more than 30 kilometres to avail themselves of any health care. Just 28 per cent of Indians in urban areas corner 66 per cent of India's available hospital beds. Mind you, India is still largely a rural country, with around 70 per cent of its population living in rural areas. Therefore, if you think about it, Hridaychak is actually very lucky; the nearest health facility is only 3 kilometres away.

On 2 October 2014, retired police constable Jameel Khan of Hridaychak complained of a stomach ache. None of the medicines available in the village or in Kaler worked, and his condition began to worsen rapidly. Finally, the villagers decided to rush him to a hospital in Patna. A 90-kilometre-long bumpy ride. By the time they reached a Patna hospital, four hours later, Khan was dead. It was Mahatma Gandhi's birth anniversary that day.

~

At about 1 p.m., when the winter sun was shining bright, some villagers accompanied me to the local school. The building was dilapidated, children were out playing, the teachers were crowded into a staff room that had an uneven floor and crumbling walls. Sunlight filtered in through the roof; if it rained, the room would get its fair share. Stored in one corner were sacks full of rice and some lentil meant for the students' midday meal. From class one to eight, some 470 children attended the school.

Mohammed Fakruddin, the school principal, had weak legs because of a polio infection in his childhood. Still, he cycled 10 kilometres each way to get to work. 'Schoolteachers are the government's tool for everything; from conducting census to elections, we have to be out there,' he lamented. He also had to look after several administrative duties, including midday meal cooking, repair works, distribution of government-allotted books and so on. He got Rs 24,000 a year for general administrative expenses. Chalks, dusters and other items were to be bought with it, and, if possible, it had to cover repair works too. 'When I find time I also teach,' he said.

Every political and administrative change in the state government sends tremors through the school. When Nitish Kumar, the chief minister of Bihar, resigned in May 2014, the resultant reshuffle and chaos meant that payments for the school reached three months late. As for contract teachers, who are not regular government employees but make up a significant part of the state's teaching community, their meagre salaries are usually paid in five- or six-monthly cycles.

One of the villagers recalled that the school building had been comprehensively repaired two decades ago. 'It was badly damaged in the rains and there was no place for our children to study. We all came together and repaired the building,' he said. When I visited, the floors were all gone, the walls were cracked, the yellow paint long peeled off, the roof leaky, and the whole structure covered in dust.

That year, the free textbooks meant for the students did not arrive in April 2014 when the academic year started. They came only by October–November. 'Half the academic session is almost lost. We managed by using old textbooks of senior students,' one of the school's eleven teachers told me. Children in this school are actually lucky, the teachers said, because many schools in the neighbouring villages have just one or two teachers. 'In Paharpur, there is a primary school (from classes one to five) operated by just one lady teacher,' one of them said.

A recent survey by the National Institute of Education Planning and Administration (NIEPA) found that over one lakh of India's elementary schools had only one classroom. In Bihar, over 1,200 schools had no building at all. Across India, 90 per cent of these no-room or single-room schools were in rural areas. Some 27 per cent of Bihar schools were single-teacher institutions, with an average of hundred students each.

Hridaychak's teacher:student ratio, of over forty, is far higher than what the government prescribes under the Right to Education Act: thirty students per teacher. The Right of Children to Free and Compulsory Education Act, 2009, has made it every Indian child's right to access full-time elementary education of satisfactory and equitable quality until the age of fourteen. Estimates vary, but India has a shortage of almost half a million teachers and over eight million primary school-age children still do not attend school. The legislation is impressive on paper, but like many other promises of this great republic, it too mocks the expectations of the people of this village.

Hridaychak's teachers complained that the Act had dramatically reduced the quality of education. 'Earlier, we would conduct regular exams, assess students rigorously, and if someone was bad, ensure that the child improves,' one of the more vocal teachers said. The Act stipulates that no child can be held back, expelled or required to pass a board examination until the completion of elementary education.

How then do they assess the students? 'We grade them,' he said.

A woman walked into the room, lit a stove and boiled some water. She added milk, tea and sugar, and boiled it over and over again. We were served tea, but the children's midday meal was nowhere in sight. 'The serving time varies a little, a few minutes this way or that,' the principal explained defensively.

To his right was a small window through which you could see the barren village farms. The window's iron railings were twisted. 'One night someone broke the wooden door of the window, bent those railings and entered this room. They stole one-and-a-half sacks of rice,' the principal said. How desperate the thief must have been to steal rice meant for children, I thought.

Everyone in the room was vocal about the many ways in which the government and its indifferent bureaucracy had been snatching what should rightfully have come to the children of Hridaychak. The government is so distant, unreachable – and that was at the centre of their collective grouse.

In New Delhi, all discussions are now about transforming India into a manufacturing hub, building smart cities and strengthening the country's IT power status. A new government is talking about regaining India's past glory and its rightful place in the global order. But here in Hridaychak, those words mean nothing.

When the children here graduate from middle school in class eight, the nearest high school is more than 3 kilometres away in Kaler, and that is if they trek their way through the farms and desolate land. During monsoons, they will have to roll up their pyjamas and trousers to wade through stagnant water to get there, drenched in rain. Even an umbrella is a luxury for most families here. In summer, after school, Hridaychak's students dip their handkerchiefs in water and place it on their heads to hold off the searing sun before they walk to a hamlet that is midway to home. By the time they reach there, the handkerchiefs are dry. They quench their thirst, dip the handkerchiefs in water again and rush home. Only boys could manage this trek, the parents of Hridaychak believed, and thus almost no girl from the village went to high school until recently.

After the road came up and some private vehicles started plying, parents who could afford to pay for the transport started sending their daughters to Kaler's high school. Otherwise, after middle school, girls stayed home and got married in a few years. The road has brought about a marginal improvement in the lives of the village's girl children.

I thought with a pang of pain and guilt about my daughter's life in Delhi. A school bus picks her up from outside our apartment complex, takes her to a school 12 kilometres away, where she has a library, science labs and many hobby clubs. That school has more than the necessary number of teachers and holds regular festivals and sends students on tours to locations within India, even abroad. She reads Harry Potter, watches *MasterChef Australia* and discusses politics with us. She inhabits a different planet. The only one to blame for the plight of the children of Hridaychak is the government; not lack of money, not lack of enthusiasm among the children, but a complete lack of willpower and compassion on the part of the government. This is the story of modern India. Except for a small number of privileged residents in its cities, the majority of Indians, those living in the country's forgotten villages, have not really enjoyed the economic boom of the rising global power.

The daily commute is only one among the many challenges that Hridaychak's children face as they attempt to find their way into the workforce and, if possible, claim their share of modern India's successes. 'We have a lot of brilliant students. But they can't reach the IITs,' one teacher says, referring to the several Indian Institutes of Technology, admission to which, through a competitive national exam, is among the most coveted achievements for those graduating from India's schools.

Ironically, Hridaychak is less than a three-hour ride from Nalanda, the site of one of the greatest higher education centres in human history. Founded sometime in the fifth century, the university survived until about

the thirteenth century, which is when the great universities of Europe were
only beginning to take shape.

In its heyday, Nalanda had over 10,000 students, over 2,000 teachers
and many pilgrims. They came from China, Japan, Korea, Indonesia,
Persia, Turkey and elsewhere. The university campus was an architectural
marvel, with eight separate compounds, ten temples, many meditation
halls and classrooms. There were lakes and parks in a compound spread
over 12 hectares. The library was a nine-storeyed building. It was not just
a centre for Buddhist religious learning, but one where modern subjects
such as medicine, history, law and architecture were taught.

Observers – among them, Nalanda Mentor Group member George
Yeo – say that the collapse of Nalanda is symbolic of the decline of
Asia and the rise of the West in the second millennium. It followed the
eventual shift of power to the West and the beginning of the modern
era of colonialism. In 2007, at the East Asian Summit held at Cebu in
the Philippines, member nations decided to re-establish the Nalanda
University. The *New York Times* said Nalanda 'represents much of what
Asia could use today – a great global university that reaches deep into the
region's underlying cultural heritage, restores many of the peaceful links
among peoples and cultures that once existed, and gives Asia the kind of
soft power of influence and attraction that it doesn't have now'.

The modern Nalanda University was established in 2010, and its
governing body comprised luminaries such as the economist Amartya
Sen, who was appointed chancellor, former Singapore foreign minister
George Yeo, Professor Wang Bangwei of Beijing University and
Professor Susumu Nakanishi of Kyoto City University of Arts. 'When
the most ancient European university, the University of Bologna, was
founded – this was in 1088 – the centre of higher education at Nalanda
was already more than 600 years old,' Sen pointed out. Even his global
standing as a Nobel Prize winner and public intellectual did not help
Sen preserve his chancellorship of the university when political change
swept New Delhi in the summer of 2014. A few months down the line,
the Narendra Modi government ensured that Sen, who had openly

expressed his discomfort about Modi's communal past and continues to do so, was out of the project.

All of these dramatic events went unnoticed and unremarked in Hridaychak. The distant past, when scholars from China or Japan may have wandered into Hridaychak from Nalanda, is not even in their folklore. The present-day dwellers of the village only have the energy to tend to their daily realities.

It was almost 2.30 p.m. and there was still no sign of the midday meal. Three women sat crouched outside the school kitchen. Food was ready, but I gathered that they did not want to serve it while I was there. What if I tasted the food? What if the food was not as nutritious as it should have been? What if I caught the school staff out for undercutting the food meant for kids?

The children chattered on. They did not seem to care too much about their own hunger or the missing amenities. I did not want to delay their lunch any further. As I left, I asked one of the children, 'What do you want to be?' The boy, in a torn sweater and inadequate winter clothes, stared at me and then looked at his friends. They all began to laugh.

Dismal as the conditions in Hridaychak were, nothing prepared me for the village's Mahadalit quarters. Matchbox-sized houses, single or double rooms in which humans and cattle crowded together. One corner was a kitchen, in another the baby was given a bath, school-goers occupied a third corner to study in, and in the middle of it all was the sleeping area. In winter, the residents of this quarter covered themselves with rice husk in the hope of some warmth.

Dr B.R. Ambedkar, the architect of the Indian Constitution and pioneer of modern Dalit politics, called untouchability 'another appellation of slavery'. Although abolished by the Constitution, the caste system – and discrimination on the basis of caste, which is illegal and punishable – thrives in India. Even as I sign off the edits on this book, a family of Dalits has been beaten up for accidentally touching the hand of a

Brahmin while handing over money for the groceries they had purchased. And reports continue to pour in about atrocities against Dalits from across India. The Mahadalits are at the very bottom of that structure, the lowest order among the Dalits.

Their quarter is at the fringe of Hridaychak, so that their homes and shadows do not 'pollute' the upper castes in the village. The recently built road runs between the houses, crosses a peepal tree and goes past the Muslim graveyard. Not one of these houses has a bathroom. So every morning, preferably before sunrise, men, women and children sit along the road to the graveyard and defecate. Most of them carry a bottle of water to clean themselves. Many also relieve themselves after sunset. However, the road is almost sacred for their Muslim neighbours because it is the path of the believers' last journey. The defilement of the road has often led to tension between Muslims and Mahadalits.

The Mahadalits have suggested a solution: build a road from their quarter out of the village in another direction. For them, the road is as much a lavatory as it is an access to the outside world. But this would require a few landowning Muslims and upper-caste Hindus to give up some of their land, and they refuse. So, for now, the sacred graveyard road continues to be lined with excreta.

Successive governments in India have covered up the true story of the missing toilets with averages and total numbers. The Modi government claims that it will end open defecation by 2019. Many governments before this one have set similarly ambitious targets. Yet, according to UNICEF, about 65 per cent of rural Indians relieve themselves in the open – sometimes on the road to a graveyard, risking communal tensions and violence. Almost 600 million Indians, mostly in rural areas, are without toilets, a problem that is fast becoming an India-only one. Bangladesh, for instance, recently declared that it has almost ended open defecation. Every morning and after sunset, India must look like a huge open latrine from above – bare bottoms by the railway tracks, behind bushes, along roads, next to graveyards, and anywhere there is some open space.

If one were to look at the last national census of 2011, the situation is even more worrying in the northern states, especially Bihar and Uttar Pradesh. In Uttar Pradesh, which has a population of over 200 million, a staggering 77 per cent of rural households did not have a latrine. In Bihar, 81.4 per cent of rural households did not have bathrooms in their premises. The national average for India's rural areas shows that over 67 per cent did not have access to toilets, while in urban India, the figure is 12.6 per cent. A significantly larger proportion of the population has mobile phones in Bihar and Uttar Pradesh.

The government in New Delhi has launched a Clean India Campaign, and many of its leaders, including the prime minister, have been seen symbolically cleaning a patch of pavement. Film stars, social activists and other famous personalities have all cleaned other little patches of pavements, either on social media or during specially arranged photo-ops. But in Hridaychak, cleanliness is a matter of life and death in the constant battle with deadly diseases.

A trek to defecate or urinate can be life-threatening too. Women who are attacked, molested or raped while out to relieve themselves would be in the thousands, but only a few first information reports (FIRs) are filed. In the regional-language media, almost every other day, there are reports of this. The English press in India's metropolises do not even consider this daily news trickle as worthy of a snippet.

In the Union budget for 2016–17, the Modi government has allocated Rs 11,300 crore for the Clean India Mission, which aims to make India free of open defecation by 2019. The government has increased by 150 per cent the budget for the mission for rural areas – from Rs 3,600 crore in 2015–16 to Rs 9,000 crore in 2016–17. In rural areas, the target is to build 1.25 crore toilets per year and a total of twelve crore toilets by 2019. As of early 2016, only 95.23 lakh were completed, at least on paper. It's worth wondering how many of them are in use – or, indeed, how many actually exist. India's social welfare programmes all look very impressive on paper, but on the ground it is a vastly different story.

Chamkalo Paswan is an articulate and angry old woman with a wrinkled face and sunken eyes. We were standing in front of her house in the Mahadalit quarter. 'Where is the sarkar (government)? Is there something like that?' Not once in her life has she received any assistance from the government. 'Our children do not get scholarships and uniforms, boarding schools meant for them have all become hotels. Our children get nothing,' she said.

It is not that the government does not impact her life at all. From the government-run anganwadi, where her grandchild studies, the family is supposed to get 1.5 kilograms of rice and 500 grams of lentil once a month. That is the incentive offered by the government to get the family to send its children to the centre. But she gets only 1 kilogram of rice and 250 grams of lentil. Through the public distribution system, they are also entitled to 25 kilograms of subsidized rice every month; only 18 kilograms reach them. 'We know what we should get, but whom do we complain to,' she asks.

In September 2014, Chamkalo's daughter-in-law was rushed to the government hospital in a nearby town for delivery. They were to get Rs 1,480 as state aid after the delivery. 'We were told the money would come into our account. We are still waiting,' she says.

Most people in the village are aware of what they are entitled to receive, but not of a single institution that they can trust and complain to.

In 2015, when the new Central government amended the Land Acquisition Bill, taking away the need for the consent of locals and Social Impact Assessment studies in many cases, a group of tribals in Jharkhand gathered one day to defecate in public on copies of the bill. They said even women wanted to join the protest. 'This was an act of desperation,' one of the protestors told local media. Such protests are almost routine in India's rural areas, but most of them go unreported in the national news, unless there is a shock value that would make it 'newsworthy': women stripping naked or men defecating together.

Whether it is an agitation demanding reservations in government jobs or calling off a mining project, underlying it all is the increasing helplessness of the ordinary Indian in the face of the gigantic, creaky and deeply corrupt governance mechanisms that run India.

Hridaychak, if anything, appears to be luckier than many. After all, Paswan is getting half her allotted ration. In nearby villages and districts, subsidized food items are often unavailable and starvation deaths have been reported. In 2010, when a few hunger-related deaths in Gaya district were reported, informal estimates said that, in Bihar alone, about a hundred Mahadalits had died of hunger that year. The deaths have not ceased.

It is not that the rural poor, and Dalits in particular, were never part of the Indian state project. In the initial years after Independence, there were concerted efforts to give the depressed classes ownership of land, and that could have been transformative. Landownership would have been a solution to many of the problems faced by the rural poor, particularly the Dalits, from cultivating their own crop to having their own toilets. Available statistics, however sketchy, show that the Dalits and Mahadalits in states like Bihar have very negligible landownership, even though the state holds on to thousands of acres meant for distribution to these very people.

Acharya Vinoba Bhave, a spiritual follower of Mahatma Gandhi, launched the Bhoodan movement in 1951 from a village in southern India to persuade India's rich landowners to voluntarily give up a part of their holdings to the landless. The movement was a huge success and collected hundreds of thousands of acres of land, and many state governments passed Bhoodan Acts. Over the years, the movement lost its steam and corruption took charge of the efforts, as with most other early initiatives of free India.

The Bihar government ordered a Bihar Land Reforms Commission in 2006, under D. Bandyopadhyay, who was credited with carrying out land reforms in neighbouring West Bengal some three decades before that. The Commission's interim report was an eye-opener on the state of affairs.

Almost five decades after the Bhoodan movement, the Commission found that there were no dependable records of the exact extent of land available for distribution to the poor. The figures, according to a state government committee that handled the issue, showed that a total of

6,48,476 acres were available, of which 2,55,347 acres had been distributed to 3,15,454 families.

The government said that about 2,78,320 acres of land were found to be not suitable for distribution because of 'improper physical characteristics', but it couldn't tell the Commission who it was that had decided all that land was of no use. Even discounting those mysterious expanses, the committee still had in its books 1,14,708 acres for distribution. That too had not yet been given to the poor, the Commission said. It recommended that the staff of the committee and the revenue department be deployed in campaign mode to finish the task of giving land to those who were meant to get it.

The Commission also found that a little over 11,130 acres meant for the landless had been distributed among fifty-nine institutions. 'From the analysis, it is apparent that someone is utilizing the Bhoodan land as his or her private zamindari,' the Commission noted. Another 15,000 acres of land had not been 'distributed formally', and thus no one knew if 'some person or a body of persons is/are utilizing such huge area for their private gain', the report said.

The Commission pointed out that historically the Bhoodan movement had suffered from many frauds perpetrated by greedy landowners. Of all such cases, in Bihar, that of Hathua Raj, a large zamindari in Saran district, is legendary. Through a simple letter, the head of this family offered to donate 1,00,000 acres of land to the Bhoodan movement. It was meant to avoid pressure from the Gandhian leader and escape the land-ceiling restrictions that had come into being as a result of the movement. The Saran district authorities notified it through a gazette notification saying that by April 1959 there were 1,03,903 acres of land available for the poor in the district. The Commission said Hathua Raj had committed a 'trick of colossal proportions'. 'A question arises as to what is to be done about such unconfirmed lands,' it said.

The Commission's sweeping recommendations, tabled a decade ago, offered no comfort to the state government, with powerful landowners and duplicitous rich ranged against it. It will surprise no one that the report has effectively been dumped.

In Delhi, Anwer and I spoke of the problems that women in his village must deal with. But he was quick to point out that, in his family, women were privileged landowners: his grandmother owned a part of the family farm, so did his mother and sisters.

In rural India, and for the poor everywhere, land is the most empowering asset they can possess, and one that women have historically been denied. This, in spite of the fact that they play a formidable role in the rural economy and agriculture. Increasingly, academics and activists are looking at the overall welfare impact that landownership can have on an individual, especially women and the marginalized communities. Based on the government's own data, Landesa, an international NGO working on land rights, estimated in 2015 that even though 85 per cent of rural women are engaged in agriculture, only 13 per cent of them own land. The situation is far worse in Bihar, where only 7 per cent of women have land rights.

'The story is not very different in our village either. Most women do not own land or any kind of property. They are at the mercy of men,' Anwer said.

In the middle of the Mahadalit quarter, surrounded by his children, Udit Raj Bansi, thirty-five, stands bare-chested, a towel thrown over his right shoulder. He is a few inches over 5 feet, with no flab on his body. His brother and he were among the first of the Mahadalits in the village to pass class ten in 1987. About five years ago, both of them were offered jobs as contract teachers under the quota available for their community. 'We even paid Rs 2,500 as bribe per person to an officer,' Bansi says, eyes welling up. They were to get a monthly salary of Rs 8,000 and were dreaming of a comfortable life. 'I have been complaining to everyone possible, but we don't know when we will get our jobs,' he adds.

Bansi's education has empowered him to vocalize what is his due. About three years ago, he went to Patna and got a few moments of audience with the chief minister and other senior officials. He complained that they were yet to get houses under the Indira Awas Yojna, a Central government scheme in existence since the 1980s – with an almost Rs 13,000 crore annual budget – which is meant to provide financial assistance to the homeless. 'They promised us a house in the next roll of allotments,' Bansi says. The next time is still to come.

A few of Bansi's neighbours have been a bit more fortunate. Some years ago, they got Rs 20,000 as a first instalment for building their own houses, and started construction. The next instalment never came, and they ran out of money. The houses remained roofless for months. Then they used wood and locally available rice straw to put up a roof, and moved in. They couldn't endlessly wait for the government. Besides, who knows if the government records claimed full disbursement of the housing scheme fund, or who pocketed it all?

Even their semi-built houses are far more comfortable than Bansi's. He and his brother, their wives and many children, are all crowded into a single-room house. Standing in this quarter, surrounded by stagnant drainage and futureless children, the words of Ambedkar ring so true: Democracy in India is only a 'top dressing on an Indian soil, which is essentially undemocratic'.

'We live like rats,' Bansi says, breaking down, unable to pretend to equanimity even for the sake of his children. Grabbing my hand, he cries: 'Please help us.'

Where the Mahadalit quarter ends, Jamuna Yadav lives in a mud house overlooking the fields. He and his wife, belonging to the Other Backward Classes or Bahujan category, have a small two-room house of mud walls and thatched roof. The outer walls are covered with cow-dung cakes. The couple tend to their cows and sell milk in the village. They don't have a bathroom, so every morning they go to the open fields with a small bottle of water.

'A few years ago, someone came and told us that the government is going to help us build toilets. They gave a few packets of cement and a couple of hundred rupees. We put our thumb impression wherever they asked us to,' Yadav says. It was probably part of the Total Sanitation

Campaign of the government, which had originally planned to provide toilet access to all by 2012.

So why did you not build your toilet? 'Is that a joke? Can you build a toilet with a few packets of cement alone?' The old man laughed.

For Yadav, until two years ago, the government was only a very distant mirage. Then it started paying him Rs 100 per month as old-age pension. Someone who claims to be from the government hands him Rs 100 every month and makes him put his thumb impression on an official document.

'Are you sure the pension is only Rs 100?' I ask him.

'I don't know. At least I am getting something.' Yadav smiles.

In his missing toilet and hardly-there old-age pension lie the tale of India's social welfare programmes and the institutionalized corruption that corrodes its democracy. According to Bihar government's Department of Social Welfare, under the Indira Gandhi National Old Age Pension Scheme, Yadav should be receiving Rs 300 every month. He even does not receive two-thirds of his benefit. There are over three million people in Bihar alone receiving old-age pension, according to the department estimates in November 2011.

Assuming that Yadav is a typical case, the pension money being pocketed by officials of the department and their political masters must be around Rs 600 million a month. And this is just one social welfare scheme in one of India's twenty-nine states and seven Union territories.

The Indian government has around forty schemes to provide welfare to its poor: uplift their economic conditions, provide toilets, drinking water, roads, schools and hospitals, guarantee employment and other assistance. It spends about 1.7 per cent of its GDP in the social sector – the health and education sectors receive 1 per cent of the GDP, while rural development gets 0.7 per cent. In the budget for 2016–17, this totalled to a whopping Rs 2,53,356 crore. All the schemes have grand names, mostly after famous Indian leaders from the past, but none of them assure a better future for the Indian poor.

No other economy is growing as fast as India's while simultaneously recording such low progress in the reduction of malnutrition, eradication of poverty, illiteracy and so on. In the Global Hunger Index in 2014, India was ranked at the fifty-fifth position, trailing neighbouring Sri Lanka and Nepal and recording only a marginal improvement from the previous year.

There have been occasional studies of the extent of corruption leakages in social welfare schemes. In 2009, a Planning Commission of India study of the distribution of subsidized food items through the Public Distribution System (PDS) found that only 16 paise out of a rupee reached the targeted poor. The remaining 84 paise went to pay salaries and as leakages and bribes and commissions for the country's bloated government.

~

A narrow concrete road runs through Hridaychak right up to the Muslim graveyard at one end of it. It passes the Mahadalit quarter and a dirty pond that has been encroached upon by many homeless Mahadalits and into which most of the village's sewage flows. A few metres down stands a tall peepal tree, the ground around it practically covered in human faecal matter. The place stinks to high heavens.

A small temple has been built adjacent to the boundary wall of the graveyard – early signs that the new communally charged India is making its way to Hridaychak. 'We went and tried to talk to them (the Hindus who built the temple) about the potential it has to create unnecessary tension between our communities in the future,' says Mohammed Tayyab, a tall man with a long beard, a broad smile and a magical cure.

The graveyard, you see, is not just a resting place for the departed, but a land of magic and power. Tayyab had returned to the village several years ago to take care of his ageing parents. Without attracting anyone's attention, he slipped into the graveyard in the night, sat in one corner and lit a small fire. Then he began to recite an Arabic prayer, occasionally throwing holy incense into the fire. Over three nights, Tayyab repeated the prayers hundreds of thousands of times, and finally he drew into himself the special powers for his cure. Or so his patients and villagers believe.

Tayyab now treats patients with arthritic pain, beating affected areas with a special rod. People from as far as Nepal visit him. Until the treatment is over, Tayyab and his patient remain empty-stomached. He doesn't charge for the cure. 'It is a blessing from Allah,' Tayyab says, looking up into the blue sky, hesitant to discuss the details of what happened in the graveyard back then. In a village still waiting for its modern hospital, Tayyab's cure may be all some can afford. He narrates many tales of the village – a link from a magical past to the miserable present – and brushes over its miseries with loud laughter.

The graveyard is an open, undulating ground with tall trees and green grass, surrounded by a white wall. The wall was built under a state government scheme about four years ago, after Anwer and other villagers found the right intermediaries to get the Bihar government to sanction the project. When the construction was under way, villagers protested that the wall was not 10 inches thick as promised, but only 5 inches. After several trips to the state capital, they were able to complain to the state minister in charge of the scheme, and finally the half-built wall was fully demolished, but not the foundation. The people of Hridaychak believe that some senior officials were part of the scam, but they have no proof. The wall was rebuilt to the specified 10 inches width but on the narrow, shallow foundation. The contractor and his workers left after the construction work was over, and the occasional visits by officials stopped after the contractor was paid.

A few months down the line, a portion of the wall collapsed. A monsoon and a few more months later, another portion caved in. Like India's rusting government machinery, the wall has been falling apart, one brick at a time. From a distance you won't see the broken parts; the long grass and stooping trees cover them. For now, there are big locks and a green gate guarding the graveyard. In Hridaychak, perhaps everywhere in India, even the dead are not safe. Meanwhile, the road that reached Hridaychak six years ago was in a shambles in 2016 when I signed off the book. Poor construction quality, lack of proper maintenance and an absent government are all actively conspiring to wipe out the villages's lifeline to the outside world.

The villagers will have to now go looking for the right intermediaries to persuade the government to repair the road and rebuild the wall, just as they are also hunting for the right people to bring them a hospital and electricity. Anwer and his fellow villagers will search for those middlemen in New Delhi and Patna, in the local markets and among political leaders. Finding the appropriate intermediary will be transformative for Hridaychak and its residents. Until then, they – like hundreds of millions of other Indians – will continue the search. For someone who can get them a bed in a government hospital, help register a police complaint, get electricity or drinking water, or a toilet.

Section One

THE MIDDLEMEN

There is a middleman somewhere out there who could do your work — getting a birth certificate, organizing government subsidy, manipulating contracts or throwing a government out. This section is a glimpse, hopefully an insightful one, into India's most flourishing industry. In every corner of this country there is a middleman. Almost every other big businessman or famous politician or consultant is a mere intermediary. The manager of your building, or your lawyer, could be a go-between. Maybe you are one.

1

Mr Fix-it Down the Street

Chaos ruled outside the house I was in. Trucks carrying ores and equipment for the mining industry plied on the road at all hours of the day and the night. In the pink-walled drawing room, blaring horns frequently interrupted conversations. It didn't help that the railway line was only a few metres away. The manned crossing where the road met that rail line was often shut, making matters worse.

In the middle of all this, Abhay Narain Rai attended two incessantly ringing mobile phones, listened to a stream of people who mostly spoke of helplessness in low volumes, and called up officials in government offices, and sometimes in the private sector too. Every day, from about 7 a.m. until he left the house around noon, this was his routine.

'Mainly, there are three kinds of issues – health, revenue and government schemes,' Rai said one February morning, after he had seen off the last of the day's visitors. Everyone in the locality knew that Rai was busy with his son's wedding; there was a reception planned for the next day. Still, four people had turned up with their grievances. 'They were really urgent – one person's mother was seriously ill and had to be admitted to a government hospital, so I called up a doctor there. The second person's son is in a private hospital which has raised a bill of

Rs 30,000. He was requesting some discount, so I called up the hospital owner. A third one wants to sell his farmland in small plots, but that is against the law, so he wants my help to keep the revenue authorities away,' Rai said matter-of-factly. He shouted across to the kitchen for tea.

Most of his family was away at the local temple to pray for the success of his son's marriage. Rai picked up a ringing phone and told his son to give the priest his reference, probably to ensure there was no delay. Even to the local gods, he had special access.

'For these people there are two options. One is to come to me and I'll call up the officer concerned and ensure that their work is done quickly. Or, they could go around those offices for several days and pay a bribe and waste time.' Rai paused and then said, 'For a daily wage worker, even a day's income lost could mean his kids will go to bed hungry.'

'Are you saying that they don't need to pay a bribe because you are involved,' I asked.

'When I am involved, the officials won't demand a bribe usually. If the beneficiary voluntarily decides to pay some money to the officials, however, they won't reject,' Rai said, explaining the rules of the game.

He lives in a crowded urban village just outside Bilaspur, a major city in the central Indian state of Chhattisgarh, where a new generation of mining barons and government-controlled companies are engaged in unbridled mining of coal, iron ore, limestone and other natural resources. A spokesperson for the local arm of the Congress party, Rai is the critical contact and an occasional saviour for the few thousand residents of Bhilha, one of the largest blocks in the country. Almost a million people crowd into Bhilha, where cheap apartments jostle with small hutments that encroach on government land. It is a typical suburb in a typical Indian city. And Rai is among its lifelines.

Bhilha's poor do not rush off to government offices and police stations to deal with their grievances, or to demand what is rightfully theirs. They go to Rai. People will even visit him before rushing their seriously sick patients to hospitals, Rai told me. For most of the residents of this suburb, he is the intermediary with the government, and sometimes even the private sector. 'Government offices intimidate our poor,' he said. 'Even today there is nobody to listen to ordinary people. The poor either need money or a source like me.'

Rai represents political leaders and other influential people at the bottom rung of the middlemen's network. They thrive as the intermediaries between ordinary citizens and corrupt and inefficient governments. These leaders assist the poor in accessing government facilities and schemes, organize government certificates that would give them access to many welfare programmes, intervene on behalf of the poor to get police to act on complaints, and so on.

These intermediaries occasionally even take up the role of the government, holding kangaroo courts and settling disputes. For the poor, the arrangement makes great sense; courts are costly and appallingly slow. According to estimates, it will take about 320 years to dispose of the over three crore cases pending now in Indian courts.[1]

It is not just the poor that these middlemen at the grass-roots level serve. They are also crucial to the local administration. Rai and his ilk help the administration gain local support for controversial projects, like widening roads or acquiring land. It is through facilitating these activities that the intermediaries sustain their political careers.

Academics have long been fascinated by intermediaries and their ability to access government institutions on behalf of ordinary citizens. However, there is not yet an adequate reckoning of the cost that these middlemen add to the already inefficient welfare programmes.

One of the studies that assessed the phenomenon of this lower-level

---

1 The estimate was made in 2010 by an Andhra Pradesh High Court judge, Justice V.V. Rao. There have been several official studies that have painted a grim picture of pending cases in India. Two of them can be found here: Thorat report: http://www.mha.nic.in/hindi/sites/upload_files/mhahindi/files/pdf/criminal_justice_system.pdf; Law Commission report of 2014: http://lawcommissionofindia.nic.in/reports/Report_No.245.pdf

intermediary is by Anirudh Krishna, a professor of public policy and political science at Duke University.[2] A career civil servant for fourteen years, mostly in India's rural areas, Krishna now spends almost six months in India doing fieldwork. He is well placed to study the system. Krishna continues to spend his time in various obscure villages, carrying out extensive research on how poor communities and individuals cope with the structural and personal constraints that result in poverty and powerlessness.

He led a team of researchers in two Indian states – Rajasthan and Andhra Pradesh – in two phases: in Rajasthan in 1997–98 and in Andhra Pradesh seven years later. 'These results show that, despite having a great deal of faith in democracy, most citizens have a hard time making connections with public service providers,' he told me.

'People's past experiences are such that a majority of people in both states – a somewhat higher proportion in Rajasthan than in Andhra Pradesh – expect that their voices will simply go unheard by public officials, including those responsible for service delivery. As a result, relatively few take the trouble to express their demands directly,' he wrote in the paper published in 2011.

Krishna identifies a group he calls 'naya netas', or new leaders, who are usually younger, educated enough to read newspapers and have experience in dealing with the government bureaucracy and other local institutions. 'Naya netas help facilitate villagers' access to powerful actors with influence over diverse aspects of social welfare, including policemen, political party organizers, doctors, health and education bureaucrats, bankers and insurance agents,' Krishna wrote in his paper. That is precisely what Rai does from his house by the chaotic road outside Bilaspur.

The naya netas, Krishna told me during a meeting, have another

---

2   Anirudh Krishna, 'Gaining Access to Public Services and the Democratic State in India: Institutions in the Middle', *Studies in Comparative International Development*, Vol. 46, No. 1, 2011, pp. 98–117.

role to play: that of being the crucial link between the voters and major national parties. 'In addition to rising education, intensified electoral competition over the past twenty-five years has assisted the rise of the new village leaders. Neither of the two major political parties in the region, the Congress and the Bharatiya Janata Party (BJP), has developed any permanent organization at the grass-roots level, and party offices are located mostly at state and district capitals. Parties rely upon suitable local intermediaries for creating support among villagers. Naya netas (along with other local intermediaries) have stepped into this organizational vacuum,' Krishna told me.

The manner in which these new leaders function varies across the country, and they don't always work within the framework of an institutional vacuum. For example, in Kerala, political parties have highly developed networks right down to the grass roots, and most people are educated and vocal. Yet, these citizens too need local political leaders to play the role of intermediaries between them and the government. Every morning, outside the houses of local political leaders in Kerala, there are dozens awaiting their turn for an audience. There are two key reasons why, even in a highly literate state like Kerala, ordinary people look for intermediaries. For one, government resources are limited and thus demand far outstrips supply, like in, say, government-run hospitals. Secondly, and crucially, many government institutions, such as the police, are brutal and corrupt. The local intermediary could help someone jump the queue or soften treatment at the hands of a government institution.

When I met Krishna over coffee in south Delhi, he elaborated on his argument. The problem in India, he explained, is that the state machinery is built top-down, unlike in the United States and other developed economies. The result of this is that, in India, the government is active and alive only up to the district level; at best, a step down. Below that, people exist in a black hole. Even political parties suffer from the same lacuna, except in developed states like Kerala, Krishna added.

The Comptroller and Auditor General of India (CAG), Shashi Kant Sharma, one of India's topmost civil servants, met me several times to explain the importance of local leaders like Abhay Narain Rai. Sharma has spent several years at the local levels as subdivisional magistrate, district magistrate, as well as the head of several departments in Bihar, where the naya netas are particularly powerful. He told me that the new intermediaries were easily identifiable. 'They come riding bikes, wear white kurta-pyjama, and are often school dropouts,' he said.

'They get something to the poor, like welfare schemes, and so have significant control over them. They bring votes to the political parties, get crowds to political rallies and also feed the political system at the ground level with money. They have an eye on a possible future political role.' In the long run, many of these intermediaries do enter mainstream politics and fight elections at the local levels. 'Even when I started my career, there used to be such intermediaries. There were full-time politicians acting as intermediaries on the side. Many others were freedom fighters or spirited people who thought of doing some good for the people. Some of them used to earn money in the process. In contrast, in most instances today, the motive is money, welfare is incidental, and political career is a definite future option,' Sharma explained. 'These intermediaries are useful though unscrupulous. Inadvertently, they help the poor and the political process.'

In some parts of Bihar, it was easy for me to identify the new web of intermediaries who have emerged. Many of them had become leaders and elected members or chiefs of village councils. The locals came up with many nicknames for them – Bolero mukhiya, Innova sarpanch – after the names of the SUVs they purchased once they had ascended to their post. The secret of their fortune is no mystery. As the chiefs of local bodies, they have an important role in dispersing a significant amount of cash and contracts to the people.

The mukhiyas and sarpanches are important cogs in Indian efforts to devolve power to the village level: Mahatma Gandhi's vision of village self-rule. According to the many committees that recommended decentralization of power and the governments that introduced it, the Panchayati Raj system would address the appalling levels of corruption at the grass-roots levels.

The Panchayati Raj operates through three layers of local governance: village, block and district. But stories from across the country suggest that India's decentralization efforts may not be as successful as its advocates want us to believe. The local members and chiefs of village councils have mostly been co-opted into the existing government machinery, so they have no incentive to fight or improve it. Of course, here too, there are many exceptions.

One winter afternoon, a local-level leader and member of a village council, who spends all his time facilitating schemes for his people, told me that their roles were irreplaceable. 'The district administration receives X amount under the rural job guarantee scheme, and officials will decide which village should get what. If I can assure them of a good commission, I get to steer that money to my village. Our people will get work for a few days, earn some money, and I also benefit.' He did not want to be named. 'We will be important as long as people are afraid of the government, officials and police,' he added.

I was travelling across Chhattisgarh in February 2015. The state was then holding local body elections. And it was clear that these elections, like elections to the Indian parliament and state assemblies, had become expensive affairs. Candidates were throwing money at people. Drunken crowds were cheering them, colourful posters and numerous vehicles announced their names.

Every political leader and candidate I met said they were spending hundreds of thousands of rupees on the election. For what, I asked many of them.

'Sir, you don't ask such questions,' one candidate replied.

Rai told me that a local candidate in his area, who was fighting for the post of sarpanch, spent Rs 35 lakh. Where did he find that money? 'He is a local transporter, and has spent his own money. He will recover it once he is in office,' Rai replied.

He explained that once these local leaders became elected representatives and acquired power, they looked for ways to recoup their investment and make some profit too, and the only way was to extract a commission from government contractors or get a cut from the government money allotted to their areas for welfare programmes. 'Even those who lose elections are on the lookout for their cut. If they are not paid, they will disrupt whatever work the elected people are trying to do.'

'Local bodies are now a huge industry,' Rai said. 'Many in our locality are now professional politicians.'

In Bihar, a panchayat chief told me that one could get members of parliament or state legislators to allocate money available for disbursement at their discretion for a commission. 'It is all set, sir. You have to give them their commission.'

The emerging evidence raises several questions regarding the efficacy of the Panchayati Raj system. Has devolution of power improved efficiency of governance and brought welfare to people? Or has it added a few new layers to the corrupt political–bureaucratic network? The evidence at hand points to the latter. For a country the size of India, decentralization is crucial; but in a deeply corrupt system, it only seems to have added a new opportunity for bureaucrats and local-level intermediaries to make more money.

Rai said that the daily existence of the poor in his area continues to be miserable. Only about 50 per cent of the families have toilets and the open space that they used to defecate in is fast disappearing. Many of the poor are encroaching upon the government land that used to be open lavatories for the other poor, to build houses for themselves.

'We don't have a primary health centre, just one high school, and not enough roads and other facilities,' Rai lamented. Unlike Hridaychak, his locality is on the fringes of Bilaspur, a flourishing city where Chhattisgarh's high court and several other institutions like the headquarters of the South Eastern Coal Fields Ltd (SECL) and the zonal headquarters of the Indian Railways are situated.

So what is the cost of these intermediaries at the grass-roots level to the system? Many studies show that only about a quarter of the money intended for the poor actually reaches them. What percentage is diverted to intermediaries then? There was no realistic data I could access. One can only guess that it must be a significant percentage of the overall budget.

It must be very expensive to sustain your public life, with so many of the poor coming to you all the time, I said to Rai.

'My social spending is very high; sometimes people expect me to pay their hospital bill, give emergency loan and whatever else. I can't afford to say no,' Rai declared. Then he told me about the local liquor contractor. 'He has the licence to run a liquor shop 2 kilometres from here, but he sells liquor in this locality illegally. I just ignore it.' In return, the liquor contractor obliges him with money.

Rai has figured out ways to make his money. 'We find the rhythm between the government and the ordinary people,' he philosophized. 'Let us say the district administration has given someone a contract to broaden the road. I help the administration and the contractor to settle issues with the local people, complete land acquisition, etc.' The contractor, naturally, pays him a fee in turn.

Needless to say, the government programmes that intermediaries like Rai facilitate do not always end well for the poor. On a November morning in 2014, with the help of local intermediaries, dozens of women were picked up and taken to sterilization camps not very far from where Rai was based. Though Rai was not involved in organizing that camp, it is the kind of programme that he regularly assists the district administration in putting together.

At the camp, tubectomy was being performed on women in a frenzy – yet another population control overdrive. Within hours of the surgeries, the women who had been operated upon began to fall ill. Over a hundred of them were rushed to hospitals in Bilaspur, and at least fifteen died in the next few hours. Investigations revealed that the doctor who conducted the procedures was under pressure to meet government

targets on sterilization, and carried out eighty-three surgeries in six hours
in unhygienic conditions. They also found that one of the medicines
that was administered contained rat poison. Some corrupt officials and
ministers had taken a hefty commission to buy the medicine in bulk
from a manufacturer. He, in turn, made up his expenses by replacing
costly chemicals with rat poison. Congress party leaders, including Rai,
aggressively protested against the BJP-ruled state government's negligence.
'We organized several protest marches,' Rai told me.

  We stepped out into the winter sun and the din of traffic. Thanking
me warmly for the visit, Rai insisted I attend his son's wedding reception
the next day. As I got into the car, his parting words were: 'I have to be
forever on the right side of the people. It's not always easy.'

2

The Mighty Typist

In a bright yellow cotton sari with a black-and-white border, feet clad in a pair of simple black slippers, Prime Minister Indira Gandhi walked into the pleasant New Delhi morning. She walked, as was her wont, briskly along the pathway from her residence to the next bungalow, where Peter Ustinov, the Academy Award–winning actor and columnist, was waiting to interview her. She was running late by thirty minutes.

As she crossed the wicket gate between the two compounds at 9.20 a.m., Sub-inspector Beant Singh, who had been guarding her for almost a decade, turned and shot her. When she collapsed to the ground after taking three bullets, Satwant Singh, a twenty-one-year-old who had been with the prime minister's security for just ten months, fired thirty rounds at her. The two men dropped their guns, and one of them reportedly shouted, 'I have done what I had to do. You do what you want to do.' The two Sikh bodyguards were taking revenge on Gandhi for ordering the Indian Army into the Golden Temple, the highest temporal seat of their religion, to flush out armed Sikh separatists in summer that year.

Rajendra Kumar Dhawan was only a couple of feet from Gandhi as she took those bullets, but not one of them grazed him. That was Dhawan's default position in contemporary India: a few steps removed from history. He was close enough to his boss to hear what she whispered, watch for her signals, keep away intruders and take down dictation. He was close enough to witness at close quarters India's struggles to evolve as a democratic nation, with all its intrigues, drama and violence. He also became the single point of contact between Gandhi and most people, including her ministerial colleagues.

Dhawan gave off the appearance of a man squeezing through the very crowded lane of history, eager to get to his mundane destination, rather than one who enjoyed the cast of colourful characters that were writing history around him. The almost silent journey of this typist exemplifies the power enjoyed by hundreds of men and women in India, many of them stenographers, who emerge as men Friday of those in power. Dhawan may be the most famous among his lot, but thousands of his ilk stand between the ordinary Indian and the powerful decision makers.

The trusted aide's primary qualification is often just his skill in peacefully, quickly and accurately typing on a QWERTY keyboard. Once he is in the office of a powerful boss, he acquires other skills, such as holding secrets, negotiating on behalf of his boss, reading the boss's mind and managing various situations for her.

These aides usually guard access to the decision maker's chamber. They pass on messages between those seeking favours and their bosses, often striking deals and collecting the booty on behalf of their employers, occasionally getting a few crumbs of it, and bringing in women or wine as required. They are expected to remain silent and to carry these secrets to their graves.

The short-statured, nondescript Dhawan became the arbiter of power between the Gandhi family and a significant part of the rest of India, including senior leaders of the Congress. His story helps understand modern India and how its gigantic, creaky engine of governance moves.

The story begins with the Partition of India in 1947. As a ten-year-old boy, Dhawan was plucked from the comforts of a landed peasantry life in rural Pakistan in 1947. The Partition of the subcontinent set off one of the biggest massacres in modern history. Millions of people migrated across the newly drawn boundaries in a traumatic exodus that continues to shape the narratives of India, Pakistan and Bangladesh. Dhawan and ten other members of his family undertook a harrowing journey to Delhi, halting first at a refugee camp in Pakistan, and then crossing the border into India. At the second halt in Ludhiana, Dhawan remembers the camp being haunted by malaria and hunger. At Kurukshetra, they were forced to halt again, because the national capital was overflowing with refugees. Days later, the family boarded a freight train and covered the 160-kilometre distance to Delhi in two days.

His family crowded into a maternal uncle's house in Karol Bagh. Here, Dhawan enrolled at a local school and completed his studies. Between 1955 and 1957, he learnt typing and shorthand, and was able to find a job as a stenographer with All India Radio. Then, in 1962, history beckoned. A relative who was already a permanent fixture in Prime Minister Jawaharlal Nehru's office, Yashpal Kapoor, took the young Dhawan to Teen Murti Bhavan, the prime minister's official residence. Nehru's daughter Indira Gandhi had just been appointed chairperson of the New York World Fair committee. Dhawan was appointed her personal assistant – and thus began his association with one of the most charismatic, controversial and influential political leaders of independent India.

In a white safari suit, Dhawan presented himself every day at 8 a.m. in Mrs Gandhi's office. 'I understood her. She knew my style of working, she knew my loyalty, she knew my hard work. I used to be there from eight o'clock in the morning until she retired for the night at twelve o'clock, 365 days of the year. During those twenty-two years, I never took a day's leave; whether on Diwali, Dussehra, Holi, I was there,' Dhawan told me in 2014. We were sitting in the well-maintained, small lawns of his house in Jor Bagh, one of Delhi's most expensive residential colonies.

As we talked about his unusual life, visitors kept trooping in, stopping to touch his feet for blessings before they carried on. One of his hangers-on brought a bundle of letters and Dhawan started checking them – most were invitations to local religious congregations. Age was definitely catching up with the man, but he seemed to be finally enjoying the leisure and privileges he had no time for in those hectic decades. At seventy-four, Dhawan had recently married, and had started writing notes on his own life. His wife Achla had been by Dhawan's side ever since she and her daughter returned to India from Canada after her divorce in the early 1990s. The two married in October 2011 and a few months later made their marriage public by hosting a reception for friends and family. 'You can call us soulmates. We have known each other so long, and I have been visiting him at home every day,' Achla told *The Indian Express*.

'There was no time to get married. If I had married I would have divorced her or my neighbour would have taken her,' Dhawan said with a faint smile, recalling that Mrs Gandhi never ever asked him about his personal matters.

By 1972, Dhawan had started handling political liaison for Gandhi. The prime minister was at the peak of her glory – through military intervention, she had created Bangladesh as an independent nation-state. In Kashmir and the north-east of the country she had managed to suppress much of the demand for independence from India, and she had captured the national imagination through her call for the removal of poverty (Garibi Hatao). But political opposition – both to her autocratic streak and to many of the decisions she made – was building up.

On 12 June 1975, the Allahabad High Court declared her election to the Lok Sabha null and void, amplifying the chorus of calls for her resignation. By 25 June, Gandhi imposed an internal emergency, suspended civil liberties, which allowed her to rule by decree. As India's democracy gave way to an autocracy, the show was run by a small coterie around Gandhi – her son Sanjay and Dhawan primarily, and a few others. 'Enough rubbish has been said about those days,' Dhawan said, refusing to discuss the Emergency. 'Whether she was in power, or out of power, I worked for Mrs Gandhi.' Clearly, he thought it quite unnecessary to engage with these moral dilemmas.

By 1977, the Emergency was revoked and Gandhi and the Congress were routed in the elections that followed. Although she was out of power and lonely, Gandhi still needed someone to type her letters. Dhawan, now a political aide, could not be demoted. She asked the Congress for a reliable and fast typist. Enter Vincent George, who, like Dhawan, went on to win the confidence of the Gandhi household; another doorkeeper who controlled access to the powerful. When I asked Dhawan about George, he replied with a poker face, 'He was alright, like any other human being.' He had very little to say about the man, though they had so much in common.

Vincent George came to Delhi in 1974 as a migrant from Kerala with higher education in search of better economic prospects. The only certifiable skill the young man had then was his ability to type fast – media reports say he won a fastest typist award in Kerala. Within a few weeks, he landed a job at the headquarters of the Congress party as a typist. His fortunes began to change when he caught the attention of Sanjay Gandhi, the younger of the prime minister's two sons.

After Sanjay Gandhi was killed in an air crash in 1980, his older brother and commercial pilot, Rajiv, joined the Congress. George was deputed to assist Rajiv, and thus was born yet another storied boss–man Friday relationship in Indian politics. As Rajiv Gandhi unexpectedly moved into the prime minister's seat in 1984 after his mother's assassination, George followed him into the Prime Minister's Office (PMO). Appointed as the youngest private secretary of an Indian prime minister, George was allotted government accommodation in New Delhi and became an integral part of the PMO. Much like Dhawan with Indira Gandhi, he controlled access to Rajiv Gandhi – from allowing someone to meet him, to even intervening during a meeting to cut it short or extend it. In May 1991, Rajiv Gandhi became the second member of the Nehru–Gandhi family to be assassinated, when a suicide bomber of the Liberation Tigers of Tamil Eelam (LTTE) blew him up during an election campaign at Sriperumbudur, near Madras (now Chennai) in Tamil Nadu. George stuck with the Gandhi family and took charge of handling all practicalities for the grief-stricken widow Sonia Gandhi and her young children,

Priyanka and Rahul. He became a bulwark for the family against the machinations of Indian politics. When it was necessary to send messages of the Gandhis' continued political relevance, it was George who operated from behind the scenes.

Within months of Rajiv's killing, the Machiavellian Congress leader P.V. Narasimha Rao made a comeback from retirement to become prime minister. It was Sonia Gandhi, refusing to enter active politics, who persuaded Rao to return. Soon, though, he began to show visible hostility towards the Gandhi family. Staying firmly behind the scenes, George organized a show of rebellion by Gandhi family loyalists. In turn, the Rao government served George with a notice to vacate the government house he was occupying. George's brother-in-law, Sabu Chacko, who worked for East West Airlines, India's first private airline, was arrested for sheltering underworld criminals in Delhi, and spent a couple of years in jail. To anyone willing to listen, George and his family pleaded Chacko's innocence.

There was no doubt that George was paying for his loyalty to the Gandhi family and there was widespread speculation that his time in New Delhi was up. But in Indian politics, there are no easy predictions. In 1997, Sonia Gandhi decided to take on a more active political role – a decision that was widely welcomed within the dynastic Congress party. With this, George's star began to rise again. But not for too long.

In 1998, the right-wing Bharatiya Janata Party swept to power. And George started facing the heat again. The Central Bureau of Investigation (CBI, the central investigative agency) filed an FIR against George, accusing him of possessing disproportionate assets. The agency said George had a mansion in a posh locality, an apartment in another colony, a commercial floor in a south Delhi locality, two shops in the World Trade Centre in Connaught Place and a 5-acre plot near Qutab Minar. It also claimed that George had several million rupees in bank accounts and other instruments. George's wife, Lilly, who was a nurse in Kuwait until the 1990 Gulf War broke out, owned two firms and showed an unusual jump in income too, the CBI said. Further, during the time that George was serving the Gandhis, he and his family were recipients of cash gifts from various sources. In November 1991 he got Rs 1.25 crore, in December he got Rs 41 lakh, Rs 70 lakh in December 1992, and Rs 20 lakh in March 1995. Though George claimed that most of his properties had been acquired using the income from his wife's firms, the CBI said the firms – Lilliens Exports and Diana Agencies – operated only for a couple of years.

To the Gandhi family, however, these alleged financial indiscretions were pardonable in view of his unquestionable loyalty. To date, he remains an important figure at 10 Janpath, Sonia Gandhi's official residence. On 20 January 2015, a trial court in Delhi dismissed the disproportionate assets case against George. After the CBI cases, however, George has gone under the radar. But even today, he holds the key to the Gandhi family's many secrets, and thus to those of India's recent decades.

George's career differs from Dhawan's only in that the latter also built up a long political career as a senior leader of the Congress party.

The ebb and flow of Dhawan's fortunes were linked entirely to Indira Gandhi's. On 31 October 1984, when Mrs Gandhi was assassinated, Dhawan, Sonia Gandhi and other officials rushed her to the All India Institute of Medical Sciences hospital, where she was soon declared dead. Dhawan's trademark white safari suit was drenched in blood.

'I got a fresh set of clothes from home,' Dhawan said, recalling that morning. As leaders and important officials began to crowd into the hospital where Gandhi's body lay, he had to be around. With his intimate knowledge of the Gandhi household, the government and the Congress, Dhawan had a crucial role to play at that traumatic moment. Rajiv, Indira Gandhi's forty-year-old son, was sworn in as prime minister that same evening. Dhawan was among the small number of people at the Rashtrapati Bhavan, where the president swore him in.

The generational shift in the Congress played out in dramatic ways for Dhawan. Rajiv Gandhi appointed a sitting Supreme Court judge, Justice M.P. Thakkar, to probe the assassination of his mother. And, by the end of 1984, two months into office, the young prime minister had shunted Dhawan out. Rumours of the aide's complicity in Indira Gandhi's assassination were growing by the day.

'I wish one of the bullets had hit me, so that I wouldn't have had to face the wrath of a sitting Supreme Court judge. Obnoxious comments and remarks were made about me,' Dhawan said. He and his family were put under surveillance, their phones tapped and every visitor to their house questioned. Overnight, Dhawan was reduced to a national pariah in a city where he had been one of the most powerful and sought-after men for decades.

In his 312-page report, Justice Thakkar said the Central government should ask appropriate agencies to investigate the alleged involvement of R.K. Dhawan in the assassination. The report of the inquiry commission said that there were 'reasonable grounds to suspect the involvement' of Dhawan, accused him of telling lies to the commission and being complicit in the crime. 'There is no escape from the conclusion that there are weighty reasons to suspect the complicity or involvement of Dhawan in the crime,' the report said. The government appointed a Special Investigation Team to probe Justice Thakkar's conclusion, but it couldn't substantiate any of those claims. It also turned out that Thakkar was unduly influenced by Dhawan's rivals in the government and party.

By 1989, Rajiv Gandhi brought Dhawan back to public life. He remained a prominent Congress leader under Sonia Gandhi too, and, as of 2016, he is a member of the Congress Working Committee (CWC), the highest decision-making body of the party.

'They tried their level best to get me removed when Mrs Gandhi was alive. Those people – M.L. Fotedar, Arun Singh, Arun Nehru – they all tried to get me removed,' Dhawan told me, naming senior Congress leaders. He is not known to have listed his enemies in the past, at least in public.

Dhawan said ordinary folk wouldn't understand his relationship with the Nehru–Gandhi family. 'I carried the body of Pandit Nehru, Sanjay Gandhi, Indira Gandhi and Rajiv Gandhi ... four bodies of the family were carried on my shoulders,' he said softly, staring me in the eye as if to assess whether I understood the significance of what he had just said.

He was at Teen Murti Bhavan when Nehru died and also in the special train to Allahabad that carried Nehru's ashes in 1964 for immersion at the confluence of the rivers Ganga, Yamuna and the mythical Saraswati. He carried Sanjay Gandhi's body in 1980 after he was killed in an aircraft crash. He was there next to Indira Gandhi when she was shot dead in 1984. He accompanied Sonia Gandhi to Tamil Nadu after Rajiv Gandhi was assassinated in 1991 and brought back his mortal remains. Dhawan recalled those times in that same muted voice.

The man who started out as a typist to Indira Gandhi has, over the years, been probably the only outsider present as fate and history played truant with the family's fortunes, and in turn with the fledgling democracy. The Nehru–Gandhi family has ruled India for forty-four years of its seven-decade life as a free country. R.K. Dhawan was there, right in the middle, throughout – with the exception of the early years of the Nehru period and some parts of Rajiv Gandhi's tenure. There isn't another insider who could throw light on the workings of the inner sanctums of Indian democracy as he could. We discussed his plans to write an autobiography.

'I have not made up my mind about what to write, what not to write.'

You have seen a lot?

'Of course, I have seen a lot.'

Are you tempted to reveal the secrets of the Gandhi family?

'No, never,' he said firmly.

As I took his leave and drove out of Jor Bagh, I thought about how he must have come to own the house. It's not something I asked him.

Unexplained riches, metamorphoses and mysterious fortunes are all part of the lives of our politicians and their trusted aides. There are many who have thrown away government jobs to become personal assistants to political leaders; there are trusted aides who have risen in politics because of the blessings of political leaders.

For example, when on 15 February 2016, a mob of lawyers and
supporters of the ruling BJP attacked journalists and academics in a court
complex near India Gate, the most recognizable face among the attackers
was that of O.P. Sharma. He had spent most of his life as a shadow to
India's finance minister, Arun Jaitley, and had recently become a member
of the local legislative assembly. Across India there are many who have
emerged from shadows of their bosses to build such political careers.

When I was a reporter covering the Delhi local government in the
1990s, a lanky young man with a foreign MBA degree joined the personal
staff of the transport minister in the Delhi government run by the BJP.
While he was with the minister, sitting mostly in the minister's room,
Ajay Singh looked like he was just preparing official communications,
fixing appointments and occasionally firefighting for his boss. After the
government lost power, Singh moved to work with Pramod Mahajan,
a senior BJP leader and a rising star in Indian politics. Mahajan, a
flamboyant politician who raised big finances for the party and managed
election campaigns, was murdered by his younger brother in 2006, two
years after his party suffered a surprise defeat in the national elections.
After the BJP lost power and Ajay Singh his official position with
Mahajan, the young confidant's life took another turn.

In 2004, he surprised the business world by taking over a defunct
private airline with a still-valid Air Operating Certificate and launched
the highly successful low-cost airline, SpiceJet. In June 2006, two months
after Mahajan was killed in Mumbai, rumours about the BJP leader's
mysterious wealth began doing the rounds. Ajay Singh told news agency
IANS: 'It is a whole lot of rubbish that Pramod Mahajan's money is
parked in the airline and that I was his point man. You can check the
account books, the shareholders are listed.'

The youth-turned-aviation entrepreneur, the old man who lives in a
mansion and the typist with many properties are all mere glimpses of the
influence wielded by the fortunate aides in the Indian system. If you want
the Indian system to work for you, it is critical that you understand the
power of the personal assistant, even in this touch-screen era.

This person carries the boss's family and business secrets, probably some of India's most scandalous stories, and whims and fancies of famous men and women, almost always to their deathbed. India's most colourful and important moments are lost to public record. There are exceptions, though – men who will tell a few tales. And they give us an idea of how much these assistants really know, how far their influence goes.

Take the case of M.O. Mathai, a confidant of Jawaharlal Nehru, and predecessor to Dhawan and George.

When Mathai landed at Anand Bhavan – the imposing residence of the Nehru clan, now a government-run museum – he had just finished serving the US troops in World War II. In his book, this is how Mathai describes how he came by the job: 'Soon after my arrival in Allahabad early in February 1946, Nehru returned from Malaya. I had already told him during my previous visit to Allahabad that only after a week of my being with him would I be in a position to say in what way I could be of any use. I took less than a week. I discovered that Nehru so far had not had any adequate secretarial assistance. He even had to file his own papers. Those connected with his books, royalties and general finances were in a hopeless mess. I told him that even a superficial assessment of the situation had convinced me that the best way I could be of help to him was to render him secretarial assistance and added that I had decided to do this disagreeable work for a year. He was immensely pleased.'

By the time he was forced out of the job in 1959 because of allegations of misuse of power, Mathai, Mac to friends and the Nehru family, probably knew all the secrets of the first family of India: the prime minister's habits, his weaknesses and his secret life. Mathai held on to the secrets of Anand Bhavan and Teen Murti Bhavan, which had become Nehru's official residence, up until the 1970s. Then he decided to write.

The 1970s was a sensational decade. Nehru's daughter Indira Gandhi had wielded immense political power, abused democracy and had been electorally humiliated. This is when Mac decided to publish his memoirs of the Nehruvian era. In the preface to *Reminiscences of the Nehru Age* (Vikas Publishing House, Delhi, 1978), which is now out of print, Mathai writes:

'Before I started writing this book, I suspended from my mind all personal loyalties of a conventional nature: only my obligation to history remained.' He rummaged through the Nehruvian era with no inhibitions, tearing apart a host of giants of Indian history, peppering it with salacious details and with a candour that is uncommon in India. Many have questioned the veracity of Mathai's claims, but no counter-evidence has been produced to date. One reason could be that Nehru's private papers are today in the custody of Congress president and head of the Nehru–Gandhi family, Sonia Gandhi.

Apart from his descriptions of India's political landscape the book is also an insight into the powers of a politician's aide. Once, after a scandal about a minister's liaison with a woman became public, Mathai writes, 'I rang up the minister and he came in the afternoon to my office. It was a Saturday when parliament was not in session. He confessed to everything. I gave him a piece of paper and asked him to write out his resignation from the Council of Ministers addressed to the PM. As I dictated slowly, he wrote, "I hereby tender my resignation from the Council of Ministers for personal reasons. I shall be grateful if you will be good enough to forward it to the President for his acceptance."' Mathai then asked the minister to meet him on Monday morning in parliament, along with another member of parliament. When they met, Mathai writes: 'I told the minister that where hormones were concerned I had no right to pass judgement on anyone; but I added, "You have committed the inconceivable folly of entering your name and that of the woman in hotel registers everywhere as 'Mr and Mrs'. Some people have egged her on and sent her to Delhi to blackmail you. I suggest that you buy her silence. Your good friend Malliah [the member of parliament who was accompanying him], I am sure, will succeed in persuading her to quietly go away from Delhi. Malliah should decide the amount to be given to her."' The mistress was silenced, and the minister pleaded his way back into Indian politics and went on to scale greater heights.

In London, sometime between 1947 and 1951, Indian high commissioner V.K. Krishna Menon hosted a reception at India House.

It was attended by the then British prime minister Clement Atlee and others. Mathai writes: 'Nehru stood in a corner, chatting with Lady Mountbatten all the while. Krishna Menon turned to me and said that people were commenting on it and requested me to break in so that Nehru could move about. I told him that I had no locus standi, he was the host and it was his duty to make the PM circulate. Krishna Menon did not have the guts to do the right thing. Two other similar parties were in the offing elsewhere in the next few days, and I did not want a repetition of the PM being glued to one person. Later, in the evening, I sent the PM a handwritten note about the incident which, I said, resulted in unfavourable comment and needless gossip. I did not wish to embarrass him by talking to him personally about this matter. He was too big a man to take my note amiss. It had the desired effect and the other two parties went off well.'

After Mathai resigned, Nehru admitted: 'My broad appreciation of Mr Mathai was of efficiency, integrity and loyalty, at any rate loyalty to me; but also a person who acted foolishly often in small matters; and sometimes rather threw his weight about. But I never doubted his integrity and I have had no reasons since.'

No one in the Nehru household would have expected Mathai to write about the many things he had silently heard and witnessed. Mathai said Feroze Gandhi, Indira's husband and father of Rajiv and Sanjay, 'could not be accused of possessing any eagerness for studies. Throughout his life he retained the handwriting of a child.' He also wrote about Feroze's affairs with various women.

Mathai's two books – the second book is *My Days with Nehru* – are peppered with stories of India's most towering personalities, their petty clashes, affairs, rumours, paramours and all. He even claimed to have burnt some of Mahatma Gandhi's personal papers that had been handed over to Nehru after the Mahatma was assassinated in 1948. By Mathai's own admission, among the papers were details of Nehru's sister Vijaya Lakshmi Pandit's elopement with Syed Hussain, a charismatic journalist who died in Egypt years later, lonely and broken-hearted.

But it was in his writings about Indira Gandhi that Mathai was at his most damaging. 'It was amusing and pathetic to see her attempting to put herself two steps higher than her father while she was Prime Minister. Poor fish! I suppose most women are overburdened by illusions.'

Among the most controversial legacies he left behind was a chapter titled 'She'. Many argue that it wasn't written by him. I met with one of the key players in the publication of Mathai's books. He told me that the chapter was indeed part of the original manuscript that Mathai had sent from Madras through a lawyer friend who lived in Delhi. However, Mathai's publisher, Narendra Kumar, who was then with Vikas Publishing, was not keen on publishing the chapter, and returned it.

'She' contained many lurid details about what Mathai claimed was his over-a-decade-long intimate affair with Indira Gandhi. There is little evidence to corroborate Mathai's claims or to trash them as fantasy.

In 1981, when Mathai died of a heart attack in Madras at the age of seventy-two, the *New York Times* called him 'one of the most powerful Indian officials during the Nehru era'.

Mathai, who crossed every boundary that may have been set for personal assistants, had a peaceful enough end. Not all have been so lucky.

In 1993, the minority government of prime minister P.V. Narasimha Rao deployed every possible strategy to garner support in parliament as it struggled to hold on to power. Among the political manoeuvres was giving huge bribes to Opposition members who were willing to be bought. Four MPs from Jharkhand Mukti Morcha (JMM), a regional party, took bundles of cash to vote in favour of the government.

As word began to spread about the fortune that the MPs had landed, many in their camp began to bargain for their share. Among them was Shashi Nath Jha, private secretary to JMM chief Shibu Soren. By the next summer, Jha had disappeared. After years of investigation, CBI exhumed his remains from a village near Ranchi in 1998 and accused Shibu Soren, among others, of murdering Jha.

The fear of retribution, including death, is all too real for the assistant. During my research, I met an old man who was, for a few decades, personal assistant to one of the country's senior-most members of parliament. After endless cups of tea, he opened up. That both of us shared a mother tongue, Malayalam, helped.

He told me about a round of bribes – not the one that resulted in Jha's murder – that was being circulated in New Delhi for the survival of another minority government. One evening, the government's agents landed up at the MP's official residence with a huge bag full of cash. After the visitors took their leave, the MP and our narrator locked the gate, shut all the doors and windows of the ageing white mansion. They broke the tiled floor of the house and dug the ground beneath. 'We kept the bag in a hole, spread sand over it and cemented it,' he recalled. To hide the amateur cementing, they pulled an old carpet over it.

After the new government survived the confidence vote in parliament, and the political dust settled, the floor of the bedroom was dug again. The cash bag was taken by road to the MP's hometown hundreds of kilometres from New Delhi, accompanied by the leader himself and his security guards. A distillery was constructed with the money.

'You are now retired, far from all that chaos. Why don't you tell me all your experiences on record?' I asked.

'I am old. I want a peaceful death,' he said.

3

Arms and the Middleman

It was a powerful Indian defence delegation that landed at the Ben Gurion International Airport on the outskirts of Tel Aviv that day in November 2008. Defence Secretary Vijay Singh, the senior-most civil servant in the Ministry of Defence (MoD), was leading the delegation, and among its members was a future air force chief, Air Marshal N.A.K. Browne. The delegation was in Israel to review the terms of pre-negotiated deals and to discuss new opportunities for collaboration. On their radar was a proposal to jointly develop a new family of medium-range surface-to-air missiles (MR-SAM) for the Indian Air Force based on the Barak-8 missile system, already under development for the Indian Navy.

The delegation was whisked away by a group of senior officers from Israel's MoD. The warm reception was symbolic of the unusual strengthening of India–Israel relations since both sides established formal diplomatic contact in 1992. Though India had recognized Israel in 1950, New Delhi was cautious. In principle, India was opposed to a religious state, primarily because of its own experience of Partition in 1947, and there were concerns regarding the sensitivities of its large Muslim population. Indians, including Mahatma Gandhi, sympathized with the Palestinian cause – the exception being Hindu zealots who staunchly supported the creation of a Jewish state.

In recent decades, business considerations rather than emotional politics have driven India–Israel relations. The defence delegation's visit was of crucial importance to Israeli defence firms, whose fortunes had come to rely heavily on Indian orders. The world's largest importer of military ware by the second decade of the twenty-first century, the Indian military accounts for almost 50 per cent of Israel's foreign military sales. India has placed over Rs 60,000 crore worth of orders with Israel's defence and space firms starting in 1999, when Israel had quickly and quietly assisted India in the Kargil war.

The delegation was driven to the city centre and checked into a luxury hotel. An officer who was part of the delegation told me that he picked up the briefing folder kept on the study table in the hotel room and began to leaf through it. Among the many papers was a white envelope that contained a wad of $100 bills, easily amounting to several thousand dollars.

'What is this?,' he asked his liaison officer, who had been deputed by the Israeli government.

'Sir, for your local expenses,' he responded without missing a beat.

My contact, generally known for his integrity, told me that he returned it promptly to the liaison officer. 'Throughout the trip no one discussed the envelope. I didn't feel like asking the others what they had done with theirs,' he recalled a few months later, as we sat in his office in New Delhi's imposing South Block complex, which houses the offices of the prime minister, and those of the defence and external affairs ministries. Not that a few thousand dollars was a significant amount by the standards of the Indian defence sector.

Though I had known the officer for a long time, we were now meeting to discuss a set of questions I had sent him a few days earlier. I wanted to quiz him about the haste with which Dr Manmohan Singh's government had signed a deal worth almost Rs 10,000 crore for joint development of the MR-SAM to defend against aerial intrusions. This was one of the business deals the delegation had discussed a few months earlier in Israel. The deal contained an unusual 6 per cent 'business charges' and many other skewed clauses, and was concluded just days ahead of the announcement of the Indian elections of 2009.

After initial efforts at giving me a formal explanation, he finally admitted how complex defence deals were and how pervasive was corruption. 'The only thing you can do here is to ensure you are clean and the file is clean. You cannot control anything else,' he said. That was when he told me about their trip to Israel to finalize the MR-SAM deal and other projects, where he was offered the more-than-generous cash 'stipend'. As I stood up to leave, the officer had two requests: not to drag him into any controversy and, more importantly, not to forget 'national interests'.

National interest can be interpreted in many ways in New Delhi's circles of power. It could mean the causes espoused by sectarian interests, or the high moral ground taken by the corrupt to cover their tracks. National interest can also be an excuse to clamp draconian colonial-era rules on those trying to bring in transparency.

In modern India, national interests are served by men and women who operate below the radar, ensuring that multi-billion-dollar deals in various sectors are not derailed, and that the Indian economy continues to spend and expand. Ensuring that a clean deal goes through is a difficult game and a corrupt deal is even more complex. This means that even the most transparent Western firms operating in sectors such as defence, construction, highways, power, oil and natural gas are forced to engage people who have a deep knowledge of the systems. These are the players who will deploy tactics, often illegal, to ensure that the company wins lucrative contracts.

Professional middlemen manage and manipulate huge contracts, run large offices, hire retired government officers and other such experts to manage the system, and are on a first-name basis with not just Indian leaders but many key players around the world. They have offices not just in India, but in cities around the globe. These are people who have sophisticated financial strategies to cover their tracks, who might be among the biggest account holders in many of the tax havens of the world.

They are also the least known players in the Indian system – and the most important. They play a critical role in sustaining many Indian political parties by pumping them with black money, yet do not figure in the list of their donors. Even if criminal cases are registered against them, the most credible evidence will eventually just disappear into thin air.

These are not the political fixers down the street or typists guarding their bosses but men, and occasionally women, who can swing multi-billion-dollar deals, manipulate files and procurements throw governments out and swing global opinions. The most powerful middlemen in India sometimes decide the very fate of the country's democracy.

At the highest levels, middlemen can make or break a company's prospects in the market. From the moment a contract proposal is prepared, the middleman's influence is visible. The parameters detailed in a bid are often tweaked to qualify their client; trials are manipulated to bring up their client to the list of winners; negotiations are deftly manoeuvred to the best possible situation for the client; and the final parameters ensure that political decisions go the right way. Not everyone involved in the selection is on the payrolls of the agent. However, at every stage, there are key people on the take. For those who do their bidding, the rewards are huge – scholarships for their children in famous Western universities, sports coaching camps for children in foreign locales, a villa in Portugal, millions stashed in a secret account in a tax haven, and much else.

To understand these powerful middlemen, one must shed preconceived notions about intermediaries in a free market. This is not just someone doing quantifiable work, like assisting a client to make sense of the market or identify the best partners, help efficient transfer of technology, protect intellectual properties, complete legal requirements, or otherwise assist in navigating the system. In India, that aspect is only a small part of the intermediary's work – the key engagement is beyond it, and below the radar. He must ensure that the system keeps working, a contract is not scuttled, decisions are taken in time and a particular company wins a contract.

In short, he must ensure that the government keeps running in the sinister and corrupt way that has become the norm. It would be no exaggeration to say that these powerful intermediaries play a critical role in ensuring that the Indian government does not grind to a halt, its armed forces modernize regularly, that highways are constructed, and the economy keeps growing at a robust rate rather than stagnate. In a perverse way, these middlemen are the answer to an inept and stagnating government.

The middleman, or intermediary, is actually a legitimate function in any modern economy. The defence industry is a particularly good example to understand what differentiates an Indian middleman from his counterparts in most other economies. In this sector, the intermediary normally provides a set of legitimate and important services, mostly to a foreign company that finds it difficult to navigate the procurement process of the host country. He could, for instance, be assisting a small firm which cannot afford to open a dedicated office in a country that is carrying out small-sized procurement. In most countries, offsets – stipulation to procure or spend a significant part of a contract in the buyer country – are integral to defence contracts, and a local intermediary plays an important role in executing them. These intermediaries are paid legitimate fees, and often a part of their fee is built into the contract making them offset or maintenance partners.

There is another critical function to be carried out in a fiercely competitive economy, which is to ensure that a company's views, not always wrong, are heard and understood by decision makers. For this function, the United States of America has a flourishing lobbying industry, and several economies officially permit lobbying with the government. Their task is not to pay bribes or manipulate, at least not officially.

In the Indian economy, middlemen play out their roles in the dingy back rooms of decision making. They carry bribes, pay whoever needs to be paid, intimidate someone if required, and ensure that their clients have insider information on a contract from the very beginning of the process. They provide undue and unfair advantage. India has no formally recognized lobbying industry, nor does it allow agents in government contracts. But influential middlemen are an essential ingredient in any major government contract.

Some of India's richest businessmen make their big profits playing the role of intermediaries. It is not uncommon for a foreign diplomat or executive to ask one about a particular industrialist – quite likely, he has offered his services to help swing a mega deal. At the highest echelons of Indian decision making, it is hard to figure out who is a mere middleman and who is a mere industrialist.

Consider the mining industry. A company cannot be successful in the mining sector unless it manages a whole cast of actors, across governments and regulatory bodies in local and national politics. Ujjal Kumar Upadhaya (also written as Upadhyaya) is a little-known businessman based in Kolkata. But, at one point, he controlled an astonishing 1.7 billion tonnes of coal deposits through his company EMTA (originally called the Eastern Mineral and Trading Agency), the third largest reserve of coal in India. The way he has come to dominate coal mining in India is part of local lore. Upadhaya stitched up joint ventures with mining utilities run by state governments and managed to secure a monopolistic status in most regions where his company operated. The Indian CEO of a global mining company once met Upadhaya regarding a major project that had been stalled. The CEO recalled, 'He was very warm, but also clear that we wouldn't be able to get the mine operational without pleasing everyone in the food chain.' Upadhaya had dropped into the CEO's office on the advice of a mutual contact. He made an offer to the CEO: take on the contract and hand it over, and Upadhaya in return would pay a fixed profit to the global giant.

Why was Upadhaya keen on running a mine, and how was he confident of offering a fixed profit to the licence holder? There may be no clear answers. It could well be that he was confident of his capacity to manage the Indian system and run a smooth business. Some mining sector insiders point to the lucrative smuggling of coal within India and to Bangladesh and Nepal, and a deliberate downgrading of the quality of coal to boost profits. There are other manipulations too that bring windfall profits. As he took his leave, Upadhaya told the CEO that he could get support at the topmost rung of the Central government. Perhaps that was a boast, but there is no denying the influence people like Upadhaya wield in the Indian economy.

When I was ushered in to meet a senior official of a European military consortium on an afternoon in February 2009, he was already a little high on wine and a little low because of the Indian heat. We were an earshot away from the thunderous take-offs and landings of the world's leading fighter aircraft at Aero India, a biennial aviation exhibition in Bangalore, now called Bengaluru. All the major aircraft manufacturers were present to exhibit their latest to impress India, which had put out a Rs 60,000 crore contract to acquire 126 fighters for the Indian Air Force. Taking off and landing with fury were the finest and most expensive fighters in the world: F-18s and F-16s from the United States, MIG-35 jets from Russia and Euro fighters made by a European consortium. A host of business and transport jets were also vying for the attention of potential buyers. Aero India has become one of the world's largest aviation shows, thanks to the country's status as the largest importer of military-ware and its growing club of billionaires who prefer private transport in the sky.

The European official had known me for some time and was relaxed and open. He was visibly upset about the failure of his consortium to win a major contract in India for almost a decade. 'I would blame it all on Choudhrie,' he declared. Their long association with Sudhir Choudhrie had come to a bitter end because a haughty senior executive in the company had not liked the methods and practices of the most powerful arms dealer in India. The European executive was not the first, and definitely not the last, to confide his fear of, and loathing for, Choudhrie.

Yet, since they cannot overtly engage in back-room negotiations, power brokers such as Choudhrie become critical. Almost every foreign firm operating in India has middlemen assisting them in some form or the other. Some of them, fearful of backlash and punishment back home, are careful not to be seen to be engaging middlemen. Instead they deploy expensive consultants, or structure their bribes through layers, via trusts and tax havens.

Firms from countries where anti-corruption laws are relatively lax tend to be opaque, because they can run their business without too much fear of prosecution by their respective governments. Not surprisingly, they tend to be among the foreign firms that most often pocket the big government contracts.

The middlemen operating at the highest levels of the Indian economy enjoy monopoly, if not complete control, over the sectors they operate in. The huge resources at their command give them the power to prop up governments and political parties. Senior civil servants who are not corrupt say that all they can do is ensure that they remain clean personally. The CEO of a foreign defence firm told me once that he had to spend a million US dollars just to get an appointment with a defence minister some years ago.

Every aspect of economy – and not the defence sector alone – where the government has a role is trapped in the crushing embrace of high-level corruption. The defence sector, however, is most instructive in our attempt to understand the power, influence and growth of powerful middlemen like Choudhrie.

Let's begin with a brief history of India's military modernization.

Since Independence, India has been heavily import-dependent for defence equipment, and in the initial decades, up until it collapsed in the early 1990s, most of the purchases were from the Soviet Union. In the next decade, India did not make many purchases. Then the Kargil conflict with Pakistan in 1999 churned things up. India went back to the global arms bazaar with such vengeance that, by 2012, it had become the world's largest importer of arms. Arms dealers flourished, weaving cosy relationships with political leaders, senior military and civil officials, as well as other stakeholders in the system. There has been much speculation about where they meet, how they benefit and how such huge kickbacks are moved around. To date, no Indian investigation agency has been able to nail a major arms dealer or senior official for paying bribes or accepting them. Many big names have been dragged into public scandals in the defence sector, but none went so far as conviction.

This is surprising in a country where a single defence scandal dramatically changed the political landscape in the 1980s. On 16 April 1987, a Swedish newspaper broke a story alleging that artillery manufacturer Bofors had paid kickbacks to people in several countries, including Sweden and India, to secure a Rs 1,500 crore contract the previous year from the Indian Army to supply 410 155-mm calibre howitzer guns. Those close to the incumbent prime minister, Rajiv Gandhi, were accused of receiving kickbacks. In the huge political upheaval that followed, the Congress party lost the 1989 election by a significant margin. However, it has had no visible impact on India's voracious appetite for foreign military-ware.

By 2012, India had displaced China as the world's biggest importer of arms, as the Middle Kingdom took a sharp turn towards self-reliance. According to the Stockholm International Peace Research Institute (SIPRI) – the most dependable assessment data available – India's share of the volume of international arms imports increased from 7 per cent to 14 per cent during 2009–13 compared to the previous five years. Informal estimates say that India could end up spending around Rs 6,70,000 crore on importing arms during this decade alone.

Indigenous military production accounts for a pitiful 30 per cent of the country's total armament requirements. The Indian government's Defence Research and Development Organization (DRDO) has been a massive failure, despite the eulogies that the political and bureaucratic class regularly pay it. It has not been able to successfully master a single major military platform, except missiles. India does not have an indigenous battle tank or a fighter aircraft, both mainstays of its military operations.

Military manufacturing here has insipid factories churning out crude products and working at the lowest end of the value chain. The few sophisticated systems that they make involve importing parts from abroad, assembling them into systems and stamping their tag on it. A few private players are now beginning to take baby steps in the weapons manufacturing industry, but it is too early to assess their effectiveness.

The abject failure of its indigenization efforts, combined with the recurring conflicts India has had to deal with – several with Pakistan, one with China, and the many insurgencies – is what has turned the country's military into a highly sought-after shopper in the international arms market. Many firms in the United States, Israel and Europe, including Russia, have come to depend on Indian orders to sustain their profits. These foreign companies, in turn, need deal makers to ensure that the procurement process stays on track and to provide them with the smokescreen of deniability regarding the paying of bribes.

In the corridors of the MoD, most officials speak of Choudhrie with reverence. A former defence secretary recalled that someone once wanted to introduce him to a certain 'Mr Choudhary' at a party. 'I didn't know which Choudhary it was, but for a moment I was mortified,' he said. While Choudhary is a common surname, the unusually spelt Choudhrie bothers are honest officials.

Choudhrie's footprints can be found in arms sales not just in India, but also in China, Indonesia, Israel, several European nations and in some African countries. In Israel, the state has used court interventions to prevent journalists from writing about him.

He is admired – and loathed – not just for his ability to swing deals, but also for scuttling those of his clients' competitors.

In December 2007, when a European firm was just a few days away from signing a deal to supply helicopters to the Indian military, the order was summarily cancelled. Unsubstantiated media reports claimed that there were agents involved and deviations from technical stipulations. Much later, two of the senior officials on the deal admitted to me that they were tricked into cancelling the deal by a mid-rung civil servant handling the issue. 'Once he put down in writing that the media has raised questions over the integrity of the deal, none of us could say anything,' one of them said. 'The golden rule (to protect one's honour) is never question a written comment about the integrity of a decision.'

A few months later, Finmeccanica of Italy ended up winning a lucrative contract to supply twelve helicopters meant to fly India's VVIPs, even though there were significant deviations from tender requirements. Allegations flew thick and fast. Later, it tumbled out that the Italian company had paid several million euros to a network of people, including a former chief of the Indian Air Force, to secure the contract.

Documents filed in February 2013 in an Italian court showed that Finmeccanica's former CEO, Giorgio Zappa, had made an interesting confession. During questioning at the prosecutor's office in Naples on 22 May 2012, Zappa said that Choudhrie – who had been their agent for a long time in India – had been removed recently, only to be replaced by less careful, more garrulous foreigners, who inadvertently exposed the scandal.

The Finmeccanica scandal is not an isolated business malpractice. It is the norm.

Every foreign executive working in India has stories of encounters with middlemen. One American executive, who has worked in India for a decade now, tells me that he is often tempted to write a book about navigating Indian contracts, and reveal the real picture of what goes on and how rampant corruption is.

Another one, who headed a fighter-manufacturing firm in India, said this of his time here: 'I have worked around the world, but there is no market more complex and corrupt than India.' He was leaving the country for good, after unsuccessfully trying to win a major contract in the decade that he spent in the country.

The exact timeline is fuzzy, but many believe that the Choudhrie family's foray into defence deals began sometime in the 1970s. An uncle, Baljit Kapur, who was among the early fighter pilots of the Indian Air Force, was an influential mentor. Kapur left the air force to join Hindustan Aeronautics Limited (HAL), the state monopoly in military aviation that assembled Russian fighters, French helicopters, British Jaguars and other aircraft bought by the Indian military. He rose to become HAL chairman with – media reports of the time speculate – the blessings of the then prime minister Indira Gandhi.

The Choudhrie brothers – Sudhir, Amrit and Rajiv – grew up in socialist India, with its slow growth rates and tight government controls. They realized that there was money to be made by helping companies deal with India's infamous red tape. Their first deal as middlemen is believed to have been a major fighter aircraft contract that the Indian Air Force signed with a European firm in the late 1970s. There are, of course, no documents tracing their involvement – only hearsay and claims by some of those involved in the deal.

Once they entered the big league, the Choudhrie brothers were quick to create a web of contacts across the political, bureaucratic and military hierarchies. Their close friendship with a senior Congress leader, who was a trusted associate of Indira Gandhi, is well known. Sudhir Choudhrie's officially known business associates include Colonel R.S. 'Pickle' Sodhi, a renowned polo player married to former Miss India Nafisa Ali, who has been active in politics.

Secretiveness, indulgence, warmth and force of personality is required for wheeling and dealing in government contracts. Sudhir and Rajiv Choudhrie made a particularly good team. A leading middleman who made his fortunes in the 1980s recalled his impression of the Choudhrie brothers, whom he met now and then at the Delhi Golf Club: 'Rajiv was very warm, but Sudhir was always aloof.'

Rajiv passed away in 1997, but the business did well under Sudhir's care. He courted politicians of all hues, expanded his reach, had some run-ins with the law, moved to London and came to be politically influential in other countries as well.

Choudhrie had a quiet and peaceful run until the summer of 2001, when 'Operation West End' broke. The web news portal *Tehelka* posted secret recordings of military officers, civil servants and politicians to show that Choudhrie was involved in fixing major defence deals. The government of the day, led by the BJP, began a witch-hunt against *Tehelka* instead of the arms dealers. Only after it lost the 2004 elections was the scandal dealt with. In 2006 and 2007, the CBI opened several cases against those who figured in the *Tehelka* revelations, including two against Choudhrie. Not that the new Congress-led government managed to nail Choudhrie.

On 1 February 2006, the CBI filed a preliminary inquiry against, among others, R.K. Jain, the national treasurer of the Samata Party, a regional party led by the then defence minister George Fernandes and Sudhir Choudhrie, director of Magnum International Trading Company. It would investigate anomalies in the army contract for the upgrading of 130-mm field guns to 155-mm calibre with kits imported from Israeli defence contractor Soltam Systems. The total contract was worth a little over Rs 208.15 crore. By April 2007, the inquiry became a full-fledged criminal investigation.

In December 1992, Soltam had submitted a proposal to the Indian MoD, offering to upgrade the field guns. The upgrade would have helped the army standardize ammunition that was produced under licence from Bofors, which would, in turn, have reduced the cost of operations, provided greater range for the guns and increased lethality. The government began reviewing the proposal without the requisite open tender process. From then on, Choudhrie was at work, or so the CBI suspected.

The FIR that the CBI filed was a rare graphic description in an official document on high-level corruption. It is crucial for understanding why people like Choudhrie get paid staggering commissions in such contracts. They ensure that the government toes their client's line, scuttle mandated procedures and keep the contract on track in the face of opposition.

The FIR said that the trial gun sent by Soltam was 'an untested and unproven prototype'. At the Pokhran firing ranges in Rajasthan, where India had carried out nuclear tests, the gun achieved a range of 39 kilometres with its own ammunition, but with the Bofors ammunition, the range was only 29.5 kilometres. The trial team also reported various problems during the firing. 'The various wings of the Army, including the DRDO, raised serious objections and stressed the need for modification of the Soltam gun and another round of comprehensive confirmatory trials after such modifications,' it said.

However, all these warnings and recommendations were ignored and an evaluation report was prepared and accepted. Proposals from companies in erstwhile Yugoslavia, the Czech Republic, Slovakia, Austria, Finland and South Africa 'were rejected on one pretext or other' by the army and the MoD, the FIR said. 'No effort was made to shortlist the various possible sources and a single vendor situation was deliberately created,' it alleged. Choudhrie's fingerprints were all over the deal.

The other offers were better and more affordable, but the army and MoD officials pursued the Soltam offer. On 12 July 1999, the BJP-led National Democratic Alliance (NDA) government's highest decision-making body, the Cabinet Committee on Security, chaired by the then prime minister Atal Behari Vajpayee, approved the proposal. Among other fabrications, it falsely claimed that the gun was capable of firing the Bofors ammunition to the stipulated range. The CBI accused army headquarters of using incorrect facts to justify the pricing to the Cabinet Committee. It did not say, however, if the senior ministers of the day were aware that they were approving blatant lies.

On 7 March 2000, a contract was signed with Soltam. The CBI claimed that Choudhrie received over Rs 67,00,000 as commission from Soltam for the contract worth Rs 208.15 crore. That was, of course, only the amount that the CBI managed to track; the total commission would have been much higher. In defence deals in India, the average commission for middlemen can go up to 10–11 per cent of the total deal. The central investigation agency claimed that 'unknown officials of the Indian Army and the MoD abused their official position and entered into criminal conspiracy' with Choudhrie and others.

By 2010, though, the CBI sang a different tune before a trial court, where it said there was no evidence to prosecute Choudhrie and others in the case. The CBI also indulged in some odd obfuscation. Choudhrie's payments from Soltam were 'received in pursuance to an agreement executed in London in June 1999 by which MITCO (Choudhrie's firm) was appointed to represent Soltam and promote their products – electric and non-electric stainless steel kitchen utensils'.

I am yet to meet anyone who is aware of Choudhrie's deals in the kitchen utensils business.

Months later, in August 2011, the judge closed the case. Almost two months later, intelligence agencies reported that Choudhrie, who had shifted base permanently to London sometime in 2006, made his first known visit to India in years.

It was much the same story in another high-profile CBI investigation in which Choudhrie's name allegedly figured, though only indirectly. His relative and former business partner, and another of India's formidable arms agents, Suresh Nanda, was named accused in the FIR related to the Barak missile scandal filed on 9 October 2006. Nanda is a former naval officer and the son of one of India's most celebrated navy chiefs.

In the Barak FIR, the CBI said that Choudhrie and his companies, including Magnum International and Eureka Sales Corporation, had a close business relationship with Israel Aerospace Industries, which was the primary supplier of the Barak anti-missile system for the Indian Navy. The FIR alleged that Choudhrie's companies 'have received a number of suspected remittances to the tune of millions of dollars from M/s IAI, Israel during the year(s) 1998 to 2001'. What it did not say was that Magnum International was a company in which both the Choudhries and Nanda were shareholders.

Despite the high-profile nature of the case, and what the CBI then claimed as credible evidence, by December 2013, the agency was once again shutting the case down, claiming it could not find any substantial evidence to prove the alleged conspiracy. Though this was typical of CBI investigations, it was truly surprising that no one else raised any questions about the case, not even the Opposition. Ironically, the Opposition – led by the BJP at this time – was in the middle of an aggressive campaign against the ruling coalition for widespread corruption, but remained unusually silent on this case.

The Nanda family – perhaps even more than the Choudhries – captures the all-on-sale ethics of Indian society.

Admiral Sardarilal Mathradas Nanda was born in British India on Manora Island outside the port city of Karachi. After working for the harbour authority of Karachi, he joined the British navy during World War II. When India became independent, he opted to be part of its navy and held several important positions. He was elevated to the post of chief of naval staff in March 1970, and led the force to a glorious victory during the 1971 war, which resulted in the liberation of Bangladesh from Pakistan. But in 1987, almost fifteen years after he retired from service, Nanda was accused of being an arms dealer.

In 1999, his grandson Sanjeev Nanda became the news. Sanjeev drove a newly imported BMW car over several people in Delhi early in the morning of 10 January 1999 while returning from a party. Six people died. In court, the young man's high-profile lawyers argued that it was not Nanda's car that mowed down those people.

On 30 May 2007, the news channel NDTV ran a hidden-camera operation showing defence lawyer R.K. Anand and public prosecutor I.U. Khan working to win over a key witness to the accident, so that he would lie in court and save Sanjeev. This was a rare glimpse into how even the courts can be deflected for the right fee. Lawyers on both sides can collude, politicians across the spectrum can come together, as long as you have the right amount of money to fork out.

Over the years, Suresh Nanda, his son Sanjeev, and the rest of the family have lived the life they wanted, hosting lavish parties, hobnobbing with political, military and bureaucratic top brass and ignoring the law. They are often to be found in a hundred-year-old colonial bungalow only a few hundred metres from the parliament. They also own one of the city's most celebrated hotels, the Claridges, where diplomats enjoy special concessions, and Indian street food has been elevated to gourmet levels. Even their purchase of the hotel from T.N. Khanna's family over a decade ago was made possible by money funnelled through Mauritius, a tax haven preferred by India's murky rich – among them Sudhir Choudhrie.

Whenever the law threatens to catch up with the Nandas, they seem to merely buy their way out of trouble. On 8 March 2008, Suresh and

Sanjeev and their chartered accountant, Bipin Shah, were caught passing on a bribe to income-tax officer Ashutosh Verma in a room in Mumbai's Marriott Hotel. A few days earlier, the CBI's surveillance team had caught on camera the income-tax officer admitting that his lifelong earnings could not have matched even 10 per cent of what he got for helping the Nandas suppress their tax obligations. When the story broke, the memory of the Nandas' efforts at buying off the Indian legal system in the car crash case a few months ago was still fresh. Once again, public outrage washed over them; once again, it left them untroubled.

The fact that they can operate with impunity in spite of the criminal cases lodged against them is almost surreal. Everyone has known what the Nanda family's real business is ever since the HDW defence scandal broke in 1987 and central agencies raided Admiral S.M. Nanda and others, accusing the war hero of being an arms dealer.

Officials of the German firm HDW, who were then supplying diesel submarines to the Indian Navy, had confirmed to the Indian ambassador in West Germany that they had paid a commission to the Nandas and some others to secure the submarine deal. Central investigators, including the CBI, raided Admiral Nanda's home as well as the properties of other family members, and charged them with receiving kickbacks. When I met Admiral Nanda sometime in early 2000, in an overheated room in his mansion in Defence Colony, he told me that his rivals had taken revenge on him by sending the investigators to his house when a family celebration was under way. He spoke of the editor of my newspaper with great affection. It turned out that the London edition of the newspaper for which I worked was owned by the Nandas.

The HDW case dragged on in the courts, reached the Supreme Court of India, and was finally closed fifteen years later with the CBI saying it had no concrete evidence to prosecute the Nandas. No surprises there. In the 1980s, the HDW allegations, along with the Bofors scandal, kicked up India's first true national outrage against corruption. It quite possibly changed the course of politics for years, wiping out the dominance of the Congress party and creating the new narrative of coalition politics comprising smaller regional parties. In 2014, when Prime Minister Narendra Modi swept to office, ending the three-decade old dominance of coalition politics, another round of national outrage over corruption and public immorality had a big role to play in his success.

In recent years, digitization has opened up new avenues for journalists and researchers to look back at transactions that are several decades old, see through the secrecy of tax havens and global conspiracies, and provide fresh narratives about what really happened in the dark corners. Digitization is also dramatically altering the way investigative journalism is done. It is not surprising that the major global scoops of recent years have centred on digital databases supplied by whistle-blowers.

Like many of my contemporaries, I have been trying to figure out how databases in several countries can speak to each other, and track money trails and see if new narratives can be found. I often spend days and much money trying to map the trail of financial transactions. In one of those searches, some friends in Europe guided me to startling details that raise disturbing questions about the way the HDW scandal was investigated and closed by the Indian agencies.

What I found about the Nanda family's business dealings in London and elsewhere in Europe demand that the CBI reopen the HDW investigation and look at the fresh evidence that is available. A host of official documents I accessed from an official database of the European tax haven of Liechtenstein, a rich German-speaking Alpine principality, and London reveal an interesting story that the Nandas have never narrated in public, and the CBI was either not aware of or deliberately ignored.

The sum of my findings is that the Nanda family has been the financial beneficiary of an establishment set up in Liechtenstein in 1987, the Mandura Anstalt, around the time HDW representatives told the Indian ambassador that they had paid a commission to middlemen. An establishment, or *anstalt*, is an autonomous fund under Liechtenstein laws whose founders need not be the beneficiaries. This means that Company A can park money in an establishment and Mr B can draw all the money from it.

The commission in the HDW deal, the representatives had said, was 7 per cent of the $380 million contract, which would have worked out to Rs 32.55 crore (approximately $36 million based on the 1981 exchange rate).

Who started the Liechtenstein anstalt and how much money came into it are not known – at least I could not figure it out. But some money from the anstalt was used to buy a property in an upscale London neighbourhood. The Nandas have claimed it as their official residence in filings with the British government over the years. Trusts or anstalts started in Liechtenstein in later years were also used by the Nandas to fund two companies in the UK, as well as to buy a second property. It is not clear if the money from the trusts was used for any other activity.

This information – available to me after just a few days of exploring financial databases – raises very uncomfortable questions about the quality of the CBI's investigation into one of India's most high-profile scandals. It also most definitely calls for reopening the investigation into the HDW bribery allegations, as well as into the financial transactions of the Nandas, moving money into India.

The trail of cash payment from mysterious entities in a tax haven for the purchase of properties in various cities around the world is hardly a singular phenomenon. If anything, it is a growing trend. An investigation in November 2012 by *The Guardian* and the International Consortium of Investigative Journalists showed that 'anonymous buyers are taking over more and more blocks of luxury housing, particularly in the capital [London]'. They were all using tax havens to route money. 'In 2011 alone, more than £7 billion of offshore money flooded into potentially tax-exempt purchases of UK houses, flats and office blocks. Most buyers snapped up property in central London, helping to explain why prices there have defied the recession,' the investigation said. It found that the majority of these buyers used British Virgin Islands (BVI), a major tax haven that is popular among Indians and accounted for £3.8 billion of the total deals in 2011. BVI is, in fact, a favourite stash location for Sudhir Choudhrie's earnings as well. Most of the Choudhrie family's companies in the UK are owned by Harberry Investments, based in BVI, according to their filings in the country. However, it is in a tiny island, closer home to India, that most stories of machinations by the Indian rich lie.

Mauritius is a little island nation of over a million people and just one-hundredth the size of the Indian economy, but it has been the biggest source of foreign direct investment to India for years. This bizarre trend has flourished thanks to Mauritius's own secretive financial regime and a bilateral tax agreement, the Double Taxation Avoidance Agreement, which allows all investments from Mauritius to enter tax-free into India. Many foreign investors and several Indians have set up companies on paper only in Mauritius and use it for tax avoidance and moving money around. It is no surprise then that most of Choudhries' and the Nandas' businesses in India have significant investments from Mauritius.

In 2003, Suresh Nanda and his family bought Claridges Hotels and have since expanded the business. Apart from its flagship hotel in New Delhi, it operates hotels and resorts in the national capital region, in the Himalayan hill station of Mussoorie and near the Bharatpur bird sanctuary in Rajasthan.

Over the years, Claridges Hotels has seen several million rupees coming into it from a Mauritius-based firm, Universal Business Solutions. In 2007, Universal Business Solutions acquired shares, of face value Rs 10, at a premium of Rs 2,390. In January 2009, it acquired another lot of shares in Claridges Hotels at a premium of Rs 3,690.

In a very similar pattern, Choudhrie has also brought significant amounts of money brought into India to start a very successful construction company, to fund a defence firm, to build luxury hotels and so on.

Despite the care taken by these players, details of their dealings spill over sometimes. On a tip-off from a civil servant, I spent several months tracking one of the Choudhrie family's business deals, and what I discovered was probably a unique instance: documented evidence of transactions between a powerful military leader and an alleged arms dealer.

According to the trail that I was able to establish while working on this book, in 2005–06, the family of former army chief (1990–93) and then Punjab governor, General Sunith Francis Rodrigues, sold one of their companies to a firm promoted by Choudhrie. The deal happened when Choudhrie and his firms were under investigation by the CBI for their alleged involvement in manipulating arms deals in India.

In transactions between 2005 and 2007, the value of a plot owned by a company of General Rodrigues, Zuari River Agrotech, was valued upwards almost a hundred times. Zuari was originally started by General Rodrigues in 1994 with the name Zuari Tigers Aqua. He held ten shares and another retired army officer, Captain Anil Bhalla, held a single share. Zuari had a plot of land valued at Rs 19.78 lakh. In 2005–06 Zuari claimed an addition to its assets, by revaluing the land to Rs 9.06 crore.

On 17 February 2006, Zuari was amalgamated with Crystal Island Park, a company started by the former army chief's son, Mark Rodrigues. All assets, liabilities and reserves of Zuari were taken over at their book value of Rs 10.88 crore by Crystal Island Park.

Within days of the amalgamation, its ownership was transferred to a company called Grandeur Real Estate. On 22 April 2006, Mark transferred his 1,29,030 shares in Crystal Island Park to Grandeur Real Estates; his minority partner Ashok Chawla also transferred his 20,970 shares. Thus, the full ownership and control of Crystal Island Park was given to Grandeur Real Estate, a company in which Sudhir Choudhrie, his son Bhanu and nephew Dhruv had been directors since 25 August 2005. Grandeur was started in 2004 with 99.98 per cent capital brought in through Mauritius.

According to annual returns filed by Crystal Island Park, after its annual general meeting on 23 June 2006, Sudhir, Bhanu and Dhruv Choudhrie, and some of their business associates, came on board as directors.

In 2006–07 Alpha G: Corp Development Private Limited, the flagship company of Choudhrie and his business associates in real estate, acquired shares in Grandeur Real Estates and became the ultimate holding company of Crystal Island Park. Alpha G: Corp has extensive interests and construction activities in Punjab, Haryana and other states. At the time these transactions were being formalized, General Rodrigues was the governor of Punjab (2004–10).

During 2005–06 and 2006–07, Crystal Island Park also received Rs 4.36 crore unsecured loans from Grandeur Real Estate. Crystal Island Park paid Rs 1.75 crore to Mark, who said it was the payment for cleaning up the 75-acre site, building a pontoon, dredging, etc.

Within a year of the takeover, the land valuation was brought back to Rs 19.78 lakh. The company said in its annual report for 2006–07 that it 'has reclassified its land amounting to Rs 9,05,92,000 from fixed assets to stock in trade at original cost, i.e. Rs 19,78,421'.

When I asked Choudhrie and Rodrigues for clarification, I received aggressive legal notices. Eben Black, head of media and director of DLA Piper, a London-based legal firm that represents Choudhrie, cautioned me not to make 'unfounded and unsubstantiated allegations, which are not only inaccurate but, we believe, deliberately and highly damaging to Mr Choudhrie and his family'. This in itself was a rare occasion: Sudhir Choudhrie's representative was speaking to a journalist on allegations against him. Black said Choudhrie 'strongly denies that he has ever been involved in arms dealing'. His client 'does not operate' Alpha G: Corp and is 'only one of the directors'.

Alpha G: Corp, which was rebranded as AlphaCorp by the time I finished writing this book, took over the Rodrigues family firm and officially distanced itself from whatever had happened in the run-up to the takeover, including the increase in asset valuation. Its company secretary Abhay Sharma told me this in a written statement: 'Alpha G: Corp has no knowledge or information of business or transactions of Crystal Island prior to the acquisition of Grandeur. Indeed Grandeur was not at all an Alpha G: Corp Company at the time Grandeur acquired the shares of Crystal Island. Alpha G: Corp came into the picture much later and undertook its acquisition based upon its evaluation of projects and valuation by registered experts. Alpha G: Corp has had no dealings with Mr Mark Rodrigues, either on account of share purchase or dredging activities.'

General Rodrigues, now leading a retired life, said he had no idea either. 'I don't know anything. I was appointed the Punjab governor in 2004 and we were based in Chandigarh. I knew nothing; it was all Mark's business. After all, they live their own lives,' he told me over the phone one evening in 2012.

Mark Rodrigues, now based in New Zealand, said he wasn't aware that the alleged arms dealer was behind the deal. 'We didn't know the Choudhries were involved. His name never came up, and he was never part of the due diligence.' He said Grandeur Real Estate, which bought his firm Crystal Island Park, seemed legitimate. 'We would not have done the deal if we had known that the Choudhries were involved,' Mark said on the phone during an interview in April 2012.

Through a Goa-based lawyer, Mark later responded to my queries saying that the transaction had taken place fourteen years after the retirement of General Rodrigues as army chief. 'He (General Rodrigues) has never been a shareholder, director, manager or employee of the company, and has not been concerned with any decision-making regarding the company. The company itself was set up around six years after he retired as Chief of Indian Army Staff, and therefore any insinuation that it is concerned with arms deals or any similar transaction is entirely incorrect and irresponsible,' Advocate Menino Pereira said on behalf of Mark.

General Rodrigues, on his part, said that to the best of his knowledge his son's sale of Crystal Island Park was a 'straightforward transaction; it doesn't matter if blue, grey or black bought it'. He added, 'I am what you call a "poor chief". I had to work for six years after retirement because we couldn't manage within my pension. It is known to everyone, the whole history speaks for itself.'

The entire transaction happened when General Rodrigues was the governor of Punjab and chief administrator of Chandigarh. It may just be a coincidence, but during this period, Alpha G: Corp had several construction projects under way in the region. Also, Alpha G: Corp was able to resolve a dispute over the conversion of land use and obtained all the necessary clearances for a mega shopping mall in Amritsar. Now, this particular business transaction is a rare one, because it is actually available on record. Traditionally, the dealings of powerful middlemen and their contacts within the government are hard to trace, because they are most often routed through tax havens. Over Rs 20,00,000 crore of global wealth is based or hidden in locations that provide secrecy to the owners of the real wealth and nil or negligible tax liabilities. Estimates show that the majority of accounts in the web of tax havens around the world are either former British colonies, or partly controlled by the United Kingdom.

Money stashed away in tax havens has been a significant political issue in India for a very long time, but no political party has been able to properly investigate it or nail culprits, nor has the CBI made any headway in its inquiries into the issue.

Indeed, the CBI exemplifies India's appalling failure when it comes to tracking high-level corruption.

The agency maintains a classified list of 'Undesirable Contact Men' with whom the government is not supposed to do business, and whom officials are not allowed to entertain. When the agency circulated the list to ministers and senior officials in 2012, there were twenty-three people on it. Sudhir Choudhrie topped the list; just below him was Suresh Nanda. The CBI considered Choudhrie to be among the most powerful people manipulating government decision-making processes in the defence sector. It said that these 'unscrupulous persons should not be accepted as accredited representatives' with government departments. All government departments 'will issue directions to their officers to be careful and cautious in dealings with unscrupulous contact men whose names are on these lists, to avoid associating with them socially and accepting hospitality and gifts from them'. The agency's note said it will 'exercise an unobtrusive check on the activities of such contact men and try to collect information about specific instances of malpractice in which they were involved'; and the departments are also to keep a watch over officials who may deal with these undesirable men and warn the CBI chief of any suspect dealings.

The twenty-three people on the rogues list, however, continue to engage in manipulating various government departments, where contracts are often worth several billion dollars and the fortunes of many multinationals are at stake. Yet, they are only the tip of the iceberg: the list could actually be very, very long if a proper audit of the intersection between business, politics and governments were to be carried out. What empowers these middlemen, what allows them to be so blatant, is the assurance that the Indian economy, especially the government sector, is dependent on them to keep the wheels moving, and the fact that most politicians and civil servants are on their payrolls. They are also comforted by the fact that the Indian criminal justice system is weak, and that they will walk free even if they are caught.

Every time a senior government official's appointment is announced, such as that of chairman of a government-run enterprise or a nationalized bank, there are stories of how much it was worth, and who paid whom on whose behalf. These appointees then grease the wheels of Indian politics and favour industrialists with huge loans and special attention. Corrupt officials are propped up by high-level middlemen, the kind of men who are on that CBI list of undesirable contact men.

Is it surprising then that the CBI has not been able to nail corrupt leaders and bureaucrats and middlemen? In recent times, investigative reportage and analysis of cross-border financial transactions have only reaffirmed the widespread belief that the CBI and other central agencies are at best powerless, at worst mere tools in the hands of a corrupt political establishment. These investigations lay bare the systematic manipulation of public expenditure by middlemen, the erosion of democratic accountability, and the weakening of Indian policy and governance.

In 2012, Vigilance Commissioner R. Sri Kumar cited an internal study to say that the CBI's conviction rate in corruption cases was a shocking 3.96 per cent. The CBI analysed 264 corruption cases in which 698 people were accused, including 486 government officials. On an average, the CBI took more than thirteen months to conclude investigations and just eight out of the total accused were convicted after twenty-six years of investigation and trial, Sri Kumar said. 'There is no certainty of punishment for corruption and that is why corruption has increased,' said Sri Kumar, who, as a member of the Central Vigilance Commission, was officially tasked to supervise the CBI.

Invited to deliver the CBI's annual lecture series on 15 April 2014, Gopalkrishna Gandhi, a respected civil servant and a grandson of Mahatma Gandhi, spoke about public perception of the agency to its 3,000-odd officers. In his characteristically mild manner, he said, 'The CBI has a very mixed image. Not all of it is flattering. It is seen as the government's hatchet, rather than honesty's ally. It is often called DDT – meaning not dichlorodiphenyltrichloroethane, the colourless, tasteless and odourless insecticide it should be – but the "Department of Dirty Tricks".' The investigations are often a joke, and mostly a tragedy. The agency routinely closes cases prematurely for 'lack of evidence'. The few high-profile corruption scandals that the CBI investigated more thoroughly have mostly ended in a humiliating defeat in court. The accused walked away even though the entire system was convinced of their guilt.

Political parties are aware of the simmering anger among the people. Corruption has become a focal point for civil society mobilization as well. Governments, though, have responded to the embarrassing failure of the CBI and other agencies by creating more institutions, rather than putting in place policies to improve the existing ones. In recent years, at least two commissions have been set up to carry out specific investigations – one for terrorism cases, the other for black money.

Every major Indian scandal has a common element: tax havens where kickbacks are exchanged. When it emerged that illegal commissions worth Rs 360 crore were part of the Finmeccanica deal to sell VVIP helicopters to India in 2010, filings in Italian courts revealed that most of the money trail went through tax havens such as Tunisia, Mauritius, Dubai and Singapore.

The practice of siphoning off 'black money' – the illegal earnings of India's rich and powerful – has many dire implications, including a crippling effect on the country's efforts at fighting poverty, illiteracy and other socio-economic challenges, scuttling national security priorities, fleecing the public exchequer and stymieing competition.

The BJP, which was the main Opposition party in 2011, constituted a task force to study the phenomenon of black money and released a report later. The following year, the UPA government presented a white paper on black money in parliament. The presentation of this ninety-seven-page report was among the many actions that the government promised. Finance minister Pranab Mukherjee, who became the thirteenth president of India a year later, admitted in the report: 'There is no doubt that manifestation of black money in social, economic and political space of our lives has a debilitating effect on the institutions of governance and conduct of public policy in the country. Governance failure and corruption in the system affect the poor disproportionately. The success of an inclusive development strategy critically depends on the capacity of our society to root out the evil of corruption and black money from its very foundations. Our endeavour in this regard requires a speedy transition towards more transparent and result-oriented economic management systems in India.'

The white paper quoted a report by the World Bank in July 2010 that estimated 'shadow economies' of 162 countries from 1999 to 2007. It said that the weighted average size of the shadow economy (as a percentage of official GDP) of these countries in 2007 was 31 per cent, compared to 34 per cent in 1999. For India, these figures were 20.7 per cent and 23.2 per cent respectively. The government admitted that its own Department of Industrial Policy and Promotion (DIPP) found that the foreign direct investment from Mauritius between April 2000 and March 2011 was 41.8 per cent of the entire amount received by India.

'It can be seen from this table that the two topmost sources of the cumulative inflows from April 2000 to March 2011 are Mauritius (41.8

per cent) and Singapore (9.17 per cent). Mauritius and Singapore with their small economies cannot be the sources of such huge investments and it is apparent that the investments are routed through these jurisdictions for avoidance of taxes and/or for concealing the identities from the revenue authorities of the ultimate investors, many of whom could actually be Indian residents, who have invested in their own companies, through a process known as round tripping' – that was the government accepting the reality.

The big problem is that there are no reliable estimates on how much is siphoned off, where it comes from, or what proportion of it may be linked to criminal activities. Even the government does not know how much of this black money comes from criminal proceeds and what percentage is 'just' tax avoidance. Many of India's successful businessmen have over the years obtained the status of 'non-resident Indians' to avoid paying income tax and answering uncomfortable questions about their income and investments at home and abroad. According to an estimate by the research agency New World Wealth in March 2016, India saw the fourth-biggest outflow of high-net-worth individuals globally in 2015 with 4,000 millionaires changing their domicile. Ironically, much of the information we have on how the Indian system actually works comes from the result of investigations abroad – the result of foreign firms trying to win contracts in India coming to the attention of authorities back home.

Bribes are spread far and wide, and reach every level of the food chain, from political leaders to the attendants guarding the doors of government offices. With almost everyone benefiting from the largesse, a conspiracy of silence sets in. And that, more than anything else, explains why India's corrupt procurement system rarely sees the emergence of whistle-blowers.

On 28 May 2014, on its first day in office, Prime Minister Narendra Modi's BJP government announced its first significant decision: the constitution of a special investigation team (SIT) led by a retired Supreme Court judge to look into black money. In his high-decibel campaign against the ruling UPA government prior to the general election, Modi's most frequent reference was to black money. He rode the gigantic wave of anti-corruption that had built up around the country. While the movement itself was mostly apolitical and civil-society-driven, Modi was its biggest political beneficiary as he unleashed the most expensive campaign India had ever seen: chartered aircraft, helicopters, holograms, media campaigns, unabashed social media and Internet strategies and the like. It was hardly surprising then that, on his first day in office, Modi announced the setting up of that SIT.

Ironically, the biggest black money case that has come up before the SIT so far is that of the Adani group, promoted by Gautam Adani, one of Modi's closest associates. It is in his chartered aircraft that the soon-to-be prime minister zipped around India, accusing the incumbent government of not fighting corruption. The Adani group allegedly took out over Rs 5,000 crore to tax havens, using inflated bills for the import of power equipment from South Korea and China, the SIT on black money was told by the Directorate of Revenue Intelligence (DRI) and the Enforcement Directorate (ED).

According to a senior ED official associated with the SIT, if the Adani case reaches its logical conclusion, the group will have to pay a fine of around Rs 15,000 crore. 'It is a watertight case,' he said, about the trail of documents showing how the group diverted Rs 5,468 crore to Mauritius via Dubai. The Adani group vehemently denies any wrongdoing. Modi, after his rhetoric-filled ride to power, has been silent.

Since Modi's ascension to office, what has happened in the ED, which had registered a preliminary case against Adani in Ahmedabad and was handed details of DRI findings, is illustrative. The officer heading the Ahmedabad branch of the directorate was raided by the CBI, which accused him of possessing disproportionate assets. It failed to prove anything at all, despite months of investigation. The two senior-most officers in the Mumbai regional office, who oversaw the investigations in Ahmedabad, were forced out of the agency. The tenure of Rajan S. Katoch, who was heading the directorate when the case was opened, also ended abruptly. Apart from the Adani case, the Ahmedabad ED investigators were also pursuing some of the biggest money launderers of Gujarat.

While I cannot prove bad faith in all those abrupt transfers, it must be said that there has been no credible evidence that the Modi government is working to bring back black money to India. Or indeed that it will pursue the biggest black money case yet to emerge here.

4

The Insiders and the Outlaws

I answered the call on my phone. The diplomat sounded frantic; it was important that we meet immediately, she said. It was evening – the most chaotic hours in a newspaper office – and I was rushing to meet a deadline. Still, I paused to wonder about her tone. This was not her way. Till then, she had always contacted me days in advance, and we had met for leisurely lunches.

The next morning, I stopped by at a coffee shop to meet her. She was already waiting.

She started off without the usual pleasantries: 'You know, we are confused. Some people in the government and the party are so enthusiastically backing the deal, we don't know what they are expecting in return.'

Her country was at a very advanced stage of negotiating a multi-billion-dollar deal between the two governments, for which the supplies were to come from private companies. The surprise official announcement of the deal during a summit meeting between the Indian prime minister and his counterpart had set in motion hectic activity. A host of players got into the act: an Indian billionaire who was hoping to do a part of the deal, a high-profile PR executive and various other outsiders.

However, what was surprising to the foreign country, and my diplomat acquaintance, was the overenthusiasm displayed by a couple of key people. One of these was an important functionary of the party in power and was known to enjoy the prime minister's confidence, and the other was a retired government official who had been appointed by the new government to an important post.

The party functionary had voluntarily offered the diplomat's colleagues all-out support for the deal. 'He is very enthusiastically backing the deal, is available to us any time of the day and is following the deal very closely,' she said. The government functionary, meanwhile, insisted on discussing the deal during a visit to the other country. 'We were surprised because it was not his remit. Of course, we were happy,' she admitted.

Yet, all this was also confusing. 'What do they expect in return from us?' The diplomat began to lay down the possible options: are they expecting money for themselves, or the party? Most importantly, how should the topic be broached? 'Should we just go ahead and ask them what they expect? Or, do you know a better way?' Later in the evening, the president of her country was landing in New Delhi for meetings and the embassy was preparing briefing notes. The most crucial agenda on the table was, however, unresolved: they still did not know the kind of bribes that needed to be paid.

I had no answers. But I was familiar with the situation. Even when you have the right intermediaries to reach the right officials and other interested parties, and even when they promise to take care of the interests of the key people in the ruling party and the government, there is always that last hitch when you are trying to swing a large deal with the government. How do you know what the ministers or the key functionaries in the government who are pushing your deal are expecting? How can you be sure that everything the professional intermediary says is true? How can you be sure that the payments will reach the parties they are supposed to? That last question is the one that plagues the senior executives of global companies engaged in business with the Indian government the most.

Imagine that you are one of those executives. You have expensive consultants and middlemen who manage the system for your company. When you need to meet a senior civil servant or a minister, the consultant will arrange it, and you have almost free access to the minister whose department is to award you the contract. The minister even meets you at his official residence and receives you warmly. Will the minister then demand a bribe directly of you? Well, no.

In fact, the minister, indeed any key functionary, will almost never tell you what his demands are, unless he is a rookie in the games of the Indian democracy. That is what his trusted man is for. To get to that trusted man, to know the specific needs of the ultimate powers that be, that is the final obstacle, the most critical aspect of dealing with the government at the highest levels.

The previous chapters of this book were my effort to understand this phenomenon and the middlemen that drive it. To solve the puzzle that is the Indian system, we will now examine an entirely different kind of intermediary. These are the men and women who appear and disappear in New Delhi depending on the party in power.

This is not an easy chapter to write because there is very little evidence available; the people I describe here live entirely in the shadows. However, in New Delhi, on an hourly basis, you hear gossip about the key contacts to a new government. They are the most crucial cogs in the system, the ones who stitch up the final pieces in a deal. These intermediaries tell the professional middlemen and companies involved in a deal how to pay, where to pay, who should benefit and in what proportion. His or her word is final.

There have been a few occasions when the role of such people was recorded by investigation agencies. Of these, the story of an Italian businessman who was a prominent face in New Delhi for over two decades is the best documented.

In 1987, allegations emerged that Bofors had paid bribes to procure an artillery contract from the Indian Army. Among the men who received kickbacks was Mr Q, according to the private diary of the managing director of Bofors, Martin Ardbo. Later, it emerged that Mr Q was Ottavio Quattrocchi, who was based in Delhi as the representative of Snamprogetti, an Italian engineering company that was part of the oil and gas giant Eni.

Evidence soon emerged that in the tender floated by the Indian Army in 1984 to buy howitzer guns, it was the French Sofma gun that was probably on top of the selection list. The then army chief too favoured it. However, the contract went to Bofors, overruling the army – that is what Quattrocchi was capable of pulling off in New Delhi in the 1980s.

Born in fascist Italy just before World War II broke out, Quattrocchi landed in New Delhi sometime in the 1960s to work for Snamprogetti. Sonia Gandhi was one of the few Italians in town. Soon enough, the Quattrocchi family and the young Gandhi couple got to know each other.

Did the Gandhis benefit from Quattrocchi's deals? There is no evidence. But we do know that Snamprogetti pocketed innumerable government contracts across India during the period that Quattrocchi was in India. One estimate said that he swung some sixty projects worth Rs 300 billion from across Asian countries, mainly India, for Snamprogetti. From gas pipelines for the state-controlled Oil and Natural Gas Corporation Limited in Hazira to plants for various public sector units producing fertilizers, Quattrocchi was on a roll. As he pocketed contract after contract, word spread that he was the man for any big deal because of his proximity to the ruling family.

That is the kind of final intermediary I am talking about here. They work through proximity to the most powerful politicians of the day. These men and women are not professional middlemen; most often they are executives heading engineering companies, full-time politicians, think tank heads, and are most often the relatives of those in power, like a son-in-law maybe. When the political party is no longer in power, they go back to doing whatever they were doing earlier.

The Bofors scandal cost the Congress party dearly. In 1989, Rajiv Gandhi was humiliated in the elections. Quattrocchi, though, was unaffected. The Congress and the Gandhis continued to protect him, not just in India but around the world as he fled the law. He may well have enjoyed their patronage until he died.

In 1993, after he was officially named as the operator of an account into which Bofors had deposited slush funds, the CBI moved to impound his passport and question him. Just hours before his detention, late one night in July 1993, Quattrocchi took a flight out of India.

The Hindu, where Chitra Subramaniam and N. Ram led an unparalleled investigation into the scandal, reported that Quattrocchi was paid about Rs 8.4 crore through AE Services, an agent for Bofors, and probably more. That was a significant amount in those days, but it is not clear if he shared it with the Gandhi family or the Congress party.

In the summer of 2003, Interpol found two accounts in the bank BSI AG containing around Rs 16 crore and Rs 4.8 crore, and the CBI got the accounts frozen. Quattrocchi's repeated attempts to defreeze them were turned down by British courts. That the CBI acted so decisively was probably a result of Indian realpolitik: a BJP-led coalition was in power at the time.

In the summer of 2004, another political change swept India and the Congress was back at the centre after years in the wilderness. Quattrocchi's fortunes turned too. In December 2005, the Central government deputed a senior law officer to personally visit London and defreeze the accounts. Within weeks, both accounts were emptied out.

That was not the end of the story either. On 6 February 2007, based on an Interpol alert, Quattrocchi was detained in Argentina, but the CBI put up only a feeble fight for extradition, thus letting him get away.

Under Congress rule, the very might of the state protected Quattrocchi. In April 2009, the CBI asked Interpol to withdraw the international red-corner notice against the Italian. In March 2011, a Delhi trial court discharged Quattrocchi in the Bofors case. The magistrate noted that the CBI had failed to provide any legally sustainable evidence despite twenty-one years of investigation. He added that while the total amount of bribe in the scandal was only Rs 64 crore, the CBI had spent a whopping Rs 250 crore on the case. Quattrocchi died of a heart attack on 13 July 2013 in Milan.

The rise of an Italian middleman in New Delhi is atypical. Most often, the men and women who have the final say on government decisions are from within the families of the ruling parties. In recent years, two sons-in-law have been under public scrutiny for allegedly playing such roles.

Ranjan Bhattacharya, a hotel management executive, came to national attention in 1996, when Atal Behari Vajpayee led India's first right-wing government to power. Married to Vajpayee's foster-daughter Namita, Bhattacharya was appointed an officer on special duty (OSD) to the prime minister. His first stint in high office lasted only thirteen days, because the Vajpayee-led BJP government failed a no-confidence motion in parliament.

Bhattacharya, one of the youngest general managers of the Oberoi group, which runs luxury hotels around the world, had left his job in the late 1980s to start his own venture.

In 1998, when Vajpayee returned as prime minister, Bhattacharya was beginning to be acknowledged as a key figure in the national capital. Senior journalist Prabhu Chawla wrote in the news magazine *India Today* in April 2001: 'Their [Mrs and Mr Bhattacharya's] social circle began expanding to embrace the likes of hotelier Lalit Suri, industrialist Nusli Wadia, journalist Vir Sanghvi, newspaper owner Shobhana Bhartiya. In short, people who mattered and who liked the idea of putting a modern face on power. Politicians were only peripherally in the reckoning, the exceptions being Samajwadi Party's Amar Singh and Arun Jaitley, Vasundhara Raje and Mahajan from the BJP.'

At the time Chawla wrote that article, the Vajpayee government was beginning to face the heat over many of its decisions. 'A complete misfit in the BJP's somewhat austere social milieu, Bhattacharya was an unlikely candidate for the grand title of "extra-constitutional authority". But he has acquired a reputation of being a deal maker who former BJP president Bangaru Laxman believed is involved in "this and that",' Chawla wrote.

Chawla was uniquely placed to assess Bhattacharya's rise in New Delhi. As editor of *India Today*, and because of his own past as a student activist of the party, he had insider knowledge. 'So far, the exchanges have been political, but over the past few months, particularly after the Government inexplicably modified its telecom policy to favour some operators, the whispers have centred on Bhattacharya's ability to influence big government decisions and key appointments. Namita, on the other hand, was the dominant figure at the dining table, influencing Vajpayee's perception of people. So far, no one has produced evidence to link Bhattacharya to any deal. But the image of a fun-loving son-in-law dabbling in government decisions and "this and that" has stuck.'

He went on to say that the 'Great Indian Family Disease', which infected many major Indian politicians, was now haunting the bachelor Vajpayee.

Bhattacharya remained below the radar. A rare interview that he gave to the now-defunct *Sunday* magazine in July 1998, sometime after Vajpayee returned to power, speaks volumes.

You don't have any say in fixing his appointments?
I do not fix appointments. He has a private secretary who does that for him. And his appointments are fixed out of 7 RCR (prime minister's residence) or South Block. And not out of 3 RCR, where I stay. And one more thing. Mr Vajpayee has been PM for a hundred days now. I have been to South Block only once and that was to wish him when he became prime minister. I have been to 7 RCR only about four–five times – and that is only a hundred yards away from 3 RCR.

But you don't have to be physically present to fix appointments.
True. But I don't fix any appointments.

The charge is that you also take money to fix appointments.
(Laughs incredulously) Why should anyone take money to fix appointments?

Why not?

The best thing would be for you to see his (Vajpayee's) list of appointments through the last three months. You will see the kind of people who go to meet him don't need to pay any money. They are mostly bureaucrats and politicians.

What about industrialists?
I'm not aware of any industrialists.

What about the charge that you and Pramod Mahajan made money on the Maruti deal?
Mr Mahajan and I had nothing to do with the Maruti settlement.

In the summer of 2004, when the BJP government suffered an unexpected defeat and the Sonia Gandhi-led Congress coalition swept to power, Sonia Gandhi chose Dr Manmohan Singh to be prime minister. However, it was not long before Robert Vadra – another son-in-law, this one married to Priyanka Gandhi, the daughter of Rajiv and Sonia Gandhi – and his undue influence began to be spoken of. Over the decade that the Congress-led government was in power, there was no concrete proof of Vadra's involvement in manipulating government contracts. However, several people who had major dealings with the government continued speaking about his influence. He would occasionally make an appearance at a glamorous evening party or in a lifestyle magazine, but there was little else to show for his influence.

What emerged eventually was that Vadra had amassed crores in a matter of a few years, thanks to the benevolence of DLF, one of India's biggest construction companies, and the support of Congress-ruled state governments.

Colonel Kushal Pal Singh, a former army officer and chairman of DLF, is the face of India's construction boom. He told senior journalist Shekhar Gupta in a television interview in November 2011: 'In my terminology, what I call bribing is in two parts: one, where you give money to somebody to facilitate quicker disposal. Second, you give money if somebody asks you to do a wrong job. Now in my terminology, bribing is to do a wrong job, which I have never done in my life.' The celebrated journalist sought no further clarifications. Singh has never spoken in public about what exactly Vadra did to merit the benevolence showered on him.

In October 2012, anti-corruption activists Arvind Kejriwal, Prashant Bhushan and Yogendra Yadav claimed that Vadra's assets had swollen from a mere Rs 50 lakh to Rs 300 crore. 'In the last four years, Robert Vadra has gone on a property-buying binge and has purchased at least thirty-one properties mostly in and around New Delhi, which even at the time of their purchase were worth several hundred crores (of rupees),' Bhushan alleged at a press conference.

The activists said DLF was giving Vadra cash as well as selling him properties far, far below the market rate. 'Who will even register an FIR against the son-in-law of the ruling dynasty of the country,' Bhushan asked pointedly.

Kejriwal, who went into politics and stormed to power in Delhi soon after, said the deal was simple: DLF sold land and properties at very low rates to Vadra across India; in return, DLF received favours from the Congress governments at the state level.

Vadra's fortune is simple to explain. In 2004, when the Congress party and its allies swept to power, Vadra was running a business of exporting inexpensive costume jewellery. By 2007, he had ventured into real estate and registered a firm called Sky Light Hospitality with just Rs 1 lakh as paid-up capital. The company bought 3.5 acres of agricultural land near a highway in Gurgaon for Rs 7.5 crore. The land could only be used for agricultural purposes, after all. However, a couple of months later, Vadra applied to the Congress-ruled Haryana government to permit him to convert the agricultural land for commercial use. The approval came promptly, and the price of the land shot up sharply.

As the land conversion was taking place, DLF began advancing crores of rupees as unsecured loan to Vadra's companies. In 2012, DLF bought back the land for Rs 58 crore. The process was simple: DLF advanced

Vadra the money to buy cheap agricultural land, which he converted to land for commercial use using political influence and sold back to DLF for a huge profit.

By 2012, Vadra was holding properties worth over Rs 300 crores, including a significant stake in a five-star hotel in the national capital.

During the ten years that the Congress-led UPA alliance ruled India, Vadra's fortunes may have soared, but there was still no concrete evidence that he had played a major role in swinging any big deals.

The capital's grapevine listed others who played critical high-level intermediary roles. Needless to say, there is hardly any documentary proof of their involvement. The name of an entrepreneur who is a member of parliament was often heard in connection with major defence deals. His own conduct, including an aggressive embracing of military issues, further fuelled the suspicion that he was indeed the man who facilitated a major defence deal with a European firm that ran into tens of thousands of crores. This man and others like him are the most powerful brokers of India's faltering democracy.

In recent years, every time details of shell companies in tax havens have emerged in public, there have been enough clues about how and where the ultimate intermediaries and the powerful politicians parked their money, and how they moved it back to India. In recent documents that have emerged about secretive firms and accounts in Panama, Liechtenstein, or HSBC Geneva, there have been rough indications of how this is done. The big Indian story, of the most powerful intermediaries and beneficiaries of corrupt government procurements and public contracts, is yet to emerge. However, the digital revolution will surely push out more specifics in the coming years.

In early 2016, as I was giving the final touches to this book, a new government was in power under the leadership of Narendra Modi. No major scandals had erupted so far, but the ominous signs of what was in store were everywhere. Foreign businessmen and key corporate leaders were whispering the name of the son of an important BJP leader who is now a key government functionary. He was, apparently, taking undue interest in a deal. One day, not very far in the distant future, we might hear of a new scandal. Who can say?

The only certainty in New Delhi's corridors of power is that deals are being struck somewhere, and that professional middlemen and political go-betweens are stitching it all together: which tax haven, how many fake companies, export or import firms, NGOs or trusts, who will get what and in what proportion. They are perpetually at war with the rapid digitization that India is seeing, which will promote transparency, and in constant search of more devious ways and dark corners to collect and store their filthy lucre.

Section Two

THE VERY PRIVATE
PRIVATE SECTOR

This is an instructive manual on how to do business and succeed in modern India. The three chapters here are merely illustrative, of course. An enterprising soul could come up with an entirely fresh, uncharted trajectory – India is the land of endless opportunities.

5

Battle for the Skies

'Thank God,' Farukh Ahmed Barkatalai Sheikh murmured as the dark blue Mercedes Benz finally came alive. It was the evening of 13 November 1995. A balmy wind from the Arabian Sea swept across Bombay, India's commercial capital, as neon lamps began lighting up the winding roads running through the neighbourhood of Bandra. One of the city's original settlements, Bandra is now home to movie stars and other nouveau riche.

The young driver was distressed that the newly imported Mercedes wouldn't start, delaying the departure of his boss, the managing director of East West Airlines, Thakiyuddin Abdul Wahid. Meanwhile, other colleagues in the private airline's corporate office were arranging for another car to take Thakiyuddin back home – just over a kilometre down the road, after a sharp bend where a white cross still forlornly stands. The house was an elegant duplex apartment with huge glass windows overlooking the Arabian Sea. Eventually, Thakiyuddin left with Barkatalai.

The forty-year-old Thakiyuddin had wrapped up yet another hectic day, reviewing daily operations and discussing expansion plans for India's pioneering airline. The final assignment of the day was a long meeting with his pilots about the proposed introduction of two Boeing 737-400s on a lease-purchase agreement from the Swedish aircraft-leasing firm Kolding. At around 8 p.m., he spoke to Faisal, his younger brother and one of the directors of the company, for the second time that day. Faisal was in Europe to collect the two aircraft, and had flown to London for a break from the freezing bleakness of Dublin, where the aircraft were being readied at an Air linkers facility. Thakiyuddin was concerned about the delay and sounded impatient during the five-minute conversation. He wanted Faisal to leave the nitty-gritty of interiors and other fittings for later, and to make sure that the aircraft reached India in the next couple of weeks. Having deposited about Rs 13 crore as an advance for the deal, East West Airlines was betting their next round of expansion on the two machines.

At around 8.30 p.m., when Sajeena had called her husband, Thakiyuddin had said he would be home for dinner after his meeting with the pilots. Their children, Shehnaz, eight, and Saahil, seven, were waiting impatiently for Appa to come home. He was an indulgent father.

It was almost 9.25 p.m. The car had reached as far as Dr Abbas Sajun's clinic when a red Maruti van reversed out of a narrow intersecting road and blocked the blue Mercedes's path. Three armed men ran out of the van, one wielding a hammer, and started towards Thakiyuddin's car. The man with the hammer began to break the windscreen. The other two began firing into the car. Thakiyuddin tried to duck behind the seats, but was still showered with a volley of bullets. He shouted frantically at his driver, 'Reverse, reverse!' But there was little room to manoeuvre on that narrow road.

The assailants ran back to their van and drove away. After the initial shock, Barkatalai regained his senses and rammed the Mercedes into their van, but the assailants got away. As they drove off, he saw in the rear-view mirror that his boss was bleeding profusely. He turned the car around as quickly as he could and drove back to the office, crying out for help as he pulled in. At the office, an East West employee got in the car with them and Barkatalai turned around again, rushing to the nearby Bhabha General

Hospital. By the time Thakiyuddin was wheeled into the emergency ward at around 9.55 p.m., he was dead.

The murder threw the improbable rise of East West Airlines into a tailspin. It was also further proof of the criminal underworld's deep tentacles in Bombay. Many in the Bombay Police and Indian intelligence agencies were not entirely surprised by the murder. They had long suspected that the airline was involved financially with Dawood Ibrahim. The underworld don was by then hiding in Pakistan after accusations of masterminding thirteen blasts in Bombay in 1993, killing 257 people.

One senior police officer involved in investigating the murder told me that they had several pieces of evidence to show that Dawood partially financed East West Airlines. Thakiyuddin also figured among the top targets of Dawood's rivals – Hindu members of Dawood's gang who had split from the Muslim don in the wake of the serial blasts. The Bombay Police had warned Thakiyuddin only a few days earlier about the threat to his life. The officer opened his leather-bound investigation notes diary from the 1990s, which showed Thakiyuddin's name as the top target of Chhota Rajan, Dawood's rival don.

In retrospect, it is clear that the murder was a telling statement about the sinister side of India's economic liberalization, which sliced through India's traditional fault lines, and the many layers of chaos beneath it. More than two decades have passed, and fresh evidence has been accumulating in the secret vaults of the security establishment. Then it was yet another underworld killing, but now the broader context is obvious: economic liberalization built on a shaky foundation of immoral politics, criminal gangs, dubious finances and criminal elements. Heart-warming stories of first-generation entrepreneurs succeeding in the information technology industry and news of philanthropic initiatives by business honchos cannot erase the big picture, which is that a significant portion of Indian business still thrives on criminal links and activities. It is no coincidence that India's most successful businessmen find themselves not just on the list of the world's richest people, but also at the cross hairs of Central and state regulators, auditors and investigators.

In many ways, Thakiyuddin symbolized the new breed of entrepreneurs who ushered in the country's impatient break with five decades of socialism. They were ambitious, swashbuckling men fuelled by a hunger for success. These new high-fliers were even more willing to bend and break the rules than their socialist forerunners, and they had greater opportunities to do so as well. In a land spilling over with corrupt politicians and bureaucrats, lax regulatory controls and easy money from shady sources, they found fertile ground.

Many of the richest men and women today made their fortunes after liberalization. The storied rise of Dhirubhai Ambani from gas station attendant to billionaire owner of the Reliance group is held up as proof that the system works for everyone. He was at the vanguard of a new class of Indian capitalists, but by no means the only one. Gautam Adani started with a commodity-trading firm in 1988 and went on to build ports, power stations and a host of other businesses. His annual revenue shot up from Rs 3,300 crore in 2000 to over Rs 47,000 crore in 2013. Grandhi Mallikarjuna Rao started the GMR group in 1978 and tried his hand at twenty-eight different businesses, reaping the rewards once the economy began opening up in 1991. Today, Rao's GMR group is a leading player in the construction of roads, power projects and airports.

Thakiyuddin too began his working life in the days before liberalization, if not on quite the same scale as G.M. Rao.

Taki, as he was fondly called, hailed from Odayam, a fishing village some 50 kilometres from Thiruvananthapuram, the sleepy capital of Kerala. Thakiyuddin was one of eleven children, many of whom went on to amass fortunes in the Persian Gulf and in Bombay. His father, Haji Abdul Wahid Mussaliar, was a prominent local businessman and Islamic scholar. He built his fortune supplying fish, cashew and other local products to cities across southern India and as far as Sri Lanka. Mussaliar would buy huge catches of fish, especially a popular type of anchovy, and dry and ship them before the day's end. It was a risky business because selling the entire catch was contingent on having a sunny day. When he managed to dry and ship the day's catch, Mussaliar made a huge profit. On other days, the entire catch would go to waste. But the business model clearly worked for Mussaliar; he was the first man in his village to own a car.

Thakiyuddin was an enterprising child. As soon as he returned from school, he would rush off to his father's seaside warehouse, a two-storeyed wooden building where Mussaliar stored his dried fish, and from where he loaded the stock on trucks and shipped it. Next to the warehouse, spread across the seafront, the day's catch lay drying. In a reckless moment, the father had pawned that warehouse to a relative so that he could borrow money to expand his business. Soon, the warehouse and office were gone. A small resort stands on that spot now. Mussaliar's wealth vanished into thin air soon after, and the family went through a rough patch.

The hard times didn't last long. The oil boom that began in the late 1960s in the Persian Gulf needed workers to sustain its construction business and oil exploration. Kerala was among the first places the Gulf sheikhs began recruiting workers from, and Odayam's Muslims were among the earliest beneficiaries – among them, the Wahid brothers. By the 1970s, there were hardly any men left in Odayam willing to plunge into the Arabian Sea to bring back its natural bounty; fishing huts were soon replaced by colourful concrete homes. The sleepy fishing village had entered the global economy, as would the rest of the country in the not-so-distant future.

The story of the Wahid family's turnaround began on an afternoon in Bombay's crowded old airport sometime in the early 1970s. A young moustached man stooped to pick up a leather wallet from the floor and ran after a strapping Arab in a long white tunic who was striding towards the entrance of the airport. The youngster stopped the Arab, and handed over the wallet. 'Sir, you dropped it.' The other man muttered a thank you and, as an afterthought, handed over a visiting card. 'Call me if you ever need any assistance,' he said and turned to catch his flight back to Bahrain. The young man returned to the city, excited and inspired by this chance encounter.

'Sir, this is Nasiruddin,' he said over the payphone a few days later, having called the number on the visiting card. Cutting to the chase, the Arab asked Nasiruddin Wahid if he would like to visit Bahrain. Nasiruddin readily agreed and, a few days later, arranged all the documents he needed to obtain a visitor's visa. With that, he embarked on his first trip abroad to visit Ahmed Mansoor Al A'ali. Only when he arrived at Al A'ali's bustling office did Nasiruddin realize that the courteous Arab was the son-in-law of the chairman of Bahrain's largest employer and a member of Bahrain's royal family. The influential son-in-law's Ahmed Mansoor Al A'ali group was also among the biggest recruiters of Indian labourers. Nasiruddin's new patron was, in fact, returning home after a round of recruitments in India when the two met. Within minutes of being ushered into Al A'ali's office, Nasiruddin was offered a job in the administrative division, but he told Al A'ali that he would rather recruit Indian labourers for the group. 'You don't have a licence, investments, or even an office – nothing! How will you do it?' The young man promised to arrange everything and report to his new boss at the earliest.

Back in Bombay, he found an acquaintance who was an employee of Air-India, the state-owned international carrier, to assist him with a soft loan and contacts. This man was a powerful link to various arms of the government. The young and ambitious Nasiruddin was learning an important lesson in doing business in India: if you know the right people, anything is possible. He managed the licence.

That done, Nasiruddin returned to Bahrain and signed a contract with the Al A'ali group. He began sending recruits to the group, a process that included arranging their visas, flight tickets and ensuring a smooth walk through the Bombay airport. It was not planned, but the labour exporter was also learning the intricacies of the airline ticketing business, which would build his fortune later.

By the early 1980s, the business was flourishing and he could no longer manage alone. He decided to woo his younger brother Thakiyuddin to the business. At the time, Thakiyuddin was comfortably settled in the

United Arab Emirates (UAE), working as a manager in a local department store, having won the confidence of a local who owned a chain of them. Nasiruddin took Thakiyuddin to Bahrain, where his benefactor wooed the younger Wahid brother with the promise of wealth and bright prospects. Their father, Mussaliar, also urged Thakiyuddin to return and partner with his older brother to create a new family business.

Ultimately, that is what convinced Thakiyuddin to give up the comfort and safety of the life he had built for himself in the UAE and take a chance to recapture the glory days of Odayam. Their younger brother Faisal told me during one of our meetings in Mumbai that Mussaliar had one piece of advice for them: 'Think beyond Odayam.' Thakiyuddin realized that as an employee of a Gulf sheikh, he was destined to lead a middle-class life. The opportunity Nasiruddin presented him with had awoken his entrepreneurial instincts. Moreover, those were exciting times. India was beginning to change.

Sometime in 1981, Thakiyuddin and his elder brother arrived in Bombay with a small suitcase and checked into Hotel Stiffles – a backpacker's paradise, where one could get a room for the night for just a few rupees.

When Jerry Camarillo Dunn Jr, whose writings have delighted generations of *National Geographic* readers, came to India in 1970, he checked into Stiffles: 'This ramshackle rat-hole was located only a block from the luxurious Taj Mahal Hotel, but it was a world away. The Stiffles' guests – rock-bottom budget travellers who came to this hippie Hilton from Europe, the United States, and Australia – spent their days lounging on rickety balconies, watching the street scene, and sipping Fanta sodas. In the late afternoon the sun would hit the palm trees out front, turning them to gold. The Hotel Stiffles had its own crumbling tropical charm, something out of a Somerset Maugham story.'

The Wahid brothers rented an office in the city's Dadar district and began to work towards growing their new business, East West Travel and Trade Links Private Limited. Thakiyuddin split his time between Ajman in the UAE and Bombay.

The business grew briskly. In 1983, East West took over a travel agency recognized by the International Air Transport Association (IATA) and by 1985, the company had four offices in Bombay alone, and was beginning to spread its operations across India. Soon, it was opening an office in a new city every six months. By 1986, it had become the biggest ticketing agent for Air-India, Gulf Air and several other airlines, issuing tickets through a network of over a thousand agents. It had also by then recruited thousands of Indians for several firms in the Persian Gulf, including Saudi Arabia's Bin Laden group.

As their company grew, the Wahid brothers were confronted with the realities of doing business in Bombay. Success depended on dealing with a mix of dodgy politicians, underworld racketeers, corrupt police, zealous bureaucrats, unscrupulous financiers and untested business partners. (Over two decades after liberalization, things haven't changed very much.) Thakiyuddin's first experience of this was during a critical conversation with Gulf Air, an important client for East West's growth prospects.

'*Kalli walli* (let it be),' the airline's unrelenting young Arab representative kept repeating, practically dismissing Thakiyuddin. East West had sought him out to secure the right to become Gulf Air's exclusive general sales agent (GSA) for all of India. Thakiyuddin was becoming exasperated with the airline's tough stance over the appointment of its India GSA. He, like others, had assumed that East West was the natural choice for the role since they were already issuing over 75 per cent of all Gulf Air tickets sold in India. However, the Gulf Air representative insisted that the airline chairman wanted Rs 50 lakh upfront as a 'personal fee'. It became clear to Thakiyuddin that arguing would do no good; if he did not pay up, they would lose the business. He hurried back to the office and frantically began to assemble all the currency he could get his hands on, from his various offices in the city and from bank accounts. With the help of a few trusted employees, Thakiyuddin managed to fill a large suitcase with 50,000 banknotes, neatly assembled into bundles, each holding 100 notes. Without consulting anybody – not even Nasiruddin, who was away in Bahrain – Thakiyuddin drove across to the Gulf Air office to deliver that personal fee.

Confident that he'd secured the platform for East West's future growth, Thakiyuddin began to take care of the practicalities: he arranged a bank guarantee, found a dedicated office for Gulf Air and began planning the strategy to consolidate East West's grip on the airline ticket market. But he was in for a rude surprise. One morning, he opened the newspaper to see a front-page article about Gulf Air appointing Jet Air, a small-time travel agency, as its exclusive GSA for India.

Jet Air was led by Naresh Goyal, who had started his professional life as an assistant in a ticketing firm in New Delhi. He had taken charge of Jet Air sometime in the late 1970s. A short man with a thin moustache and a broad smile permanently etched on his face, Goyal would eventually become an iconic figure in India's aviation industry. At the time, however, Jet Air was a small travel agency working with a handful of African airlines.

Despite being humiliated in the Gulf Air episode, Thakiyuddin didn't back down. His family was aghast, but by then, Thakiyuddin had become the aggressive leader of their business. He had to be trusted. His first instinct was to call the Gulf Air representative and ask him to return the fee he had paid. If not, Thakiyuddin threatened, he would complain to the Indian authorities. Needless to say, Thakiyuddin never saw his money again – complaining to the authorities was, of course, pointless.

Then, one bright summer day in 1987, Goyal walked into East West Travel's office. About a year had gone since Jet Air won the GSA contract. He greeted Thakiyuddin, hands folded. 'I would have been destroyed had I not won the Gulf Air GSA,' Goyal said. According to Goyal's narrative, he wasn't even aware that East West was in the reckoning, and he had staked his entire savings on winning the GSA. But Thakiyuddin was convinced that the Jet Air owner had played dirty, and that the Gulf Air representative was part of the conspiracy.

Thus began one of the greatest rivalries of corporate India of those days.

With Gulf Air in his pocket, Goyal didn't look back. He soon became the GSA for Kuwait Airways and began to pick up business with several new partnerships. At first, Thakiyuddin sought to curtail Jet Air's rise: he funded a suit by Gulf Air employees against their transfer to Jet Air. He gave up soon because East West now required all his attention. Even though Jet Air's star was rising, it paled in comparison to the soaring fortunes of East West, which dominated airline ticketing in India. By the late 1980s, East West had recruited over 75,000 Indians to go to work in the Persian Gulf, and was issuing around 600 airline tickets a day. As East West was taking off, India was undergoing momentous political upheaval, and that presented the Wahids with a golden opportunity.

The 1980s were a decade of both promise and turmoil. After Indira Gandhi's assassination, Rajiv Gandhi, then just forty, became the country's youngest prime minister. He realigned India on the global stage, turning away from the Cold War mindset and stepping up engagement with the United States. As a sign of his ambition for India as a regional power, he sent the Indian Army to Sri Lanka, though with disastrous consequences. On 13 June 1985, Gandhi summed up his vision before a joint session of the US Congress: 'India is an old country, but a young nation; and like the young everywhere, we are impatient. I am young and I too have a dream. I dream of an India, strong, independent, self-reliant and in the front rank of the nations of the world in the service of mankind.'

During his time in office, Rajiv was determined to end state monopolies and support the private sector. He reduced tariffs and tackled overall bureaucratic controls, and famously unleashed a revolution in the telecom sector, which was symbolized by the yellow public call office (PCO) booths mushrooming by the thousands across the country. That aside, Gandhi pushed many measures in the face of opposition from the old guard of his party: among them, the Panchayati Raj system to devolve power to the lowest level of Indian society, incentives to private sector to make them profitable, and subsidies to increase private industrial production. Though not a communist regime, India was firmly in the

Soviet camp, following many of its economic policies, dependent on Moscow for its military modernization and finding grand capitalist conspiracies too. However, the young prime minister struck a different tone, kick-starting processes that would eventually lead to the economic liberalization programme that is still under way. He took particular interest in the aviation sector, as he himself had been a commercial pilot with the state-owned Air-India.

The rise of East West, Jet Air and other pioneers in the airline ticketing business was a precursor to the emergence of privately owned airlines. The leap from ticketing to flying aircraft needed a helping hand from the government – such a move still would. Even in 2016, government blessings and permits are vital. The many ways in which the government can throttle an entrepreneur are mind-boggling: denying security from local police, not repairing a public road outside the factory complex, licences, electricity, imposing draconian labour laws and complex duties – the list is long. The government's abundant help is needed not just to start and run a business but also to keep its Kafkaesque tentacles off the enterprise's back.

Thakiyuddin and his family had long-standing Congress connections. He had even been a student leader of the party during his college days in Kerala University. With that and through social acquaintances from Kerala, Thakiyuddin was able to befriend Gandhi's powerful private secretary Vincent George, which in turn enabled him to meet the prime minister himself. During those meetings, Gandhi urged him to consider launching an airline, or so Thakiyuddin claimed.

In 1989, under a new Open Sky policy, the government began issuing air taxi licences for capacity building of the Indian aviation sector. Until then, the Indian skies had been monopolized by Air-India for international routes and Indian Airlines for domestic ones. Over twenty licences were issued in the first wave, and most went to big Indian business houses such as the Tatas and the Birlas. East West, now under the firm leadership of Thakiyuddin, even though his elder brother Nasiruddin remained chairman of the company, was among the recipients. By this time, Thakiyuddin had got to know Rajiv Gandhi well and had built up his contacts with the right people in New Delhi. Then the tide turned.

It was a hot and humid day, 21 May 1991, and Tamil Nadu was gripped by election fever. Gandhi was campaigning in the state. The indications were that he was riding back to power after being in the wilderness for almost three years. He was wading into the crowd late in the evening in Sriperumbudur, 40 kilometres from Madras (now called Chennai), when a bespectacled young girl, Thenmozhi Rajaratnam alias Dhanu alias Gayatri, dressed in a yellow salwar suit and a green shawl, stepped forward to touch his feet reverently. As she bent down, Dhanu pressed the trigger of a bomb fitted in her belt filled with about a kilogram of RDX and pellets. The woman assassin from the LTTE instantly killed herself, the Gandhi family scion and fourteen others.

As the news of Rajiv Gandhi's assassination spread, Faisal Wahid, who was studying in Bombay then, called Thakiyuddin to break the news. It was late in the evening. A heartbroken Thakiyuddin locked himself up in a room for days, grieving. He was mourning an idol, but not only him; he was also grieving the loss of the Wahid family's most important patron in India's complex and corrupt power structure. Ministers and government officials would oblige the Wahids because they had access to Gandhi; this privilege saved them precious time and money. Licences that could take months or even years to obtain could be had in a matter of days. Back then, access to the Gandhi family guaranteed success. Rajiv's premature death was, therefore, a blow for East West and its prospects.

When Thakiyuddin finally emerged from his mourning, his family members say, he was determined to start an airline as a tribute to the erstwhile prime minister. That a modest family from an obscure village in Kerala ended up starting India's first privately owned airline encapsulates the hope and promise of India in the early 1990s – and also its many darker sides.

A few weeks later, Thakiyuddin hired two pilots, including one of Gandhi's former flight instructors from Indian Airlines. The second pilot was a nephew of Datta Samant, the fiery trade union leader of Bombay who led the year-long textile workers' strike in 1982, which tolled the death knell for the city's historic textile industry.

East West Airlines was taking tentative but crucial baby steps, building the company around politically connected professionals. When Thakiyuddin needed a third pilot, he hired one of Gandhi's favourites, the one who used to fly the prime minister's special Air-India aircraft.

In contrast to the optimism running through the East West office, and India's airline sector generally, the global aviation industry was in turmoil in 1991 because of the Gulf War and a hike in oil prices. The iconic Pan Am succumbed to mismanagement and folded dramatically on 4 December 1991, leaving hundreds of passengers stranded in aircraft and terminals. Earlier that year, both Eastern Airlines and Midway Airlines had shut shop in the United States.

As with any crisis, it was also a time of opportunity. The bankruptcy of these US carriers left a fleet of over a thousand Boeing 737s sitting idle across the country. Any company willing to pay an advance deposit and rental anywhere between $100,000 to $120,000 a month could get their hands on a fully functioning Boeing 737. It was as if the gods themselves were conspiring to get East West Airlines off the ground.

Thakiyuddin tied up with Guinness Peat Aviation, a commercial aircraft sales and leasing company set up by, among others, Tony Ryan, the Irish billionaire who later founded the hugely successful low-cost carrier Ryan Air. India's move to open its skies was a beacon of hope for a depressed industry; soon, aircraft leasing executives from across the world flooded Bombay. East West was assiduously courted; many executives tried to persuade the Wahid brothers to lease aircraft from them. It was almost as easy as hiring a taxi in Bombay. The only paperwork required was an Airline Operating Permit; everything else could be negotiated.

East West Airlines started with a total investment of just Rs 35 crore, which the Wahids were able to secure relatively easily, in spite of the fact that they were starting an unproven business in a newly liberalized market. Such was the optimism at the time that East West was able to get sufficient capital to start off, including Rs 10 crore from Fairgrowth Financial Services, Rs 15 crore from the Industrial Development Bank of India (IDBI) and another Rs 10 crore as a personal investment from Nasiruddin. The eldest brother continued to split his time between Bombay and Bahrain, while Thakiyuddin settled into running the company. The Wahids signed a lease for a Boeing 737 from Guinness Peat Aviation at a monthly rental of $110,000. The Wahids' travel agency, East West Travel and Trade Links, became the holding company of the new airline.

Many in the company wanted the first flight to be on 25 December 1991 to coincide with Thakiyuddin's birthday, and preparations were on in full swing for the launch. Faisal was in Dublin to collect the aircraft. On 12 December, Thakiyuddin called him, sounding unusually downbeat. 'We have a problem,' he said. In the rush to launch the airline, they had overlooked the fine print of India's import regulations, which stipulated that a 33 per cent countervailing duty would be assessed on the total value of any aircraft brought into the country. The duty alone would have far outstripped the leasing cost and put immense stress on East West's modest operating budget.

Thakiyuddin and Nasiruddin travelled to the capital to lobby with policymakers about lifting the duty. But they found a different New Delhi. Though the Congress was still in power, it was shorn of Gandhi's charismatic leadership. P.V. Narasimha Rao was prime minister. And he wasn't exactly fond of the Gandhi family and, by extension, of those to whom the family had extended patronage.

The Rao government was also carrying out a massive restructuring of the economy to avoid balance of payment troubles, trying as best as it could to usher in a free market economy. Spearheading this economic revolution as finance minister was Dr Manmohan Singh, an economist who had returned to India from Geneva, where he had headed the South Commission, a grouping of developing countries. He would later become one of India's longest-serving prime ministers between 2004 and 2014. Sympathetic though he was, Dr Singh told Thakiyuddin that he couldn't waive the duty. The minister suggested that East West pay part of the duty under protest. He pointed out that, since the aircraft were being leased, East West could recoup the duty when they returned the aircraft. Thakiyuddin took the advice and East West paid around Rs 3 crore as duty under protest, allowing the airline's first aircraft to finally land on Indian soil in January 1992.

Early in the morning of 28 February 1992, several politicians, journalists and friends of the Wahid brothers assembled to board the country's first privately operated domestic flight in almost four decades. There were also about forty fare-paying passengers. Under the terms of East West's air taxi operators' licence, the company couldn't publish its timetable or its fares, so word of mouth was the only way to entice passengers. For a country just waking up from its socialist slumber, East West represented the promise of glamour and faster connectivity. 'Indian Airlines better watch out,' screamed a leading national newspaper the following morning.

At 5.30 a.m., the Boeing 737 took off for Cochin (now Kochi), the commercial capital of Kerala, the home state of the Wahid brothers. After the Cochin stopover, the plane turned around and returned to Bombay with passengers who had boarded at Cochin. Back in Bombay, the aircraft took off for Mangalore in coastal Karnataka after collecting new passengers. On the first flight to Mangalore, there were about a dozen fare-paying passengers and a host of Faisal's friends from the film industry, including, he said, Sushmits Sen, Amir Khan and Faisal Khan. As with most of the Wahid brothers' decisions, there were strong emotional as well as symbolic reasons for selecting Cochin and Mangalore for East West's first flights. Thakiyuddin travelled frequently to Cochin, which was close to his boyhood home, and to Mangalore, his wife's birthplace, and could never find tickets on Indian Airlines.

At the East West corporate office, it was a time of great excitement, exuberance and also irrationality. The airline was setting new standards for domestic flights, making headlines with its impromptu magic shows, ice-cream festivals and live music performances. The hubris extended to how

Thakiyuddin ran the company: compared to monthly salaries of around Rs 25,000 for Indian Airlines pilots, he offered East West pilots an eye-popping Rs 1,00,000 a month. When there was just a single fare-paying passenger from Mangalore one day, the manager suggested that the flight be cancelled, but Thakiyuddin would have none of it. In India's celebrity-obsessed political and business environment, he was the new entrepreneur to be courted, and he often obliged his many suitors with preferential seats and chartered flights. Many politicians were to be his guests on East West flights. In turn, he had no qualms about aggressively courting them in turn to overturn the countervailing duty. Eventually, he collected the signatures of 125 members of parliament for the abolition of countervailing duty, including almost all the MPs from Kerala. Thanks to the campaign, Dr Manmohan Singh gradually brought down the duty, first to 18 per cent, then to 8 per cent, before finally scrapping it altogether a few years later.

East West hit its stride in its maiden year – quite a feat, and not just by Indian standards. Its 1992 revenues were over Rs 130 crore, with a Rs 8 crore profit – a stark contrast to the loss of over Rs 150 crore suffered by Indian Airlines the same year. East West tickets were on an average 20 per cent cheaper than in Indian Airlines, and its flights were soon full. By mid-1992, the company had added three more aircraft to its fleet, with the stated aim of adding another two every six months.

Towards the end of 1992, the pilots of the state-run Indian Airlines and Air-India announced a strike demanding better salaries and working conditions. Government efforts to negotiate yielded nothing, as the pilots adamantly stood their ground. Thakiyuddin and Nasiruddin were summoned to New Delhi to a meeting with the then prime minister Rao and Madhavrao Scindia, the civil aviation minister. At that meeting in the PMO, Scindia did most of the talking. The government, he said, was clear: East West had to operate as many flights as possible, on whichever routes possible, to break the back of the striking pilots. 'The government will offer you all possible assistance,' Scindia promised in front of the prime minister. Given the looming crisis, Rao, famous for his pouting lips and silence, reluctantly nodded.

Buoyed by this call from the government and the prospect of access once again to the highest echelons of power, Thakiyuddin took a gamble and decided to more than double his fleet. Within hours of the meeting, he was on the phone with two leasing companies, and in a few days, seven brand new aircraft were pulled out from under their nitrogen covers and repainted in the colours of East West. By January 1993, the East West Airlines fleet had more than doubled from five to twelve aircraft. One of the company's key advisors, a veteran British Airways executive, threatened to resign, calling the reckless expansion a suicide mission. But Thakiyuddin overruled him. With the pilots' strike continuing without an end in sight, and New Delhi anxious to see East West pick up the slack, Thakiyuddin felt he held all the cards. Only, as with any political favour, this one too would come at a price.

Not content with relying on the Wahids, Scindia had simultaneously leased a few three-engine Tupolev-154s from Uzbek Airlines with pilots to fill part of the gap in the number of aircraft on domestic routes. In the dense fog-covered airport of the national capital on 9 January 1993, one of those Tu-154s landed in a bizarre manner, hitting its left wheel on the runway first, then skidding and flipping over and breaking into three pieces as it went up in flames. The 163 passengers and crew aboard escaped miraculously. The instant public outcry, led by the striking pilots and trade unions, forced Scindia to resign.

The toast of the Indian elite, the Wahids were safe from the religious riots raging across Bombay in 1992 – it had started after the Babri Masjid demolition by Hindu fanatics on 6 December that year – but not from the uncertainties of national politics. The promises that Scindia had made to East West Airlines disappeared with him. Rao seized on this crisis to sever ties with the Wahids, whom he saw as Gandhi protégés.

The competition in the Indian skies was also intensifying. Naresh Goyal's Jet Airways took to the sky in May 1993. For an airline that would go on to become the country's most successful private airlines, its launch wasn't very auspicious. During the maiden flight, one of its Boeing-

737-300s landed at the wrong airfield in Coimbatore, Tamil Nadu. In contrast to the 737-200s that East West flew, Jet's Boeing-737-300s had low-hanging engines, which increased the risk of accidents. Goyal started vigorously poaching East West staff and went on to adopt several of his rival's strategies.

By mid-1993, the Income Tax Department, the Department of Revenue Intelligence and other agencies began to aggressively pursue East West. The security establishment had already told the government that the Wahids were mixed up with the Dawood Ibrahim gang, and that there was definite evidence against them. Many suspected that the Wahids had fallen out of favour. 'Instead of fighting competition, we were firefighting,' Faisal later recalled. Even at that point, however, the Wahids did not realize that they had already been undermined in a much more malicious way.

On 12 September 1992, assistant police inspector Krishnavtar Gulabsingh Thakur was preparing to stretch out on a couch and grab some sleep. His colleagues, constables P.G. Javsen and K.B. Bhanawat, were fast asleep just outside Ward 18 of JJ Hospital, with their .303 rifles resting against the benches. Inside the ward slept Shailesh Haldankar, a member of the Arun Gawli gang, which competed with the then dominant Dawood gang. Bombay's underworld directly or indirectly controlled many businesses, including construction and Hindi films, and were a significant force in local politics.

Haldankar was fast asleep, assured of police protection against possible revenge attacks. Only a few days before, he had stunned the city by gunning down Dawood's brother-in-law, Ibrahim Parker. Parker's killing had infuriated Dawood. For him, it was both a challenge to his authority in Bombay and an emotional setback.

A couple quietly walked into the hospital campus around 1.30 a.m. and carried out a detailed reconnaissance of the facilities, undisturbed for over an hour. They left the hospital premises and reported to Dawood's six handpicked hitmen that Haldankar and his associate, Bipin Shere, were in Ward 18, protected only by a police officer and four constables. They mapped out the location and the exit points from the hospital.

At 3.40 a.m., the six men walked unchallenged into Ward 18, armed with weapons, including an AK-47, a first even for Bombay's crime syndicates. The hit squad began firing indiscriminately. Haldankar was dead in no time, the policemen scrambled to safety behind overturned furniture. The hitmen noticed that Shere, their second target, was not there, even as they turned their sights on the policemen. Inspector Thakur took cover behind a couch, pulled out his service revolver and fired at them. Constables Bhanawat and Javsen began firing their rifles, injuring two of the shooters.

The hit squad fired back at the police team in an attempt to break through. Two of the constables were fatally wounded, while a third was shot in the leg. There was collateral damage: a nurse, a patient and a relative of the patient were injured. During those five long minutes, over 500 rounds were fired in Ward 18. For the Bombay underworld, which carefully avoided confrontation with the police, this was an unprecedented and dramatic attack. It unleashed far-reaching political and business repercussions locally, nationally and, eventually, internationally.

East West Airlines got caught in the crossfire.

Only months later, on 6 December 1992, the 500-year-old Babri mosque in Ayodhya was brought down. The demolition set off communal violence across India, with the riots claiming hundreds of lives. The incident triggered a serious backlash from a section of Bombay's Muslim community, including its Muslim-dominated underworld. In the months that followed, Bombay witnessed bloody communal riots, which claimed over 900 lives. It was against this backdrop that the city was rocked by the serial bomb blasts of 12 March 1993, in which 257 people died. The police blamed Dawood Ibrahim, along with the smuggler Tiger Memon, and they instantly became the most wanted men in the country. The chaos that ensued split Bombay's underworld.

On 23 July 1993, a Delhi police team intercepted a Toyota vehicle in Gagan Vihar, a crowded middle-class neighbourhood in Delhi. The occupants of the vehicle turned out to be key members of the hit squad that had ravaged Ward 18 a few months ago. According to investigators, a few hours after the hospital shootout back in September 1992, the hit squad had checked into a guesthouse of the Bombay Suburban Electricity Supply undertaking, where a private staff member of a junior minister in the Central cabinet had booked a suite for them in his own name. The minister, Kalpnath Rai, was a prominent Congress party leader from the state of Uttar Pradesh. His nephew, V.N. Rai, hosted the hit squad in the guest house, which, like many other residences owned by government or private companies, served as an alternative to hotels for travelling executives.

The Delhi Police found that minister Rai's staff had also arranged accommodation for them in the national capital. The men had even stayed at 25 Meena Bagh, the minister's official residence. And this is where the plot thickened – and ensnared East West.

During the course of the investigation, the police raided an apartment in south Delhi to recover several items belonging to the criminals, including an envelope addressed to Mohammed Farooq, a key hawala operator – a money launderer – who was known to have intimate ties to Dawood Ibrahim. The police noted that the envelope was to be delivered to Sabu Chacko, the flamboyant head of East West Airlines in Delhi. Later, investigators claimed to have also found evidence that Chacko arranged for East West Airlines to pay hotel bills for Farooq and his wife when they stayed at Hotel Hans Plaza near Connaught Place.

Chacko wasn't just an airline manager: he was also Vincent George's brother-in-law. George was the one who had introduced Thakiyuddin to Rajiv Gandhi and was later a key interlocutor for the Wahid family. Thakiyuddin had appointed the brother-in-law as head of the East West Airlines operations in New Delhi on George's recommendation. Chacko was an important, on-the-ground presence for East West Airlines as the company navigated India's complex domestic aviation regulations. He had proved himself to be an effective political operator and trouble-shooter – until Rajiv Gandhi's assassination.

With the discovery of the envelope, the knives came out: the security establishment and George's and Chacko's detractors sought to besmirch Chacko's name – and that of East West Airlines – with an apparent connection to Dawood. Years later, the Supreme Court dismissed all charges against Chacko and he moved to the United States. But in the summer of 1993, he became a convenient scapegoat.

Thakiyuddin and East West Airlines were on the wrong side of this very public case. Suspicions about their possible connections with Dawood Ibrahim were intensifying. During the interrogation of Dawood aides arrested in Delhi, the police claimed they were told that one of the don's key financial operatives had handed over large sums of money to East West over the years, Rs 5 crore just in the summer of 1992.

Then *The Times of India* published a report claiming that East West's travel division had issued tickets for the Memon family to escape from India after the 1993 Bombay blasts. Tiger Memon was the key conspirator in the bombings, who had fled to Pakistan via Dubai with his family within days of the attack.

The family's tickets were, in fact, issued by another firm, a small travel agency with a similar name: East West Travel and Tours, which continues to be a significant travel operator in Mumbai.

East West Airlines sought to distance themselves from the unfolding scandal as quickly as possible. It took out front-page advertisements in newspapers to explain their innocence and reassure customers. But the damage had been done.

Despite the adverse publicity and suspicion all around, in 1994, East West became India's first private airline to be granted scheduled routes. The government was hard-pressed to refuse East West its licence once it became clear that the company had nothing to do with the 1993 bombings. What swayed the Ministry of Civil Aviation officials in the end were the various persuasive skills that Thakiyuddin deployed to navigate the system. Becoming an officially registered airline was a huge milestone, for East West could now legally announce its routes and fares, and step up its promotional efforts to attract passengers.

The company quickly put the turbulence of 1993 behind it. It even launched an initial public offering (IPO) on the Bombay Stock Exchange (BSE) in mid-1994. The decision was not easy. BSE had suffered a humiliating meltdown in 1992, engineered by a group of stockbrokers led by the infamous Harshad Mehta, a trader who captured the public imagination with his flamboyant lifestyle and stock-market wizardry. Subsequent investigations revealed the scale of Mehta's enormous con job – manipulating stock prices, which resulted in huge losses for state-owned banks. Public trust in the stock market was shattered. Despite in-house estimates showing that the company could raise up to Rs 250 crore, East West decided on a much more modest Rs 55 crore IPO on the advice of its bankers. On the very first day, its shares were five times oversubscribed and eventually over twenty-three times. It was an overwhelming vote of public trust in the company, emblematic also of India's new pride in private enterprise.

Having raised fresh capital, East West embarked on the next phase of expansion. In late 1994, it placed an order for a new fleet of Boeing-737-400s and introduced business class on domestic routes. The plan was to lease three of these new aircraft from Malaysian Airlines, which had already placed orders for several of them with Boeing. East West pilots and technicians completed their training in Kuala Lumpur and the Boeing facilities in the United States, and East West submitted applications to import its new aircraft.

During that critical summer of 1994, Naresh Goyal dropped in to meet Thakiyuddin, the usual broad smile on his face. He complained about the trouble with his 737-300s and their low engines, and said that he was going for Boeing-737-200s, just like East West. According to Faisal, Thakiyuddin told him about his plan to lease several brand new 737-400s, and that more of these new models were available on short notice from Malaysian Airlines.

A few days later, the Directorate General of Civil Aviation (DGCA), India's central aviation regulator, sent a letter to East West stating that since the government was 'not familiar' with these new models, the

company was required to submit three copies of the aircraft manual.
The manual contained sensitive intellectual property (including aircraft
blueprints and drawings) that Boeing was not willing to make public.
The demand itself was ridiculous, Boeing pointed out, and refused to part
with them. As the three aircraft painted in the East West colours idled in
Kuala Lumpur, the DGCA showed no signs of relenting. Thakiyuddin and
Nasiruddin scrambled to lobby with the aviation ministry and pleaded
their case with higher-ups in the government. But the DGCA held fast.

Malaysian Airlines, which had received one month's rental in advance
and five months' deposit, issued a termination notice. The airline
stipulated that East West had three days to lease the aircraft and, if not,
could purchase them outright within two days of that deadline; otherwise
the contract was void. The East West top brass was helpless. India's famed
red tape had scuttled their ambitious expansion plans. A week later,
Malaysian Airlines exercised the termination of the contract and East
West had to forfeit its cash advance.

A few weeks later, the same three Boeing-737-400s landed in India as
part of Jet Airways' fleet. The Indian aviation market was stunned. After
just a few weeks of operation, passengers reported some of the tail paint
was peeling off, revealing East West colours beneath. Naresh Goyal didn't
boast of his coup, but to East West it was a clear second warning of the
man's ruthlessness. Even if this were true, one can't really blame Goyal,
because he too was only learning to navigate the Indian bureaucracy.
Anyone who understands the system realizes that it wasn't just enough
to know a powerful Gandhi, or a few senior political figures; you needed
to reach every level of governance, from the attendant outside a senior
functionary's office to the highest office.

By mid-1995, East West found itself at the crossroads: its expansion
plans had been thwarted, competition was heating up and rivals were
poaching its staff. At a board meeting in the last week of May, Faisal
recalled Thakiyuddin saying, 'We don't need to pretend: Naresh Goyal
has been after us. Damania Airlines [the other major private player] is with
us. We need to fight him.' Thakiyuddin laid out a road map to take on

Jet Airways. As a first step, he said, the company needed to hire someone well versed in the workings of the aviation industry – from outside the family, perhaps a foreigner – to lead the company's day-to-day operations. East West would have to be restructured with a view to long-term growth. Finally, Thakiyuddin believed, it was essential that East West increase its fleet of aircraft. He declared an all-out offensive against Goyal's Jet Airways.

The battle in the skies was heating up.

Thakiyuddin hired Price Waterhouse to advise East West on its restructuring and on hiring a CEO, CFO and other top executives. The company also made plans to lease Boeing's advanced version of its 737-400s. Just a few days after that fateful board meeting, however, Thakiyuddin got a call from a Boeing vice-president, an old acquaintance. 'Taki, we have an issue. A 737-400 has had a structural problem in India. We need an engineer to fix it and you are the only one who can do it.'

Thakiyuddin agreed to help, mindful that his staff of Boeing-certified engineers were sitting idle since East West lost their order of 737-400 aircraft from Malaysian Airlines. He realized only later that the Boeing executive was talking about one of Jet Airways' recently acquired 400s that was originally meant for East West. He called his trusted aides to consider this delicate situation. Most argued against giving any assistance. Taki, however, saw an opportunity to position East West as the white knight of India's domestic fleet of Boeings. He instructed his engineers to help Jet Airways and launched a nationwide media campaign declaring that East West was equipped to help other airlines. Jet Airways retaliated by saying the competition was still flying older aircraft.

Then things took an unexpected, nasty turn. One day in June 1995, Thakiyuddin received a surprise visitor. Damodaran was one of Naresh Goyal's close confidants and a well-regarded marketing brain in the fledgling Indian aviation market. A fellow Malayali from Kerala, he told Thakiyuddin that he was fed up of working with Goyal and wanted to join East West Airlines. The meeting concluded with the East West chief assuring Damodaran that he would get back to him in a few days. Despite opposition from several staff members, Thakiyuddin decided to hire Damodaran. The latter started putting in place new marketing strategies for East West, and from day one became an integral part of the company's strategy sessions. Then, about four months into his tenure with East West, he failed to turn up in the office. He was untraceable for many days after: his mobile phone was turned off, and when an East West executive called his house, his wife feigned ignorance about his whereabouts.

A few days later, Thakiyuddin was busy in the office when the phone rang at around 7 p.m. Naresh Goyal was on the line: 'Taki, my man is back with me. Don't ever try that with me again!'

Their rivalry turned ugly. Thakiyuddin was now convinced that he ought to push ahead with his new strategy.

His determination began to pay off. 'The last two quarters of 1995 were our golden period. Our revenues almost doubled and we were making a very strong comeback,' recalled Faisal. In fact, in October 1995, East West recorded its highest-ever monthly revenue. The Wahid family tied up with Marriott International to open their first hotel in India on one of their properties in Kovalam in southern Kerala. Staff morale was at an all-time high. The company had signed up for the lease purchase of two more 737-400s. Finally, it looked as if it was forging ahead of the competition.

To sustain East West's growth, Thakiyuddin began looking for an equity infusion in the fall of 1995. Emirates, the United Arab Emirates' new airline, was expanding quickly and showed interest. Thakiyuddin flew to Dubai to meet the key officials of the Emirates group in Dubai. The discussions went smoothly. Both sides signed a memorandum of understanding for Emirates to invest in East West, provide aircraft maintenance and other forms of support. It was a coup of sorts. A few days later, a senior Emirates official let it slip to the media that his company was tying up with an Indian company. Though he didn't name the airline, it was obvious to everyone in the market who the Indian partner was.

Within days of the leak, the government in New Delhi announced that
no foreign airline could invest in Indian aviation companies, and that
any airline with equity investors would have to shed their ties to foreign
investors. Jet Airways had significant investments from Kuwait Airways
and Gulf Air, so everybody assumed the government had issued a well-
meaning policy intended to guarantee Indian ownership of private airlines.
It looked like a fair announcement. But, for Thakiyuddin, it was yet again
a sign that Goyal was after him.

He didn't have time to react, though. On 13 November 1995,
Thakiyuddin was gunned down on his way home. His murder plunged
East West into chronic, and ultimately fatal, turmoil. Over the next
two years, the company was perpetually in crisis and finally buckled in
1997. The investigation into Thakiyuddin's murder dragged on for two
years, and police ended up drawing the wrong conclusions, according
to intercepts that Indian intelligence has obtained over the years. That
flawed and half-hearted investigation provides a telling commentary on
the crisis that has gripped Indian institutions at all levels, not least India's
security agencies.

6

Anatomy of a Murder

Shrouded in mourning, a Boeing-737 soared into the afternoon sky on 14 November 1995. There was none of the usual playfulness typical of an East West Airlines flight; the mood inside was sombre. Right at the front, in a casket, lay the body of Thakiyuddin Wahid. Close relatives and some senior executives of the company were the only passengers on board that flight to Trivandrum.

Thakiyuddin was always the most vibrant presence on his flights, mingling with the guests, surprising them and going out of his way to accommodate their demands. One of his favourite passengers, Mother Teresa, had a free ticket on all East West flights. Indian political leaders, corporate czars, film personalities and others of the fashionable set were all frequent guests. The Wahid brothers also enforced very stringent standards of service.

Sajeena and her children, Thakiyuddin's siblings, they all sat in a daze. Just forty-five months after their first flight had soared into the skies, East West's managing director was on his last journey home. He was a few days away from celebrating his fortieth birthday.

Yet the journey was in keeping with the action-packed life and times of Haji Abdul Wahid Mussaliar's family in Odayam. It was a village where men boarded illegal boats in search of fortunes and the Islamic scholar Mussaliar placed daily bets on the sun to run his anchovy business. It was there that a young Thakiyuddin learnt his elementary business lessons while assisting his father in this daily recklessness. The Wahid brothers inherited their father's risk-taking spirit. There have always been murmurs about their ties to Dawood, and many a security official I met was convinced that East West was among the businesses in which the gang lord had an active financial interest. One senior police officer who was posted in Bombay during the period says there was 'no doubt about their proximity to Dawood'. It is an allegation that Faisal and other family members vehemently deny, demanding proof.

As the aircraft crossed into south India, the sky turned dark and a heavy downpour started. Turbulence wasn't unusual in this part of the world and pilots were trained to manage it. But within the aircraft, Aamina, one of the younger Wahid sisters, began to feel breathless. A medical team wasn't deemed a necessity on an aircraft that was on a funeral trip. Faisal, who had returned from London the previous night and was seated next to the casket, rushed to Aamina, as did others. With each passing moment, her condition deteriorated. After a quick round of consultations, the pilot declared an emergency and diverted the flight to the nearest airport, Bangalore. Doctors said it was just exhaustion and nothing more.

Sajeena found mystical signs in the diversion. Eighteen years later, I met her at one of the apartments owned by the Wahid family in an affluent Mumbai locality. Recalling those two days that overturned her life, Sajeena told me: 'Even on his last journey Thakiyuddin visited Bangalore; it was a signal from him that he wanted us to settle down there. He had been talking about shifting to the city for sometime before his death.' She moved to Bangalore after Thakiyuddin's murder. Bangalore, regarded as the Silicon Valley of India, was where East West was in the process of setting up an MRO (maintenance, repair and overhaul) facility in partnership with the state-controlled Hindustan Aeronautics Limited.

After Thakiyuddin's death, the MRO never took off, but his wife and children dropped anchor in the city a few weeks after, not very far from the airport where East West was hoping to base its MRO.

Sajeena today manages a travel house originally started by a French national and acquired by East West in its heyday. After the collapse of the airlines, most of the Wahid family went back to doing what they originally did: selling airline tickets and recruiting manpower for the Gulf region, mostly in Bengaluru, Thiruvananthapuram and Mumbai.

On the day Thakiyuddin died, an East West pilot was the first to tell Sajeena and the children that something was wrong. He said there had been an accident and they were taking Thakiyuddin to the hospital. Sajeena imagined that her husband may have had a heart attack. Soon, one by one, airline employees began to drop by. Nobody told her the truth, but they asked her to stay at home when she insisted on going to the hospital. As the evening dragged on, she began to overhear employees attending the ten-line phone booth at home telling callers about her husband's death.

It wasn't as if Sajeena did not know about the risk to Thakiyuddin's life. As the Wahid family was putting in place final preparations for the airline, 'people used to call at home and tell us "tell your husband not to start the airline",' she said. But Thakiyuddin dismissed them as intimidation strategies by his rivals.

'We were never the same again,' Faisal whispered. We were sitting in the very apartment that he used to once share with his brother's family. He spoke of many things. How he learnt about his brother's death over the phone in London from a hysterical colleague, the happy and hectic times when they ran the airline, Thakiyuddin's impressive personality, their father's dreams, his own youth of fast cars and fast business. Across the sliding glass windows of the apartment, the Arabian Sea was bathed in the rays of a setting sun and the dark rocks glowed. A couple of fishing boats were perched on the rocks, others bobbed in the waves, saffron flags fluttered atop them all. The idyllic scene hadn't changed very much in the two decades since Thakiyuddin's murder, but the city outside had changed beyond recognition.

Faisal sat on a dining chair that had seen much better days. The cushion was flat, the varnish faded. The furniture, and almost everything else in the house, had been left as they were on the day Thakiyuddin died. Faisal and his family were its only, and occasional, visitors.

A few hundred yards away, on Perry Cross Road, is a plot that Thakiyuddin had paid an advance on, to buy and build a family home. Today, behind high walls, there stands the new home of India's cricketing god Sachin Tendulkar. Thakiyuddin's move to buy the land fell through after a dispute among its owners. Tendulkar has built a 6,000 square foot, three-storeyed house, with a lap pool and a gymnasium on the top floor, and a private garden. Tendulkar paid Rs 39 crore to buy the plot and the old villa that stood on it in 2008, more than what the Wahid family needed to start their airline barely two decades earlier.

Mumbai now has new heroes and East West is a mere footnote to India's frantic growth. Except for a few old-timers, no one seems to know very much about the owners of the duplex apartment in New Jaldarshan – 1995 is that far removed from 2016 in this country.

India's socialist economy has not been replaced by laissez-faire in these decades. The government did not really withdraw from the marketplace or regulations. If anything, it found new ways to coerce and assist a new breed of business people as the scope widened dramatically. What is constant is the grip of corrupt politician–businessman–criminal syndicates on governance. It is even greater than anything the average observer of the Indian democracy can imagine, even in these days of exposés and hidden cameras.

✌

Thousands thronged the Wahid compound and narrow road in front as Thakiyuddin's body was brought home on 14 November. Next to the ancestral house stood a new mansion that the Wahid brothers had only recently built for their eldest sister. At the back of the plot lazed the half-dozen or so cows that their mother, Salma Biwi, herself tended.

There had never been a bigger crowd for a funeral in that part of the world. For the locals he was a hero, not anathema because of his alleged underworld links. Leading Sunni preacher Kanthapuram A.P. Aboobacker Musliyar led the prayers. Political leaders, prominent citizens and ordinary people walked alongside Thakiyuddin's body as it was carried along the narrow streets to a mosque about 2 kilometres from the Wahid home. The mosque was newly built – it stood by the Arabian Sea, the imposing minarets as tall as the coconut trees all around. It was a gift of the Wahid family to the local community. Completed just a few months earlier, the mosque could accommodate over 2,000 people. It had come up in place of an old, much smaller mosque, mostly made of wood, parts of which the new structure retained. The mosque was almost too grand for that sleepy village, like the Wahid family itself.

Thakiyuddin's grave is on a sloping land not far from the mosque. A year later, on 21 November, his father, who had been suffering from Parkinson's disease in the last years of his life, died and was laid to rest next to Thakiyuddin. Nobody told Mussaliar, who was in Bahrain with his eldest son for treatment, about Thakiyuddin's murder, but everyone believes he knew. His health deteriorated soon after. Back home, a few days before Mussaliar's death, when someone talked to him about Thakiyuddin in the present tense, he responded: 'You are all just lying.' One of the rare moments he spoke about his son's death. A few days later, he passed away too.

After Thakiyuddin's death, Salma Biwi's routine changed too. She was no longer interested in her cows and visitors. She would sit on the veranda of her house, singing. She sang about a hero, his naughty and enterprising childhood, the epic struggles of his youth and the great fortunes he amassed on distant shores. She finished with a heartfelt rendition about the hero's death, savagely killed by evil men one evening on a street where he was revered. Her eyes welled up as her songs drew to an end, and she would weep uncontrollably. She was narrating folklore from religious traditions, and also telling the tale of her own favourite child's improbable life. There is no shadow cast on his heroics in her narration. His morally complex life in Bombay was far removed from her own in the village, where she tended her cows, greeted village folk, and where Thakiyuddin and the other siblings came visiting regularly. She died in 2012 and was buried next to Thakiyuddin and her husband.

Small plaques give away the lay of the bodies. Overlooking the three graves is a gulmohar that bursts into flower and flame every summer. It was planted by Faisal after his brother's death. The view from the graveyard is breathtaking. The imposing mosque against a backdrop of lapping waves. The sea is a constant presence in the Wahid story. Fish from the sea made the family's initial fortune; it was also the illegal route to the Persian Gulf for neighbours and relatives; and it carried in its winds the sense of adventure and recklessness that led to the Wahid brothers' East West dream. Those winds have also carried tales back home. The family's alleged links to Dawood Ibrahim, for instance. What underlines those suspicions and provides credence to the theory is the improbability that the Wahid brothers could start an airline.

～

For the Bombay Police, the investigation into Thakiyuddin's murder was a foregone conclusion.

Rakesh Maria, then a deputy commissioner of police, a young IPS officer whose somewhat dramatic policing style was already a matter of discussion, was in charge. Only a few weeks before he began investigating Thakiyuddin's death, Maria had extensively interrogated a key hitman of Chhota Rajan, who had split with Dawood after the 1993 blasts. According to Indian investigators, Dawood had aligned with another smuggler, Tiger Memon, and the Pakistan intelligence agency, Inter-Services Intelligence (ISI), to carry out the blasts. Reverberations from those days continue to be felt in present-day India. On 30 July 2015,

Yakub Memon, Tiger's younger brother, who had returned to India from Pakistan a year after the blasts along with many of the Memon family members, was hanged on his fifty-third birthday – a decision that was widely condemned in the liberal media as serving nothing but the bloodlust of a nation. Several others responsible for carrying out the blasts are still in jail. Meanwhile, those indicted in the riots and the demolition of the mosque at Ayodhya – which was the trigger behind the 1993 revenge blasts – are yet to be punished. In fact, many of the accused continue to occupy powerful positions in Indian public life.

With the Mumbai blasts, Dubai-based Dawood lost social acceptance among India's rich and powerful. Days later, the gangster moved out of his Persian Gulf sanctuary and settled in Karachi, Pakistan. His contacts in India went under the radar. Film stars no longer wanted to dance at his parties, the high and mighty were loath to share his booth at the Sharjah Cricket Stadium, and his family became pariahs in a city they had virtually ruled. Bombay was scarred forever, and the much-romanticized don turned into India's most wanted criminal.

The sharp-edged knife of communal division that sliced through India in the wake of the Ayodhya movement penetrated deep into the underworld too. Chhota Rajan became the Hindu don and found secret admirers and supporters in the Indian security establishment. The complex, hatred-filled history of India–Pakistan had a new edge to it.

During the interrogation of the hit man belonging to the Chhota Rajan gang, Maria and his team obtained a long list of people that the gang would be targeting in the coming days because they were either business proxies or close associates of Dawood. In one of their worn-out files, you can still find the detailed list that the police team made of businesses and high-profile people who were aligned with the two dons, based on the interrogations of the shooter as well as other underworld operatives arrested over several weeks in 1995.

During a meeting in Mumbai, one of the officers in the interrogation team shared his diary with me, now worn and bound in leather covers.

Many of those in the list are today among India's leading entrepreneurs. Some are worth many crores, own TV channels, produce Bollywood films and are construction magnates. Most continue to be celebrated faces in new India. Some, like Thakiyuddin and film producer Mukesh Duggal, who was close to Rajan, have met with a bloody end.

The information regarding the Rajan gang's plan to target Thakiyuddin was promptly passed on to the local police, and a police vehicle was stationed close to New Jaldarshan. Faisal recalled that the vehicle had been mysteriously withdrawn a few days before the murder, and that a local police officer had told Thakiyuddin it was a generic threat, that he needn't worry.

For a police force that was used to seeing almost everything through the prism of underworld rivalry, there were further reasons to conclude that Thakiyuddin was a victim of the Rajan gang. Their investigations showed that Rohit Verma, Rajan's key aide who was killed several years later in Bangkok, had led the assault on the East West Airlines chief. There were telltale signs of Verma's role, including a hammer he left behind in the car as signature of his involvement. He had left behind such hammers before, and for years Bombay lived in fear of the hammer. Then, in September 2000, Verma jumped in front of assassins' bullets to save his boss. The Dawood gang had carried out a hit on Rajan, who was hiding in Bangkok then. Verma died instantly, his boss lived. Rajan continued to mark his presence in India's national narrative through occasional televised telephone interviews from unidentified places, mostly boasting about murders, disowning other killings and often rubbishing rumours that he was dead. In October 2015, he was arrested by the Indonesian police and extradited to India the following month. Rajan, whom the Dawood gang has been hunting across the globe, has found a secure place in an Indian jail.

In the charge sheet filed in a local court, the police was conclusive: Thakiyuddin had been murdered by the Chhota Rajan gang because of his proximity to Dawood, and the hit job was carried out by a gang that was led by Rohit Verma and included Joseph John D'Souza alias Joe. Rohit charged from the front while Joe was on the right side when attacking the car, the police said.

Many years later, Joe met a bloody end at the hands of the police. He and his brother, both sharpshooters, were picked up from a hideout by Bombay Police's most celebrated 'encounter' officer, Inspector Pradeep Sharma, and killed in a fake encounter in 2004. Encounters are a favourite professional tool for the Indian police. They arrest an alleged criminal, or a terrorist, and fake a shootout between the two sides to carry out a cold-blooded murder. The police has been using this tactic for a number of reasons – to terrorize and warn other criminals, to build the profiles of political leaders by showing that they were being targeted by terrorists, and occasionally to cook up stories behind bomb blasts and avoid painstaking investigations. Encounters are the easiest way to solve a case and create a sensation. Occasionally, to overcome the complex demands of India's colonial criminal laws and slow-moving judiciary, police officers also use encounters to end a real threat from deadly criminals. This is the usual excuse in most cases where policemen own up to staging the encounter.

Mumbai had become used to encounters after the serial blasts of 1993, as the police went about eliminating the underworld. Sharma was personally involved in over a hundred such killings. A generation of official police shooters emerged under the tutelage of Sharma and the late senior inspector Vijay Salaskar. Sharma was jailed in 2010, accused of faking an encounter to kill Ram Narayan Gupta, an aide of Chhota Rajan. In July 2013, he was acquitted of the charges, but another police officer, Pradeep Suryavanshi, who was leading that encounter, was convicted for murder, and twenty others, including thirteen policemen, were also convicted on various charges. Salaskar was killed by a Pakistani terrorist during the November 2008 attacks in Mumbai.

Early in 2013, Sharma agreed to meet me. As is usual for the VIP inmates of Indian jails, I met him in a government hospital on the outskirts of Mumbai, where he was ostensibly admitted for treatment. A large room on the top floor had been taken over by armed men, probably Mumbai Police personnel, who were guarding Sharma with automatic weapons. Sharma had his personal assistants, a special diet and other facilities, and a large balcony that overlooked the bustling traffic outside. He leaned back on a chair and rested his foot on a teapoy as we settled down in the balcony to talk. His bloodshot eyes didn't convey much as he spoke of a life of bullets and killings. Broad-shouldered and tall, Sharma was not comfortable with long conversations and often searched for words. But he recalled each incident and every encounter precisely.

The metropolis beyond that balcony was crowded with late-evening traffic as we discussed the bloody Mumbai of the 1990s, the underworld, businesses mixed up with the criminal gangs, his seniors and other issues. When I broached Joe's story, Sharma wouldn't discuss exactly what happened in that encounter. 'This is Mumbai, boss,' he remarked casually.

Crime Register Number 596/95 of the Bandra police station was no different from the dozens filed in Mumbai courts every month. It was yet another underworld killing. The only difference was that the victim was a high-profile, high-flying airline owner. The city's crumbling lower judiciary was already stretched way beyond capacity, handling cases of communal riots, bomb blasts and underworld battles. Communal passions ran high in Mumbai. There was even the theory that the Hindu-dominated police was by and large communal.

However, in India's inefficient, corrupt system, there are islands of excellence. You just need to know how to access them, and that often requires dubious means. My friend Zakir was able to use his extensive network in the lower courts of Mumbai to get hold of the entire charge sheet in Thakiyuddin's murder, more than a decade after it was filed in the archaic courtrooms of Mumbai with its old-fashioned filing systems. The huge bundle was revelatory.

The police investigations into the Thakiyuddin murder case had several missing pieces. In itself, this is not surprising, not in India anyway, but it was shocking in the investigation of the murder of a man of Thakiyuddin's profile. He was someone who headed a family business and was part of a particularly close-knit family, but the police never seemed to have bothered to sit down with his kith and kin. Except for a page-and-a-half-long statement from Faisal, the charge sheet has no testimony from the family. It never asked his wife if there were threats to his life. It didn't ask his brothers (Nasiruddin, Shihabuddin, Tahakutty and Faisal, who doesn't recall giving a detailed statement) or his brothers-in-law (Peer Mohammed and Najumuddin, who were also the only other family members on the East West Airlines board) if they had any inkling of a threat to his life. They didn't bother to probe if there were any professional rivalries in the fledgling airline market. The police had already made up their minds: this death fitted well with the pattern of underworld rivalry.

Missing from the police charge sheet is the story of India's cut-throat businesses and that of a grand rivalry that is now buried deep inside many official documents. It is a story that has been narrated to this writer by several unimpeachable sources in the Indian intelligence agencies.

Not that hints of rivalries and business tensions didn't figure during the investigation at all. Faisal's short statement in the charge sheet speaks of the simmering tension between his brother and Naresh Goyal. There were many others, too, who were jostling to enter the fledgling private aviation market. But the Mumbai Police appear to have summarily dismissed those possibilities.

Years later, when I quizzed Faisal about his statement to the police, he couldn't recall giving a formal statement. As an afterthought, he added that it may have been based on a meeting he had with one of the senior police officers when he returned from Thakiyuddin's funeral. 'The police never bothered to understand our side of the story,' Faisal complained. He specifically rubbished allegations of East West's proximity to the Dawood gang.

'If we were indeed funded by him, why would the airline go down (later in 1997) because of financial problems? The main allegation against us was that East West provided the flight tickets for the Memon family to get out of India after the blasts. But it was not us, and police also agreed that the tickets were provided by East West Travel and Tours, another travel company with a similar name. But *The Times of India* splashed the news on its front page, despite our clarification to them. It was very damaging,' he said.

Faisal does not deny that they were acquainted with the Dawood family in the days before the blasts, and admits that they have issued tickets to many of them. Before the blasts, Dawood had been an important and unavoidable acquaintance for most of Bombay's high-flyers. Faisal told me about how Noora, Dawood's temperamental brother, once walked into one of the East West Airlines offices with the passports of several film stars to book tickets for a flight chartered to Sharjah for a live programme. For India's biggest travel house, issuing over 600 tickets a day on an average, and with almost a dozen offices just in Mumbai, it was the inevitable reality of doing business, Faisal argued.

A Mumbai journalist who had once seen Thakiyuddin at a function organized by Noora, felt there was nothing unusual about it. 'I have seen film stars dancing, police officers paying their respects and politicians in attendance,' he told me. However, the rumours of East West Airlines being a front for the Dawood Ibrahim gang hung heavy in the air. What added to the mystery was how these Wahid men from nowhere had made such a success of the high-risk business of aviation with just over Rs 35 crore.

A few days after Thakiyuddin's last rites, Faisal returned to Mumbai, determined to find out what had happened to his brother. He was angry, sad and helpless. He went to Maharashtra's home minister, the police chief and other officials dealing with the case. They were all courteous, listened to him attentively and assured an impartial investigation. Later, when he started to piece together what had happened on the evening his brother died, Faisal came across startling facts that never figured in the police files. His first stop was Barkatalai, the trusted driver who broke down as soon as he saw Faisal, ruing his inability to save his boss. The driver recalled the evening and spoke about two young men who stood under the street light waving at Thakiyuddin as his car rolled down that day. Barkatalai recognized one of them as the relative of an East West employee.

Faisal tracked down the two youngsters, both of whom were frightened by the moribund drama and the possible torture of doing the rounds of police stations and courts as witnesses. After much cajoling, they opened up. The police had not bothered to speak to them. Faisal went to see police officers handling the case with their taped interviews. The two boys accompanied him. The youngsters were summoned and Faisal alleges that the policemen questioned the two of them very roughly for the next few minutes. The two were visibly shaken when they emerged from the session. The meeting was over in no time and the two men never returned to give testimony in court.

～

India has not been able to live down the humiliation it suffered at the hands of China in the border skirmishes of October–November 1962. That humiliation effectively finished the unblemished reign of its first prime minister Jawaharlal Nehru, forced Defence Minister V.K. Krishna Menon out of office and led to several systemic changes. To date, minor transgressions by Chinese troops along the unmarked Line of Actual Control (LOAC) between the two countries are treated almost like invasions – not just by a hyperactive media but even large sections of academics and politicians. One of the major fallouts of the 1962 defeat was the realization that India's Intelligence Bureau (IB) was not capable of gathering intelligence from deep inside enemy territories. From discussions about the failure of the Bureau, the Research and Analysis Wing (R&AW), a dedicated foreign intelligence agency along the lines of the United States' Central Intelligence Agency (CIA), took shape in 1968. But developing an external intelligence agency was easier said than done. Due to a host of factors, it was very challenging for Indian spies to physically operate in India's two key adversary nations, Pakistan and China. These challenges forced the R&AW leadership to focus significantly on their technological capabilities. They have acquired several aircraft and helicopters to fly along the border and sometimes deep inside neighbouring countries, highly advanced interception capabilities to listen in on all kinds of conversations, fairly advanced satellite monitoring capabilities, and now an increasing capability to monitor the Internet and other new technologies.

These capabilities, largely controlled from two unnamed multi-storey buildings in New Delhi, and other facilities scattered across the north and east of India, have provided big breakthroughs. Among them was the intercept of a telephone conversation between then Pakistan army chief General Pervez Musharraf and his chief of general staff, Lt Gen. Mohammad Aziz, discussing operational specifics and other aspects of an ongoing border conflict between India and Pakistan in 1999. Musharraf was on a visit to China when the conversation took place and that helped India nail the Pakistan Army's public claim that it was Kashmiri freedom fighters, the mujahideens, and not Pakistani soldiers who had crossed the Line of Control (LOC) between the two countries to occupy the strategic heights of Kargil.

Since the 1993 bomb blasts in Mumbai, R&AW has also diverted a significant part of its capabilities to track India's most wanted man, Dawood Ibrahim, and his associates, who had fled to Pakistan from Dubai and other hideouts. It didn't take them long to obtain important telephone numbers that the gang used from Karachi. Over the next several years, the agency has been successful in listening in on their conversations and has built up an elaborate profile of the state patronage that Pakistan extends to Indian criminals. R&AW's findings became key inputs – along with information provided by the Mumbai Police,

Intelligence Bureau and other agencies – for India to declare Dawood as India's most wanted and ask Pakistan to deport him to India. In dossiers presented to Pakistan during diplomatic encounters, Dawood, Tiger Memon and other aides, such as Chhota Shakeel, were all listed among India's most wanted hiding in Pakistan. A couple of years after the 1999 Kargil conflict, R&AW published a detailed dossier, running into several dozen pages, on Pakistani patronage to India's most wanted criminals. It included their phone numbers and residential addresses in Pakistan and was handed over to foreign diplomats. R&AW had also been listening in on other underworld operatives, such as Chhota Rajan, who was hiding in Thailand during this time.

Those in the know rate R&AW's technical intelligence above all other capabilities, and at par with most of their counterparts around the world. Given its lack of parliamentary accountability and the secretive nature of its budget, R&AW has been able to acquire some of the finest equipment, as well as build a trained cadre of outstanding technical intelligence operatives.

Even all these years later, one of the transcripts of this technical intelligence division – of a conversation intercepted in 2003 – is vivid in the mind of an R&AW officer I spoke to. 'It was a conversation between Chhota Shakeel and one of his men in Mumbai. He was abusing [an airline big shot] and asked the aide to go and meet him, to tell him that he has not, after so many years, paid up the promised amount for killing Thakiyuddin,' the officer recalled. He said there were a few other conversations over the years along similar lines. 'It fell into a pattern. We had reliable evidence that Thakiyuddin was killed by a rival who had colluded with and commissioned the underworld,' he said.

The conversations went into the files of R&AW, only to be revived in early 2005, when the agency got a new leadership. It had suffered a credibility crisis after news broke that one of its senior operatives, Robinder Singh, had fled to the US after operating as a CIA mole in the agency's headquarters for years. The new leadership was desperate to boost the morale of the agency and show results. At one of the review meetings, officials handling the underworld told them about the strong evidence that pointed to Thakiyuddin's murder being the fallout of a business rivalry, and that he was killed by members of Dawood Ibrahim's gang, the very same criminal syndicate to which East West had alleged financial links.

The intercepts negated the Mumbai Police's claim that Chhota Rajan's gang had killed Thakiyuddin because he was part of the Dawood camp. The R&AW intercepts were also in complete contrast to the claims of Chhota Rajan over the years. In 1996, in an interview to journalist Harinder Baweja, who was then with *India Today*, Rajan claimed: 'I gave the instructions for Wahid's killing. He was Dawood's financier in India. I got him killed because I wanted to take revenge on Dawood for the bomb blasts.'

The intercepts, however, showed that it was Dawood's gang that carried out the killing. Was this the result of Thakiyuddin trying to distance himself from Dawood? Or was it that the Dawood gang was paid a better premium by someone else? There will never be clear answers.

In early 2005, a senior officer of R&AW was on the line with the police commissioner of Mumbai, asking him to reopen the murder case of Thakiyuddin ten years after the fatal shooting. The commissioner listened attentively and politely. However, the Mumbai Police did not look into the R&AW inputs and the case was never reopened. Was it incompetence or manipulation? There is no knowing.

∾

As Faisal went investigating his brother's death and grieving for him, East West was tumbling. Meetings of the board, which was made up of the Wahid brothers and their brothers-in-law, would break down into mourning sessions. 'We were in turmoil. I should have gone after the commercial issues, but all I wanted to know was what happened to my brother,' Faisal said as we munched on fried buns ordered from the restaurant below his modest travel office. 'Everyone had a different version of the killing, and that egged me on to find out the real facts. If we had professional leadership, the company would not have gone down.' Faisal has had long years to mull over all that happened in the aftermath of the murder that changed everything.

Besides the lack of professional leadership, there were other circumstances too that conspired to bring down East West. The BJP was reaping the dividends of the communal tension created by the demolition of Babri Masjid. In the 1996 general elections, it recorded spectacular gains and a coalition led by the BJP went on to form the Central government. As noted before, it lasted just thirteen days. But in those thirteen days, an inquiry was ordered into the allegations of East West Airlines' links with the Dawood gang. It was only to be expected: the BJP had been very vocal against the underworld.

Most business houses in India do not declare allegiance to any one political party, nor do they openly fund just one of them. There are no Koch brothers in the Indian landscape. There may be barons who are aligned with one or the other party, but they manage to keep it well under wraps. Almost all of them at least pretend to be fair and political donations are always in equal measure. If there is a shift in allegiance to the rising political force, they are also smart enough to switch back to the rival camp along with the public mood.

The Wahid brothers, though, were unabashed and naive in their allegiance to the Congress. They had built no bridges with the Hindu right wing at all. This was not because their Muslim identity would have been a hindrance: at the highest levels, there is no religion, no caste. It is money and the give-and-take of favours that speak. It was the Wahids' own fault that they did not see the tidal wave of right-wing politics rising across India. And they paid for their political naivety.

When the BJP came back to power for five years in 1999, several irrefutable links between Naresh Goyal and Dawood Ibrahim's gang emerged. This time, the government did not react.

Though the 1996 inquiry was a setback and finances were strained, hope returned to the East West office in summer. By the end of May 1996, the BJP government had to resign. Everyone wanted to avoid elections, and regional political satraps formed an alliance to put together a coalition front of smaller parties, leaving out the Congress and the BJP. At a meeting of the regional parties in Delhi, Karnataka chief minister H.D. Deve Gowda wasn't the most attentive – in fact, many believe he slept through most of it. So great was the political turmoil of the time that the meeting elected this untested man as India's next prime minister. Gowda, a farmer and a wily politician who had not until then sought his political fortunes outside Karnataka, was overwhelmed and intimidated by New Delhi and its sweep of power games and politics. He needed trusted men to help him navigate the minefield.

Gowda began his stay in the national capital at Karnataka Bhavan. Helping him manage Delhi was Chand Mahal Ibrahim, who was rarely spotted without his signature Ray-Ban sunglasses and a broad smile. Gowda had plucked this little-known politician from Karnataka and thrown him into the vortex of Indian political uncertainties. Overnight, Ibrahim became an indispensable part of the capital's power centres.

Gowda was sworn in as India's eleventh prime minister on 1 June 1996, with the Congress providing outside support. Ibrahim was sworn in as a senior minister and held two crucial portfolios: civil aviation and information and broadcasting. He was a Malayali Muslim like the Wahids, and both were close associates of the Sunni preacher Kanthapuram A.P. Aboobacker Musliyar, who had led the funeral prayers for Thakiyuddin. They had several common friends and acquaintances.

Mired in gloom as it was, optimism began to return to East West. The Wahid family became close confidants of the civil aviation minister. There is, of course, no better patron than the Union minister looking after the portfolio your business falls under.

With Ibrahim's blessings, East West put on fast track an ambitious strategy to revive its fortunes. It activated contact with Singapore Airlines, which had been desperately trying to enter the Indian market and was already in talks with the Tata group to launch a domestic carrier in India. For Tata group supremo Ratan Tata, a pilot himself, it was both the revival of a key Tata legacy as well as a lifelong passion. For East West, it was a question of survival.

It was not to be. The Tata group took nearly two decades more to enter the Indian civil aviation sector – as a minority partner in Air Asia in 2014 as well as in a joint venture with Singapore Airlines. When asked in 2013 why they took such a long time to re-enter aviation, Ratan Tata was understated: 'We didn't come earlier because we chose to stay out.' The answer brushed over his big efforts – on at least three occasions – to find a toehold in the aviation market.

That the Tata group, India's foremost business house with a legacy of over a century and a half, and one that played a pioneering role in industrializing India, struggled is testimony to the overwhelming corruption and manipulation that has crept into Indian decision-making. Ratan Tata has politely referred to the matter in public, but in private he has complained bitterly about the obstacles created by rivals to prevent his group from entering the sector.

A couple of weeks after Faisal's last visit to Singapore, his eldest brother Nasiruddin called one morning asking if he had seen the newspapers of the day. 'Singapore Airlines Over My Dead Body', the headlines screamed, quoting Ibrahim. This was the very opposite of what Ibrahim had been telling Faisal, or even what he had told the Singapore Airlines leadership over the phone.

Faisal rushed to 22 Akbar Road in New Delhi, the sprawling mansion next to the Congress headquarters, where Ibrahim lived. He had never before had to wait for more than a few minutes to meet Ibrahim. But on that occasion, Faisal sat for an hour and a half in the office. When the minister did finally show up, he was evasive and said that his hand had been forced by the Congress, which was propping up the government.

According to Faisal, one of Ibrahim's assistants told him that immediately after the East West delegation visited Singapore, Naresh Goyal had visited Ibrahim repeatedly, and that the minister had taken him to meet Prime Minister Deve Gowda at his official residence at least twice. The first time they went, Goyal was refused entry by the prime minister's security personnel. Ibrahim had to call Gowda on a secure government telephone line to ensure that Goyal was allowed into 7 Race Course Road, the aide told Faisal.

For East West Airlines, the end was near. A cocktail of factors – deceptions, financial misfortunes and the lack of professional leadership – finished them.

East West was, for instance, fighting a case for violation of contractual norms in the leasing of the two aircraft through the Swedish firm Kolding. It sued PLM, the original owner of the aircraft, filing a claim of around Rs 850 crore. The case looked good for East West, but as a ruling was nearing, PLM dramatically filed for bankruptcy in the US, and all its assets were mysteriously sold off. Its company lawyers no longer turned up at the hearings.

The three aircraft owned by PLM, which were now flying for East West, were due for check and overhaul, which would at that time cost over Rs 10 crore per aircraft. After extended court proceedings and many appeals, the Supreme Court ordered PLM, or rather its original owners, to take back the aircraft.

From fifteen aircraft in November 1995, when Thakiyuddin was killed, East West was down to twelve by the end of 1996. The company lost around Rs 14 crore in the deal with Kolding; two more of its aircraft were up for major check and overhaul and its MRO proposal with Hindustan Aeronautics Limited was going nowhere. By early 1997, the fleet was down to ten aircraft. Lenders too started imposing huge costs on the company. The company took money at up to 32 per cent interest from banks, against the prevalent 12 per cent lending rate.

By the end of 1996, East West had started defaulting on its bank loans, and the lead lender, Indian Bank, declared it a non-performing asset (NPA). Other lenders followed suit, and many began to revoke the company's bank guarantees. The Central Bureau of Investigation filed a criminal case against the company for defrauding state-controlled fuel companies that supplied aviation turbine fuel. Unable to pay them in time and to overcome the crisis, the company allegedly used fake bank drafts.

East West started grounding more aircraft. The collateral damage was the travel division, number one in India until then. Because it was part of the same company, banks refused guarantees on behalf of the travel division to the IATA, which might have helped the division to scale up business significantly. As the aviation business began sucking in all their resources, by late 1996, the travel business too began to shrink.

Many still wanted East West to fly. Air Linkers offered a further grace period of six months on aircraft leasing fees. Most of the pilots and engineers had stayed back with the company despite its dwindling fortunes. But human goodwill was no match for harsh economic and political realities. One morning in June 1997, the last East West flight touched down in Mumbai.

The end of East West Airlines fitted in with the narrative of the post-economic-liberalization era: ruthless business tactics, politically influential businessmen, politicians who are on the take, ambitious upstarts and shady players.

As the curtains came down on East West, the fortunes of Jet Airways were starting to soar. Goyal – a young, hard-working man from Punjab with no known family, financial, political or educational backing – has an equally dramatic story. He remains a controversial figure, and one who continues to surprise and infuriate. But Goyal symbolizes contemporary India. Without an examination of the rise of Goyal, it would be impossible to appreciate the crisis at all levels of the Indian democracy – the oligarchy that is India's political class, the power of money to swing decisions, the meek regulatory systems that are bent and broken regularly by business interests, the elite's blatant disrespect for laws and norms, and eventually, the disappearance of even a semblance of morality from public life.

As a diverse society struggles to strengthen its institutions in the face of powerful politician–businessman nexus, it would be yet another Indian miracle if democracy survives and flourishes. If democracy continues to gasp for breath, and finally dies one day, it would be the final outcome of a collective conspiracy. It would be a death foretold.

7

The Fly-by-Might Operator

Intelligence Bureau chief K.P. Singh and his senior colleague, the joint director Anjan Ghosh, took an elevator down North Block to an official vehicle waiting in the basement on a summer day in 2002. A few hundred metres away, at the circular building housing both houses of parliament, members were agitated over a letter Ghosh had written a few months earlier.

It was a single-page note to Sangita Gairola, joint secretary at the Ministry of Home Affairs, saying that his agency had 'confirmed information of intermittent contacts between Naresh Goyal and underworld dons, Chhota Shakeel and Dawood Ibrahim, to settle financial issues. There is strong suspicion that parts of Goyal's investments may have accrued through the assistance of underworld groups, prominently headed by Dawood and Chhota Shakeel.'

Ghosh further alleged that Goyal and Jet Airways had been steady recipients of large dubious investments originating from Gulf sheikhs. 'Naresh Goyal's bonhomie and close business links with the Shaikhs have been known for over two decades. These connections are believed to have been used repeatedly not only to get direct investments, but also to get a lot of tainted Indian money laundered and recycled into business in India.

Much of this kind of money is generated through smuggling, extortion and similar illegal practices,' the letter said.

The letter of 12 December 2001 emerged in the media suddenly and caused an uproar. At the next session of parliament, there were vehement demands from members across parties to know the truth. One of the members, Raju Parmar, had asked a starred question in Rajya Sabha, which the home minister had to stand up and give a verbal answer to, and not just table a written reply. To a starred question, there could be instant supplementary questions that the minister had to answer. Parmar's question was listed for 7 May, the morning on which K.P. Singh and Ghosh were hurrying up to the parliament building.

Waiting for the two senior IB officials was India's then deputy prime minister and home minister, L.K. Advani, whose public discourses frequently revolved around the theme of how closely Indian politics was linked to the underworld. The BJP, as well as Advani, had always taken a tough position on the issue. Advani listened patiently as the two officials told him about the evidence they had of Goyal's links with the underworld. In recent months, they had at least three telephone intercepts of his conversations with Dawood and Shakeel, the officials said, adding that there was other evidence too, according to one of the officials present at the meeting.

Advani looked shaken and determined after the meeting, the official said. 'He was clear that this could not go on. I thought Jet Airways would be shut down in a matter of days,' the official said to me over a decade later. By the time I met him, sometime in 2014, Jet Airways had become a flourishing international airline, Goyal a darling of politicians and civil servants, and Advani a pale shadow of his once formidable, divisive self. One of his political pupils, Narendra Modi, would soon be the one steering the BJP to a more aggressive and popular phase.

As head of the interior securities ministry, Advani was second only to prime minister Atal Behari Vajpayee in the tumultuous years between 1998 and 2004, during which India tested nuclear devices, fought a limited war with Pakistan and had to deal with the repercussions of two major terrorist attacks: the hijack of a passenger aircraft and an attack on the parliament building. Indian political rhetoric has always been shrill on the issue of terrorism, but despite decades of struggling with it, the country has no robust responses in place to deal with non-state actors.

The hijacking of 24 December 1999 showed this up only too plainly. New Delhi was shutting down for Christmas on a mildly foggy winter evening. An Indian Airlines aircraft, IC-814, took off from Kathmandu for New Delhi, mostly carrying vacationers. A few minutes after it was airborne, five hijackers took over the aircraft and forced the pilot to fly over several countries and land at a few airports, until finally they instructed him to hangar at Kandahar in Afghanistan, which was then under Taliban rule. India's anti-hijack commandos from the National Security Guard trailed the aircraft for the most part, including over Arab skies. The government dithered on a commando operation, and they returned to New Delhi.

There are still questions about how the hijackers managed to get logistical assistance in Kathmandu and at its airport, and there is reason to suspect that local criminal elements in both Nepal and India provided active assistance to the five hijackers, who were all from Pakistan. Eventually, External Affairs Minister Jaswant Singh flew to Kandahar with three dreaded terrorists and handed them over to the hijackers. It was a bizarre twist to a harrowing tale, and typical of the deep-rooted lack of imagination in the Indian system. What if, midway through Singh's flight, something untoward had happened? What if there was a turncoat among the security detail guarding the terrorists?

Vajpayee's cabinet was divided over the barter; in closed-door meetings, Advani strongly advocated against a compromise with terrorists. However, Vajpayee prevailed with his argument that the safety of passengers took precedence over all else. Years later, Jaswant Singh would remember his flight to Kandahar with the three terrorists as a 'painful chapter', one that he wouldn't want to revisit. He did, however, admit to the foolishness of India's external affairs minister travelling with such risky co-passengers.

By the time the hijack was called off in the evening of 31 December, one passenger had been killed and the NDA government's masculine posturing on security matters had taken a severe blow. As we wound up our unusual Christmas week, my wife-to-be Priya and I stepped out for dinner in a scarred and embarrassed city. We wound up eating a tasteless New Year's Eve dinner at a packed restaurant before heading home.

Advani was determined to ensure that India was not humiliated in this fashion again. His ministry and its arms, including the Intelligence Bureau, were told to be firm and uncompromising on security matters. Within days, the Ministry of Civil Aviation and the Ministry of Home Affairs began consultations on security clearance for air operators. There was suspicion that the hijackers had inside help on IC-814. Investigators would later track the hijackers' accomplices to Mumbai and other parts of India.

On 31 January 2000, exactly a month after the hijack, civil aviation secretary Ravindra Gupta chaired a meeting on the issue of security clearance for air operators. In attendance were four senior officials, including Sangita Gairola, to whom Ghosh had written the letter linking Jet Airways to the underworld. She told the meeting that, in the light of the suspected underworld links of East West Airlines and the bizarre incident of the arms drops in Purulia in West Bengal – a Latvian AN-26 aircraft flew over India undetected and dropped several hundred AK-47 rifles and more than a million rounds of ammunition on 17 December 1995 – security agencies had already tightened the security clearance mechanism. The ghost of IC-814 haunted the meeting but nobody mentioned it, at least according to the official minutes. One of the key questions was which ministry should be the nodal agency for providing security clearance to air operators.

On 25 March 2000, Gairola wrote to the civil aviation ministry, conveying her ministry's comments to the questions raised at the meeting.

Paramount was that 'the authority empowered to give security clearance would be the Ministry of Home Affairs' and that 'security clearance would be required at every stage', such as the induction of new directors to an operator's board.

Around this time, Mesco Airlines sought permission to induct two new directors to its board. V.P. Bhatia, an undersecretary in the home ministry, wrote to the civil aviation ministry denying permission, as the two were under investigation by the CBI for forgery and falsification of accounts. In the case of the Delhi Flying Club board too, Bhatia wrote refusing security clearance to Congress party leader Satish Sharma, a close associate of the Gandhi family, because of criminal cases against him. The NDA government was sending out a clear signal: it was not willing to compromise national security, especially in civil aviation.

On 8 March 2000, the civil aviation ministry sent the details of the reconstituted board of directors of Jet Airways to Advani. It included eight non-resident Indians and five foreigners. The home ministry under Advani – Iron Man to his followers, known for his firm stand on issues – sat on it for months, even though the civil aviation ministry kept shooting off reminders. The government had given several assurances to parliament over questions from members regarding Jet Airways, and that too was weighing on him. On 4 January 2002, civil aviation secretary A.H. Jung wrote to his counterpart in the home ministry, Kamal Pande, about the several reminders they had sent on the issue. He pointed out that Jet 'continues to operate as scheduled airline, without proper security clearance for their reconstituted board'.

By 9 December 2003, Civil Aviation Minister Rajiv Pratap Rudy had also written to Advani about the issue. He pointed out that the Jet Airways matter was initially taken up with the home ministry in March 2000. 'However, despite a number of references over the past three years, a clear response from MHA has not yet been received. This Ministry has been put in an awkward position in the absence of categorical advice of the Ministry of Home Affairs.' Rudy added that the five assurances made to parliament, on finding a proper solution to concerns regarding the airline, were still pending and that the issue had figured in parliamentary committee meetings too.

At the end of three years, IB chief K.P. Singh gave a strange twist to the entire case. He claimed that his agency had earlier agreed to give Jet Airways security clearance because 'nothing specifically adverse was available at that time either against the Airlines or its Directors on the records of the IB and the R&AW'. He wrote to the home ministry: 'Whatever information has since emerged about Jet Airways or its owner Naresh Goyal from R&AW and other sources, does not seem to be of the nature that would justify the withdrawal of security clearance earlier given to the airlines.' That put an end to intelligence inquiries into Jet Airways' dubious funds and its promoter's links to Dawood Ibrahim.

These exchanges between the various departments have remained buried in government files for years, and would have been there forever, had not a contact of mine handed them over to me at great personal risk.

A handful of officers in the security establishment had spent a significant part of their professional lives tracking Naresh Goyal, the origins of his business, his questionable business deals (and those of many of his friends) across the political spectrum and the underworld. With each change of government, these officials thought tough action would be taken. But Goyal continued to flourish.

Singh's note omitted no facts. Before absolving Goyal, he said that the Jet Airways owner 'appeared to have earned his wealth through smuggling and other illegitimate means and that the airlines was probably investigated for FERA [Foreign Exchange Regulation Act] violations'. Singh also pointed out that Goyal had in the past been accused of adopting unfair business tactics to undermine rival airlines, such as purchasing of union leaders and exploiting political connections. 'Such tactics are, however, not uncommon in a highly competitive business milieu and while such traits reflect unfavourably on his professional ethics, they do not impinge on national security,' Singh wrote.

His note referred to the input given a few months earlier, detailing Goyal's links with the Dawood gang. It added that the inputs 'were mainly procured from the R&AW' and that the intelligence agency had 'indicated their inability to further develop the information already given by them' except to say that Goyal 'had earned his wealth through smuggling and other illegitimate means'. Singh didn't mention the IB's own intercepts of the conversations between the Dawood gang and Goyal – intercepts that his own agency had earlier reported to the government.

Curiously enough, the home ministry – even Advani – raised no objections, though it was only months earlier that the home minister stood in parliament to assure the house of appropriate action.

Dawood is no ordinary criminal. While designating Dawood a 'specially designated global terrorist' and freezing all his assets, the US treasury department had said: 'Ibrahim's syndicate is involved in large-scale shipments of narcotics in the UK and Western Europe. The syndicate's smuggling routes from South Asia, the Middle East and Africa are shared with Osama bin Laden and his terrorist network. Successful routes established over recent years by Ibrahim's syndicate have been subsequently utilized by bin Laden.' The US announcement also pointed out that this son of a former police constable from Maharashtra had 'consistently aimed to destabilize the Indian government through inciting riots, acts of terrorism, and civil disobedience. He is currently wanted by India for the March 12, 1993 Bombay Exchange bombings, which killed hundreds of Indians and injured over a thousand more.' It added that Ibrahim had also financially supported Islamic militant groups working against India, such as Lashkar-e-Tayyiba (LeT).

Singh's letter contradicted what Anjan Ghosh had said a few months earlier. 'It was a simple case, and there was no doubt about what the ministry's position should have been,' one of the officials who dealt with the case told me.

On the IB chief's cue, the home ministry gave up its authority to issue security clearance and instead left it to the civil aviation ministry. Of all the records I have gone through regarding security clearances for private air operators, Jet Airways' is the only case where the home ministry gave up this right.

Mukesh Mittal, a director in the home ministry, wrote to the civil aviation ministry that they had found 'certain adverse inputs against Shri Naresh Goyal, chairman of the Jet Airways', and attached a gist of the inputs on him, which repeated almost all the points raised originally by Anjan Ghosh and K.P. Singh, and reproduced Ghosh's letter almost verbatim. 'Report, though unconfirmed, ascribes this exponential growth in the company's holding due to money transfers through hawala (illegal money transfer) channels,' the note concluded.

After this indictment, Mittal's official note concluded: 'In view of this position, Ministry of Civil Aviation may please consider the proposal keeping all aspects in view and take an appropriate decision.' He added that the order has been issued with the 'approval of the Home Secretary'.

Once again, Advani did not seem to have any comments on the issue. Yet, he cannot be singled out for blame in a system where ambivalence and obfuscation – not positive articulation – mark the conduct of business.

Despite the government's almost clean chit, the intelligence agencies never closed their files on Jet Airways. As of 2015, I had confirmation that the case was very much open. The former chief of an intelligence agency said the case could never be closed. 'It is a test case for us, and it is a shame that, despite such overwhelming evidence, we couldn't take any action,' he said one evening, as we discussed the deep roots of the underworld and criminals in Indian politics and business. He argued that the extent of Dawood's network had not yet been revealed to the public.

Over the years, intelligence agencies have been gathering significant evidence of Dawood's connections with many political leaders and businessmen from his hiding place in Pakistan. He has evolved very sophisticated ways of keeping in touch with the Indian elite and businesses. A Union minister in Dr Manmohan Singh's UPA government, which was in power between 2004 and 2014, had been exchanging notes with him through a resident of south Delhi, who was also suspected to be a bookie manipulating cricket games. According to several intercepts by R&AW over the years, the bookie had been negotiating through the minister for Dawood's return to India. The don was willing to spend a few years in an Indian jail if he was allowed to return. The Karachi-based don had never felt at home in Pakistan; it was in India that he built his fortunes and followers. In these intercepts, the south Delhi resident is heard promising Dawood and his key aides that the minister would try to get the government to offer Pakistan a deal to extradite Dawood. Officially, India had been demanding that Pakistan return Dawood to India, but Pakistan continued to deny that he was in its territory at all.

A prominent regional political satrap from Uttar Pradesh used to receive messages from Dawood through human couriers sent from Mumbai, according to dependable intelligence operatives who have watched the activity closely. Dawood and his aides would send their messages to a Mumbai-based Muslim preacher, and he in turn passed on the information through trusted youngsters recruited from Uttar Pradesh. The couriers have been used dozens of times in the past decade, one of the officials claimed.

Dawood is certainly not the only criminal that the Indian political class cosies up to. While this has not been adequately scrutinized, freak police investigations, intelligence inputs or unusual spikes and lows in people's careers tell tales. The story of Sachin Ahir, a junior minister in the Maharashtra state government until 2015 and a close associate of Sharad Pawar, who was once Union agriculture minister and remains one of India's most powerful politicians, is a case in point.

In the Bombay of the 1970s and '80s, the two senior members of the Maharashtra Congress – Sharad Pawar and A.R. Antulay – locked horns. This was a time when criminal ganglords were friends of politicians and Bombay was a city of textile mills. Sachin Ahir and his elder brother Vijay started their careers as musclemen for a mill owner. Like their uncle, gangster Arun Gawli, the Ahir brothers knew muscle power.

Then the Ahirs' story got mixed up with the Pawar–Antulay rivalry. To counter Antulay's influence among Muslims, Pawar propped up Maulana Ziauddin Burhanuddin Bukhari in the Konkan region of Maharashtra, created the Konkan Mercantile Bank and handed over its reins to Bukhari. He was also given a large plot of land in the heart of Bombay to create Millat Nagar, a Muslim colony.

Bukhari was shot dead during the tense period after the demolition of Babri Masjid. Police investigation into the case established that Vijay Ahir was the key conspirator. He landed in jail, and soon his young brother, Sachin, in his early twenties then, was appointed the general secretary of the Rashtriya Mill Mazdoor Sangh (RMMS, or the National Mill Workers' Union), which was a powerful trade union of the mill workers of Bombay started by the Congress in 1945. Sachin's climb was as swift as his entry. He became the president of RMMS in no time. In 1999, when Pawar and a few others left the Congress, protesting the leadership of Italian-origin Sonia Gandhi, Sachin was among them.

Sachin's rise wasn't unexpected. The underworld has a huge say in construction, land deals and other businesses in Mumbai. It is the money flowing in from these businesses that sustains the city's politics. And there's no bigger fish in that sea than Dawood.

He lingers on in movies, politics, betting, drug smuggling, land deals, construction – and in the imagination of the security establishment. In the summer of 2013, when the police forces of Delhi and Mumbai exposed the widespread practice of illegal betting and fixing in the cash-rich Indian Premier League, they said the Dawood gang ultimately controlled the betting syndicates. Delhi Police charged several people, including former Indian cricketer S. Sreesanth, under the draconian Maharashtra Control of Organized Crime Act (MCOCA), saying that they had indulged in spot fixing during matches at the command of Dawood and his key aide Chhota Shakeel. Though the evidence was untenable, allegations of links to Dawood is an effective ploy to strengthen and sensationalize any case, and also to cover up the agencies' weak investigation skills. In 2015, a

Delhi court threw out the Delhi Police's claims. Dawood has, meanwhile, grown into an enigma, a nightmare, and an unavoidable reality of the daily existence of modern-day India.

That said, he also survives because of deep-rooted contacts within the security establishment itself. On 11 July 2005, a joint team of Mumbai and Delhi Police intercepted a car in the national capital and arrested Vicky Malhotra, a key aide of Dawood's rival Chhota Rajan, who was wanted in numerous criminal cases, including murder and extortion. Surprisingly, accompanying Malhotra was Ajit Doval, a former chief of the IB and one of India's most celebrated spies, who went on to become the national security advisor (NSA) to Prime Minister Narendra Modi in 2014. Some intelligence sources said Doval, despite his retirement, was part of an ongoing IB operation to use the Chhota Rajan gang to target Dawood. Some said Doval was acting on his own. Investigations revealed that Dawood had contacts within the Mumbai Police and that they had created an alert about Malhotra and thwarted Doval's operation. The police promptly sacked an inspector who was in touch with the Dawood gang. A few days after this drama, Dawood's daughter married the son of famous Pakistani cricketer Javed Miandad. The reception was held at Dubai's Grand Hyatt hotel. Speculation was that Doval was planning to target Dawood and his gang if they attended the Dubai reception. But Dawood turned the tables on him and one of India's most celebrated spymasters was caught on a Delhi road with a criminal.

Regarding the Dubai reception, the US embassy in New Delhi cabled to their headquarters: 'Like a bad dream, terrorist and underworld figure Dawood Ibrahim returned to the headlines of India's media in July when his daughter married the son of a famous Pakistani cricket player. An upscale wedding reception brazenly took place at the ostensibly American-run Grand Hyatt hotel in Dubai on July 23. Ibrahim, India's most wanted man for the 1993 Bombay bombings that killed hundreds, and a US Specially Designated Global Terrorist, reportedly did not attend the event. One media outlet mentioned, however, that Ibrahim, believed to be living in Pakistan, travelled on forged documents to witness the nikah (wedding) ceremony of the couple on July 9 in Mecca. The wedding and subsequent reception generated intense interest in the Indian media, which reported that Indian police and security services were shadowing business, entertainment and underworld figures from India who might try to attend the reception. In the end, no prominent Indians actually showed up in Dubai. The manner in which Ibrahim could so blatantly stage such an event has infuriated our Indian contacts.'

~

To succeed in India, it is important to have friends across the political spectrum and deep inside the system. The end of right-wing rule in the summer of 2004 didn't change much for Naresh Goyal – quite unlike the fate of East West Airlines when the Congress lost power almost a decade earlier.

Goyal had friends in all the right places. One of the key regional parties in the new ruling dispensation, the UPA, was Sharad Pawar's Nationalist Congress Party (NCP), which, according to New Delhi's political grapevine, insisted on getting the civil aviation portfolio. Praful Patel, a flamboyant businessman whose family made its fortunes in tobacco, and who is known to be a key aide of Pawar's, became the civil aviation minister.

Around the time that the new government was coming to power – when India had yet not permitted its private airlines to fly abroad – Jet Airways began applying for slots at the London, Kuala Lumpur, Singapore and Bangkok airports. When the matter came up in parliament, Patel said the airline was doing all of this at its own risk. What he did not say was that a committee appointed by the previous government had submitted a detailed road map for expansion and modernization of the aviation sector. And that an exercise had already been initiated to implement just one of the recommendations of the committee: permit private airlines to fly abroad. This was not publicly known, nor was the parliament told about it. Within months, Jet Airways became an international airline.

As Jet Airways prepared to launch its services in the US, Maryland-based Jet Airways Inc. filed complaints before various authorities, asking that the Indian company be denied permission to fly to the US, accusing it of trademark infringement. Its CEO and president, Nancy M. Heckerman, also said that Jet Airways of India was an Al Qaeda company. Her objections were marked to the Indian government by the US, asking for clarifications. Within months of the 23 May 2005 complaint, the Government of India officially communicated to the US that there were no security concerns with respect to Jet Airways.

Even as the airline was awaiting US clearance, similar queries about its links to dubious outfits emerged from the governments of Singapore and UK in 2006 after a Jet Airways employee in London, Amin Asmin Tariq, was arrested for alleged links to the foiled bid to blow up transatlantic flights with liquid bombs. New Delhi was consistent in its stand: Jet Airways posed no security concerns. Officials who had been watching Goyal and Jet Airways for years told me that the government's enthusiasm was surprising. 'Not only did the government give a certificate of good conduct to them, but it put its diplomatic might behind the company,' said one senior official in the security establishment. Another one said the political establishment may have given a clean chit, 'but the Indian intelligence agencies can never close the case'.

In January 2006, Jet Airways offered to take over Air Sahara, part of Subrata Roy's Sahara group. Much like Naresh Goyal, Roy too had made a mysterious climb up the big-stakes ladder. Starting in 1978 with a small residuary non-banking company that collected very low amounts as deposits, mostly from the poor who had no access to formal banking, Roy went on to control a sprawling business empire that owns London's Grosvenor House, New York's Plaza Hotel, newspapers, TV stations, racing teams and luxury apartment complexes. He is one of India's leading sponsors of sports and employs over a million people who greet each other with 'Sahara Pranam'. On a very hot summer day in May 2013, Roy assembled 1,21,653 of his uniformed employees in a stadium in Lucknow city to sing the national anthem and set a Guinness Book record. He wears his patriotism on his sleeve.

In March 2014, the Supreme Court of India sent Roy to jail in a running battle between the Sahara group and the country's capital market watchdog, the Securities and Exchange Board of India (SEBI), over inconsistencies in the accounting of Rs 24,773 crore that it claimed to have collected from 3.1 crore investors. The addresses of most of these subscribers couldn't be verified, and Roy's legal team was accused of trying to mislead the market regulator and courts. As of mid-2016, he continues to be in jail.

Let's return to his airline interests, though. In January 2006, Jet Airways offered to buy Air Sahara for Rs 2,300 crore in the biggest deal yet in Indian aviation history. There was concern among some analysts that Jet was overpaying. The civil aviation ministry gave in-principle approval, but concerns about security clearance came up again in the context of Naresh Goyal joining the Air Sahara board. A minister in the UPA government took aside the chief of an intelligence agency involved in the matter and told him to be meticulous in dealing with it. 'I was surprised because he was known to be a Goyal man, and here he was telling me to be firm with Jet Airways,' the official told me. As instructed, the agencies were meticulous, thus delaying the process, and as a result, the deal collapsed. Both sides filed lawsuits against each other. Strangely, a day after the deal officially collapsed, Goyal's security clearance came through, this time from the home ministry.

Sahara's ventures were running in losses, and the group had been scrambling for cash. It restarted negotiations with Jet. This time, a desperate Sahara settled at Rs 1,450 crore, almost 40 per cent less than the original offer. 'I have rarely seen Subrata Roy so helpless,' one of the key negotiators in the deal told me during a meeting in Mumbai. 'Nareshji was in complete command.'

As the Jet Airways juggernaut powered ahead, the Indian aviation market – like the Indian economy itself at that time – was exploding. In 2000–01, a total of 1.4 crore passengers flew in Indian carriers; the number jumped to 4.5 crore by 2009–10. Many of India's cattle-shed airports were overhauled and private businessmen entered the aviation business, reaping rich rewards.

Around the time that the Jet Airways–Air Sahara deal was being negotiated, the government decided to overhaul Delhi's old airport. Delhi International Airport Private Limited was incorporated with the government holding 26 per cent of the shares, the rest held by a consortium of private players, including Fraport and Malaysia Airports Holding Berhad. Leading the private consortium with 50.1 per cent stake was India's GMR group. Such public–private partnerships (PPPs) are among the defining features of India's efforts to reform its economy, especially the crumbling infrastructure. The Delhi airport symbolizes India's economic resurgence, its quest to modernize infrastructure, the partnerships that shape 'new India' and the questionable deals undermining all of it.

In July 2004, when bids were invited for redevelopment of the airport, GMR was not among the front runners. But in January 2006, it was the consortium led by GMR that was appointed to redevelop the 5,106-acre Indira Gandhi International Airport. Then, in August 2012, government auditor CAG released a damning indictment of the airport project, accusing the government of blatant favouritism to the joint venture (JV), resulting in public losses running into billions of dollars. The CAG also found that a clause limiting the JV's terms to thirty years, to be extended by another thirty years through 'mutual agreement and negotiation of terms', was mysteriously omitted from the final contract, making it easier to extend the JV contract. This was particularly ominous because it was a decision arrived at by the UPA council of ministers. The airport operator had been allowed to lease land for commercial exploitation at a far lower rate than even the amount government agencies were paying. For a meagre Rs 100 as annual rental and a one time payment of Rs 6.19

crore, the operator had been allowed to use land with earning potential of Rs 1,63,557 crore over the concession period of fifty-eight years. Each passenger flying out of the airport was, and still is, forced to pay a user fee, which was not part of the contract provisions. The forty-four-page audit report is packed with an enumeration of favours to the private consortium. The report resulted in the usual round of protests and outrage, which died out in a few days.

～

With its glittering airports and booming aviation sector, India has come a long way from the time when J.R.D. Tata set up the country's first airline. Born in Paris on 29 July 1904 – just seven months after the Wright brothers flew the first aircraft at Kitty Hawk – JRD (as he was better known) was the scion of a major industrial house in British India.

The Tatas often vacationed in Hardelot, the beach town in France where Louis Bleriot, the first pilot to fly across the English Channel in 1909, had a house. Until Charles Lindbergh crossed the Atlantic in 1927, Bleriot's was the most heroic feat in the nascent history of aviation. Bleriot's plane used to land on the beach next to Tata's vacation home – an exciting sight that must have made a deep impression on the young boy. At the age of fifteen, just as World War I wound up, JRD made his maiden flight on a Caudron Bagnet, an early French plane.

JRD was hooked – and that addiction to aviation would lead him to write and rewrite the history of civil aviation in the Indian subcontinent. About a decade after his first flight, JRD graduated from India's first flying club in Bombay as its first certified pilot in 1929. After three hours and forty-five minutes of dual flying experience, he was allowed solo flight and within a week qualified for his 'A' licence.

'No document has ever given me a greater thrill than the little blue and gold certificate delivered to me on 10 February 1929, by the Aero Club of India and Burma on behalf of the Federation Aeronautique Internationale (FAI). The fact that it bore the Number 1 added to my pride in owning it, even though it meant nothing more than that I was the first one to have qualified in India,' JRD would tell his biographer R.M. Lala several decades later.

Just six weeks after JRD got his licence, he joined hands with Nevill Vintcent, a heavyweight boxing champion of the Royal Air Force in the Middle East, to float the idea of India's first airline. The Tata group wrote on 20 March 1929 to the government to find out if it was interested in starting a mail service between Karachi and Bombay. It was, but between Karachi and Delhi, the capital of British India. Within a month of this letter, the British-owned Imperial Airways, which later merged with British Airways, landed in Karachi with India's first mail. A local connection flight to Bombay would then be handy. The Tatas sought a subsidy of Rs 1,25,000, but the government was not inclined to provide any such incentive. Between 1929 and 1931, the group wrote numerous letters to the government on the proposal, and this period tested 'JRD's endurance and patience', according to Lala.

'I think that government are treating us shabbily ... I hope that you will be able to save me this journey and to find out whether Government intend to say yes or no within the next 100 years,' JRD wrote to Vintcent on 9 December 1931. JRD's persistence ushered in the era of civil aviation in India with the Tata Aviation Service.

Decades later, JRD would recall the event: 'On an exciting October dawn in 1932, a Puss Moth and I soared joyfully from Karachi with our first precious load of mail, on an inaugural flight to Bombay. As we hummed towards our destination at a "dazzling" hundred miles an hour, I breathed a silent prayer for the success of our venture and for the safety of those who would work for it. We were a small team in those days. We shared successes and failures, the joys and heartaches, as together we built up the enterprise which later was to blossom into Air-India and Air-India International.'

JRD landed in Ahmedabad for refuelling and delivering eight pounds of mail. 'A bullock cart trundled to the runway and four gallon cans of petrol were poured into the tank of the little plane,' Lala wrote. Despite headwinds and a bird that flew into his cabin and had to be killed, JRD's inaugural flight landed in Mumbai with the 55 pounds of mail for Bombay without much trouble. He also carried mail for southern India.

The Imperial Airways aeroplane would arrive in Karachi every Friday evening and hand over the mail to Tata Aviation Service, and its Puss Moth would take off the next morning. The Imperial Airways plane would wait until the next Wednesday to allow the Tata plane to complete its circuit and come back with mail for foreign countries. The biggest trouble for the nascent operation was that the Imperial Airways plane was almost always late.

When World War II broke out in 1939, the government took over all aviation activities and put the Tatas' aircraft under its command. A De Havilland 86, the company's first four-engine plane, was commandeered for coastal operations. However, the war too was an opportunity for JRD: 'When the war came along, with the help of Nevill Vintcent, we decided to offer to build up an aircraft industry that would be useful after the war. So what should we build? Metal aeroplanes needed a lot of metallurgical materials and experience we couldn't import easily, so we decided to offer to build the Mosquito – a light, twin-engined fighter bomber. It was made of wood and could go extremely fast. The De Havilland Company built it and it was designed to carry one big bomb. It was used to bomb Berlin. We would have to import the engine, of course. The body was a fairly simple structure, very successful. The British Government said "yes" and we began to build a factory in Pune near the Aga Khan Palace.' As the factory preparations were in full swing, the British cancelled the order. JRD thought the British didn't want India to make a good aeroplane to compete with the British industry.

In 1943, Vintcent was returning to India from Britain after discussions with the government about manufacturing Mosquito planes. The former Royal Air Force (RAF) pilot took a lift in a Hudson bomber, which was shot down off the coast of France. Vintcent was lost in the Atlantic forever.

A few months after India's Independence, JRD proposed the setting up of Air-India International Limited, an international airline co-owned by the Tatas, the government and the public. The new government of free India approved his proposal within weeks, and on 8 June 1948, the first Bombay–London service was inaugurated.

Buying up dozens of Dakotas left behind by the US Air Force in its WW-II bases in India, imposing very high standards of service and working with visionary zeal, JRD rapidly scaled up the airline and established it as one of the best in the world. But then, in 1952, the government decided to nationalize the civil aviation sector, although it insisted that JRD remain chairman of Air-India International. He continued to steer the company until 1978. In 1968, the *Daily Mail*'s Julian Holland rated Air-India at the top of the airlines she surveyed. 'I left some chocolates on my seat while the plane was delayed in Rome for an hour. When I returned, they had not moved but the blinds had been drawn at the window to keep the sun off them and prevent them from melting,' she reported.

Four decades later, Air-India was rated the world's third most dangerous airline by the Jet Airliner Crash Data Evaluation Centre, based on its annual safety calculations that assess all hull-loss accidents and serious incidents in the past thirty years of operations in relation to the revenue passenger kilometres (RPK) performed in the same time. The assessment took into account international safety benchmarks, such as the IATA Operational Safety Audit (IOSA) and the Universal Safety Oversight Audit Programme (USOAP) country factor. It was a reflection of the larger malaise crippling Air-India. Employee morale was at its lowest, there were frequent strikes, the airline was struggling under staggering debt: it was as if there was a grand conspiracy to destroy the national carrier and its legacy.

During the UPA's 2004–14 tenure, some very questionable decisions were made, and these contributed to the destruction of Air-India. Overseeing the decisions was Praful Patel, the civil aviation minister whose proximity to Naresh Goyal was widely known. The government nudged Air-India to increase its orders for new aircraft from twenty-eight to sixty-eight, thus hugely inflating its debt. The state carrier, with a revenue of

Rs 7,000 crore, was asked to take on a debt of Rs 50,000 crore for purchase of the new aircraft. Then the government got the two public carriers – Air-India, which flew international routes, and the domestic flier Indian Airlines – to merge, creating chaos with the clash of two different cultures.

When Patel took over as civil aviation minister, Indian Airlines was the market leader with a 42 per cent market share. Now it is struggling for survival. Between 2004 and 2014, Air-India also withdrew from several lucrative international sectors, handing them over to private players. The airline that JRD had built up with passion and conviction is no longer recognizable.

In the 1990s, when the Tatas decided to re-enter the aviation business, JRD's successor Ratan Tata found himself up against a wall, just as JRD had in British India. Only, Ratan Tata had to contend with not just the government but also competition that manipulated the political and bureaucratic regulatory systems to keep him out. The unravelling of Tata's aviation ambitions has been discussed in a previous chapter. Here, all we need are Ratan Tata's own words at a gathering in Dehradun in November 2010: 'We approached three prime ministers. But an individual thwarted our efforts ... I happened to be on a flight once and another industrialist who was sitting next to me said: "I don't understand. You people are stupid. You know the minister wants Rs 15 crore. So why don't you pay it?" I just said: "You can't understand it. I just want to go to bed at night, knowing that I haven't got the airline by paying for it."'

In December 2012, as Tata stepped down as the chairman of the group, he indicated that it was unlikely to re-enter civil aviation because of 'destructive competition'. He was diplomatic: 'I would hesitate to go into the sector today in the sense that the chances are that you would have a great deal of competition which would be unhealthy competition ... Cut-throat competition which is done to keep you out is destructive competition. Overseas, people go bankrupt or companies go bankrupt. Here they never do, they continue to be sick and still operate. Then they are operating to kill you.'

Yet, in recent years, the Tata group has finally succeeded in entering the airline business. In 2013, Singapore Airlines and the Tatas announced the launch of their airline, named Vistara. The Tatas are also the Indian partner of Air Asia, the Malaysian low-cost carrier, which began operations in India in 2014.

~

For many in the know, Goyal's success and impressive grip over successive governments are not surprising.

In September 2012, the government announced a new liberalized FDI regime for the civil aviation sector, permitting foreign airlines to buy up to 49 per cent stake in an Indian airline. By April the following year, Jet Airways became the first Indian company to dilute its stake, valuing itself at around Rs 8,000 crore. Etihad, the national carrier of the UAE, agreed to pick up 24 per cent stake in Jet. Soon after, the Manmohan Singh government signed an agreement with UAE, expanding the number of weekly seats available on flights between India and the Gulf nation from 13,330 to 50,000. The Jet–Etihad alliance was the biggest beneficiary of this decision. When the Opposition and media questioned the haste with which the government had cleared additional seats for the crucial sector, Prime Minister Manmohan Singh was forced to issue an unusual denial. His office claimed that there was 'absolutely no disagreement within the government or between the Ministers and Prime Minister on the matter. The Prime Minister is neither washing his hands of the Bilateral Air Services Agreement nor is the Prime Minister's Office trying to do a U-turn on the issue now.' Internal documents had hinted at Singh being uncomfortable about the sudden move.

As of mid-2016, Goyal, now a London resident, continues to be a dollar billionaire and among India's richest people.

He came in from nowhere to start India's most successful private airline. There are no known public explanations for how he got the initial investment of over Rs 30 crore for Tailwinds, a company based in the tax haven of Isle of Man, from where money was routed to India to set up Jet Airways. The Enforcement Directorate, responsible for investigating financial crimes, has been trying to investigate the source of Goyal's riches. Intelligence agencies have tracked Tailwinds' links to Australia and Hong Kong, and got no further. And now, his status as a non-resident Indian allows Goyal to dodge explanations.

Goyal's story is an instructive manual on how to succeed in modern India. But he is not the only one. It could have been Thakiyuddin Abdul Wahid, had his life not been cut short by that evening shootout in Mumbai just over two decades ago. In every gathering of India's powers that be, you could point at someone randomly and there would be a similar story to tell.

Section Three

ISTOCKPHOTO

THE BIG LEAGUE

This section is about the men and women at the very top of the Indian democracy. They sit so high above us, they are practically out of sight. These are stories about the ultimate beneficiaries of the Indian democracy. But they are not representative enough – the true diversity of the nation's most successful people is hard to portray.
Success, success at any cost, success beyond all fantasy. That is the mantra that binds them.

8

Masters of the Game

At about the time that forty-five-year-old housewife Susmita Chakravarti hung herself from a ceiling fan on 4 October 2012 in her apartment near Delhi's Indira Gandhi International Airport, Siddharth Mallya had butterflies in his stomach.

Susmita was both hungry and depressed that afternoon, worried about her family's future. Her husband Manas Chakravarti, a retired air force officer, was a store manager with Kingfisher Airlines, the company run by Siddharth's father, Vijay Mallya. She had not eaten much since morning. Ignoring repeated calls from her husband, Susmita hung herself around 1.30 p.m. Alerted by her husband, their neighbours broke into their apartment and found her body.

Those days, Siddharth was also tense. He was worried about his TV debut just a few weeks later, where he was to judge models for the 'Hunt for the Kingfisher Calendar Girl: Season 4'. The Kingfisher Calendar had come to symbolize the glitz of the Mallya family and the UB group, which controlled Kingfisher beer, Kingfisher Airlines and several other businesses.

There is no reason to believe that Siddharth was aware of the existence or death of Susmita Chakravarti. It is unlikely his father was aware of the middle-class Chakravarti family either. Manas was only one of the thousands who had not been paid for six months by his company. On Twitter, where Mallya senior mostly promotes his various sports teams and their interests, Susmita did not figure anywhere. Publicly available indications are that Mallya senior was, in fact, preoccupied with his Formula One team's participation in the South Korean Grand Prix. It was to be held on 14 October. A day after Susmita's death, he appears to have flown out on his private jet to South Korea.

Of course, he had other concerns too, this liquor baron who styled himself after Richard Branson, and had nurtured and expanded with much flamboyance a business empire his father had built. At the peak of its glory, Mallya's group was a multinational conglomerate of over sixty companies, with an annual turnover of over Rs 45,000 crore by 1998–99. From selling Kingfisher beer to owning various sports teams, including in F 1 racing, cricket and football, and part-owning *The Asian Age* newspaper and the tabloid *The Blitz* – both of which I worked with for a few years in the 1990s – Mallya captured the energy coursing through a newly liberalized India.

A decade before Susmita killed herself, Vijay Mallya had even embarked on a political career. It is hard to tell if he was not sufficiently occupied with his expanding business empire, or whether he was moved by the possibility of serving society better. In 2002, he was elected to the Rajya Sabha from his home state of Karnataka as an independent candidate, with the support of local legislators from various political parties. What caused them to vote for a business tycoon, not known for either political or social activism until then, remains a mystery.

Until a couple of decades ago, Indian industrialists preferred to send proxies or prop up professional politicians in legislatures to do their bidding. Some of India's most seasoned politicians, who have occupied exalted positions in governments past and present, owe their flourishing careers to industrialists who funded and promoted their careers before the Indian economy began to open up in the early 1990s. Now, though, business magnates are increasingly occupying seats in parliament and state legislatures themselves. This is, of course, in no small measure due to the affection that political parties across the spectrum shower on them. It is also possible that the new class of rich people see no benefit in veils of pretension and seek direct access to the highest class of power.

During his first term in parliament, Mallya was nominated to the parliamentary committees on civil aviation, defence and industry. There is nothing on record to show that either the chairman of the Upper House, who is also the vice-president of India, or its members had qualms about Mallya occupying positions that clearly conflicted with his business interests.

By 2003, Mallya had launched Kingfisher Airlines – and he was sitting on the parliamentary committee on civil aviation, which had the power to summon senior officials of ministries and departments that dealt with the sector. In a country like India, where government permits are critical to any business, there is no better place for a businessman to be than the parliamentary committee that oversees the sectors where his business interests lie. According to a World Bank 2015 ranking on the ease of doing business in a country, measured on ten metrics, India ranked at an abysmal 142 of the 189 countries on the list. That is where a corrupt government and a complex (and corrupt) bureaucracy have brought India's dreams of liberalization to.

Mallya, of course, is not alone. Industrialists brazenly occupy posts on committees that have the power to influence the sectors they work in. On 15 December 2008, Rahul Bajaj, a scion of India's leading automobile manufacturer, the Bajaj group, got up in parliament to ask the finance ministry what steps it had taken to ameliorate the problems faced by the automobile industry.

Parimal Nathwani, a group president of India's largest private sector firm, Reliance Industries Limited (RIL), has been a member of the Upper House since March 2008. Where did this Gujarati win his election from? The state of Jharkhand. In January 2014, Nathwani, who is the key troubleshooter for his boss – India's richest man, Mukesh Ambani – was re-elected for a second term.

On 6 August 2009, when the Upper House was discussing the availability of natural gas at competitive prices for power generation and other national priorities, Nathwani got up to defend the Reliance group, India's top natural gas producer. The irregularities surrounding RIL's conduct in gas extraction from the Krishna–Godavari basin in the eastern coast of India were already the subject of much controversy, and many accused it of trying to push up the price of natural gas and earn undue profits.

Over the years, various parliamentary committees have been the playground of businessmen. Kalpataru Das, an MP from Orissa whose family has vast business interests in mines, sat on the select committee that scrutinized the new mining bill in 2015; Vijay Darda, whose family owned the Marathi newspaper *Lokmat*, the Hindi newspaper *Lokmat Samachar* and the English newspaper *Lokmat Times,* was a member of a committee that dealt with media regulations through the first decade of the new millenium; Chandrapal Singh Yadav from Uttar Pradesh sat on the standing committee on chemicals and fertilizers when he was the chairman of a fertilizer company in 2015; many MPs such as D.R. Meghe, P.B. Kore and M.A.M. Ramaswamy, who run private medical colleges, sat on parliamentary committees in the health sector over the years; Rajeev Chandrasekhar, who has major interests in the financial sector, was a member of the consultative committee for the Ministry of Finance starting 2009.

If businessmen do not themselves make time for the business of politics, their proxies and friends are active, openly lobbying for their narrow business interests in parliament.

In 2009, a group of health activists informed the Supreme Court that the Union health minister, Anbumani Ramadoss, had suspended production of cheap vaccines used for immunization of poor children because he wanted to help some private companies close to him. They also accused him of transfer of crucial resources to companies owned by a political associate.

Such allegations surface regularly. Over thirty MPs wrote to the government a few years ago suggesting that it replace freshly cooked midday meals served to students with packaged biscuits. India's highly successful – if also mired in corruption – midday meal scheme serves freshly cooked lunch to over 100 million poor students every day. It is a key reason why many of them attend school. It was clear that the MPs were batting on behalf of the Biscuit Manufacturers Welfare Association, but their parties did not take any punitive action against them.

According to a 2010 study by National Social Watch Coalition, 128 out of the 543 members of the then Lok Sabha were businessmen with known or potential conflicts of interest with respect to the parliamentary proceedings they were participating in. Before the national elections of 2014, at least ninety-two members of the Rajya Sabha had declared pecuniary interests in the house's register of interest, which was a step forward in avoiding potential conflict of interest. The Lok Sabha started keeping a similar register in 2011. These steps, however, are far from enough.

Apart from pecuniary interests, there are other morally compromised situations that politicians are part of. Take the case of lawyers who are also active politicians. Congress spokesperson Abhishek Manu Singhvi, for instance, appeared in cases to take on his own government on behalf of telecom firms. Among the cases he argued on behalf of the telecom firms was one in which they were suspected of not fully disclosing their revenues, a share of which was to come to the government, which had ordered an audit of their books by the CAG. During the day, Singhvi would appear in court for those companies and private interests that were suspected of defrauding the public exchequer, and by evening he would be on national television channels defending his government's decisions.

Despite the spirited legal fight put up by some of India's most expensive legal minds, led by Singhvi himself, the Supreme Court ruled that the CAG could audit private telecom companies, because they had to share revenue with the government. In March 2016, the CAG's first report was tabled in parliament and it said that the government had suffered a loss of Rs 12,489 crore because telecom operators had hidden significant revenues from the government. How did the Narendra Modi government respond? By ordering a special audit of the companies by a private auditor – taking the audit away from the CAG, one of the world's largest audit firms with unparalleled resources and credibility.

A few months before he became the Opposition leader in the Rajya Sabha in 2009, senior BJP leader Arun Jaitley, now the finance minister, gave a legal opinion to the Tata group in his private capacity. In that opinion, he harshly criticized the UPA government's move to levy a higher royalty from the Tatas for extracting coal. A few years down the line, when it became clear that the arbitrary allotment of coal mines was a colossal scandal, Jaitley was one of the loudest critics, rebuking the government and accusing it of corruption. Jaitley's private legal opinion for the Tatas did not find its way into the mainstream media.

If we turn away from legislative politics to other arenas, the story is just the same. The administration of cricket in India is a telling example. Prime Minister Narendra Modi, finance minister Arun Jaitley, BJP president Amit Shah, Congress leader Rajiv Shukla, veteran Maharashtrian politician Sharad Pawar and several others, across political divides, have been active in the administration of the lucrative game. These men, not a woman among them, run various state-level cricket bodies as personal fiefdoms. They hardly even bother to make a show of cleaning up the administration of the game, or dealing with fixing or betting and other such issues.

There is the peculiar case of Anurag Thakur, a member of parliament and son of a senior BJP leader, who was elected secretary of the all-powerful Board of Control for Cricket in India (BCCI) in March 2015. When asked if his victory and other developments signalled a takeover of cricket administration by the BJP, he told *The Mint* newspaper: 'Not really, you can't say that. It's very interesting ... I don't belong to any group. Both the factions wanted me to become president. That clearly shows it's not about the group. And similarly, if the BJP has lopsided with one [sic], then how are they contesting from different groups? There's nothing like the BJP and Congress within the BCCI.' Now, in May 2016, the same Anurag Thakur becomes the president of BCCI upon Shashank Manohar, the incumbent president, vacating the post.

Thakur's statement simplifies the political realities that shape power and influence in modern India. When it comes to sharing the pie or claiming a piece of it, there are no political divisions.

In 2000, Thakur, just twenty-five but already an emerging politician, was elected as president of the cricket association of his home state Himachal Pradesh. His father Prem Kumar Dhumal was then the state's chief minister. In November that year, during a Himachal Pradesh vs Jammu & Kashmir game in the domestic first-class tournament, the Ranji Trophy, Thakur made a dramatic entry as captain of his team. It was historic, ridiculous and a story for our times. It was probably the first – and last – time that the president of a state cricket association got himself elected as the captain without undergoing selection trials or playing any significant cricket. With that otherwise insignificant appearance, Thakur became qualified to become a member of the national junior selection committee, satisfying the criterion that only first-class cricketers could be a part of national selection panels. Since then, he has been steadily climbing the ladder of power. Today, he is probably the most powerful sports administrator in India.

Through the course of his dramatic rise in both politics and cricket, Thakur faced no significant opposition. In fact, political leaders across the divide aided his rise. So when he says there is no political divide in the business of cricket administration, he has to be believed. Similarly, there are no political divides when it comes to inducting industrialists into legislatures and politicians into businesses.

In Punjab, where the Badal family has been in power for years, there are many allegations of their stranglehold over every aspect of public life. The Badals are accused of shutting down TV channels that air unfavourable reports and of owning businesses that get lucrative contracts from the state government. In one instance, it turned out that the state power corporation under Chief Minister Parkash Singh Badal had been giving out contracts to companies owned by his daughter and her husband. Badal's relative and a member of his cabinet, who held several important portfolios, including revenue and non-conventional energy, Bikram Singh

Majithia, had his department award contracts to companies his family controlled. Over two dozen members of the Badal family and the extended clan run the Punjab government. While Parkash Singh Badal emerged in public life as a career politician, the next generation mostly consists of men and women with flourishing businesses as well as an active political life. This marriage of business and politics is visible around the country. As the state gets ready to go to polls in 2017, there are indications that its people may finally have tired of the Badals.

In next-door Himachal Pradesh, politics is dominated by a few families, such as that of Anurag Thakur. While it seems clear that they manipulate politics for personal benefits, it is hard to tell if the scions are career politicians, or businessmen who became politicians. Those lines have become blurred. It is also a fact that politics is increasingly a profession, rather than a vocation, for many public figures in India. When India's first Lok Sabha was formed, there was just one member who declared politics as his profession. Today, a quarter of its members say they are professional politicians. It must be lucrative.

The public and media discourse celebrates these young leaders, which deflects conversation about the stranglehold of an oligarchy on the country's political power and interests. It is in the Congress that the hold of an oligarchy is most visible. A decade ago, when party president Sonia Gandhi decided to inject fresh blood into it, she looked only at the old Congress families. So a new generation of well-educated youngsters became leaders overnight, thanks to their parents' undiluted loyalty to the Gandhis. They were mostly educated in the West, well spoken, well dressed and came with a deep sense of entitlement. Several senior civil servants, who have spent decades in government service and have worked under an earlier generation of political leaders, are alarmed by the fact that this young brigade believe it is their birthright to exercise power.

A recently retired civil servant told me that a young junior minister in the UPA government would pick up his personal phone with the greeting 'Yes, Maharaj speaking'. The leader is from a former royal family, and his father and other family members went on to become professional politicians, active across many states. A senior cabinet member of the UPA government told me that he had to tell one of those young oligarchs to behave respectfully with senior civil servants. Another minister said that one such princeling, who also runs a huge business empire, would unabashedly push his businesses across various departments, and one day met with him. 'I had to tell him to stop it. It was an unpleasant meeting.'

In his 2011 book *India: A Portrait*, Patrick French pointed out that many parliamentarians across parties reach high positions only because of heredity. He found that family links helped some 28.6 per cent of all MPs of the fifteenth Lok Sabha get there. In a country with a median age of just twenty-five in the Lok Sabha that dissolved in 2014, every single member below the age of thirty belonged to a family with powerful political connections. For those between thirty-one and forty, the figure stood at 65 per cent, French pointed out. Simply put, the younger lot of national leaders was there because their parents or grandparents were loyal political workers of the Congress, or the BJP.

Meanwhile, parliamentary performance has been dwindling. Loud, and sometimes violent, disruptions are now a regular feature. When members finally sit down to discuss issues, the quality of debate is embarrassingly poor. The result is that the executive has become more authoritarian. The government waits for parliament sessions to end so that it can promulgate executive orders – called ordinances – instead of working to pass bills after detailed debates. Ordinances only require the nod of the president, almost always only a formal rubber stamp.

Narendra Modi has proved no different. Take, for example, one of Modi's key ministerial colleagues, Ravi Shankar Prasad, who handles the key portfolios of law and telecommunications. In December 2014, the *Financial Times* of London reported that Prasad had been on the payroll, as a lawyer on a retainership, of Mukesh Ambani's Reliance group for several years. He is responsible for the telecom sector, where the Reliance group is investing several crores of rupees to roll out a 4G broadband network around the country. According to documents I accessed during the research for this book, even Prasad's lawyer son is a consultant with Reliance.

Central auditors have found several lacunae in the manner in which Reliance obtained the 4G spectrum, including suspected forgery. Their audit still awaits the government's response. How will Prasad take an impartial decision on the issue? Modi, who rode to power on an anti-corruption mandate, seems unconcerned.

⁓

Around the time Susmita Chakravarti was succumbing to depression, Vijay Mallya was beginning to shoulder more responsibilities. In 2012, he was nominated to the parliamentary standing committee on chemicals and fertilizers, though he was the chairman of Mangalore Chemicals and Fertilizers Ltd, one of India's biggest fertilizer manufacturers. The Mallya group had a 30 per cent stake in it.

As this book was being finalized in 2016, Kingfisher Airlines, which Mallya had started as a birthday gift to his son Siddharth in 2005, had folded up, accumulating the largest bank loan default in Indian history. The airline owed over Rs 9,000 crore to Indian public sector banks.

On 2 March 2016, when the banks moved the Debt Recovery Tribunal, Mallya slipped out of India on a diplomatic passport, which was issued to him as a member of parliament. Such are the privileges of being in Indian politics.

Kingfisher Airlines, Mallya had proclaimed, was not a business of transportation but a hospitality business. He personally selected air hostesses; in his first-class lounges at airports, liquor flowed freely and impressive food was served on board aircrafts that had entertainment systems and bright red seats. As the luxurious airline attracted high-fliers in large numbers, it was also bleeding money, and went on to take loans from public sector banks. According to documents that have now emerged, Mallya personally met with senior banking executives to push for loans. The Enforcement Directorate has since accused him of laundering some of the loan money from banks abroad.

India's mounting bank loan defaults is in itself a revolting and instructive manual about the elite. The second biggest bank loan defaulter after Kingfisher today is Winsome Diamonds group, which has failed to pay back a loan of over Rs 6,500 crore. And where is its promoter Jatin Mehta now? He is in Singapore. Promoters of the *Deccan Chronicle* newspaper submitted forged balance sheets to various banks to raise hundreds of crores of rupees, which was used to buy a cricket team and fancy cars.

What will finally come of the humongous amount that Mallya and his company owe to banks? If the past is a good indicator, nothing at all. After the media frenzy dies down, he is likely to go back to a life of racing cars, high-octane parties and beautiful people because many of India's most successful business houses of today have been loan defaulters in the past.

For all his apparent obliviousness, Mallya does have a softer side. On his website www.mallyainparliament.in, Mallya posted a poem titled 'Power of a Billion'. It does not speak highly of his poetic abilities, but two lines from it stayed with me for a long time:

'A Nation that prides itself in modern self-sufficiency
Is it real for a few – and a dream for all?'

9

The League of Extraordinary Gentlemen

February 2015. A television news channel was running a noisy discussion about the elections to the legislative assembly of Delhi, just days away. The anchor and the discussants spoke over each other. But that was not what worried Harihar Patel as he sat glued to his TV in Chhattisgarh's Gare village.

After several minutes, he turned to me. 'Do you think AAP (Aam Aadmi Party) will win?' The question dripped with hope, as if an AAP victory would bring a revolution that could change his fortunes. AAP was the new pro-poor party led by anti-corruption crusaders. The unrealistic hopes he pinned on a party of amateurs was telling. In the bleakness of his situation, it was hope alone that had kept Patel going.

It was already dark outside. In the large open courtyard of his house, a small mill was grinding wheat to flour in one corner. Two of his grandchildren were running around. He did not know how long his life would remain this idyllic.

'My house is in Gare 4/5, and behind us is Gare 4/6.'

For those unfamiliar with the ways of mining, those words mean nothing. Those in the business know they indicate some of the richest coal deposits in India. These blocks were allocated to private mining companies, including the Jindal group, for a brief while, before the Supreme Court cancelled the allotments in 2014 because of irregularities that are estimated to have cost the Indian exchequer several thousand crore rupees.

For the last two decades, Patel, a practitioner of Ayurvedic medicine, and hundreds of other people in this area have been fighting to hold on to their ancestral lands – even if their homes are now permanently coated with coal dust and fly-ash. Their fight is two-pronged. Besides trying to keep their lands, they are also battling unethical mining practices. For over a decade since India began liberalizing its mining sector and allowing private companies to own coal mines, Gare has been at the heart of a fierce competition among giant mining corporations.

As retaliation, Patel has been arrested in early morning raids, offered bribes and humiliated. He and a few others organized the residents of about twenty local villages to form a company, claiming ownership of 300 acres of their ancestral land. They collected Rs 25 lakh to bid for the coal block that is their village, but gave up the idea once they realized it was not enough, and returned the money. Now they propose to put up a solar power plant, and later a coal-fired power plant. 'We will not give up our ancestral land. Leave it to us. Whatever is below this land also belongs to us,' he said.

When a part of Gare was allocated to the Jindal group, the locals, led by Patel and other activists, challenged it at a public hearing organized by the government in another village on 5 January 2008. There, the police beat them with long bamboo sticks reinforced with iron. About 250 villagers were injured.

'Coal blocks are coming up all over, and they mine ignoring environmental guidelines. The fish in our river are mostly dead, animals are dying, our people suffer from various stomach ailments, liver and kidney problems, and bronchial asthma is very common,' he said, reeling off the village's list of complaints. Most people in the area also suffer from constant itching and burning of the eyes.

Behind us, one of the largest complexes of Jindal Steel and Power Limited (JSPL) rose into the night sky. High walls and wire-mesh fencing protected a complex that was all chimneys – some old and slim, others new and wide, the latter looking as if they were nuclear power plants.

'They have been expanding every year. Only 20 feet away, another power plant has just been completed and will start operations soon,' Patel said. 'Growth, it seems, is just for them.'

In the wake of liberalization, a new generation of entrepreneurs dreamed up audacious projects in mining, power, steel, aluminium and the like, pumping in crores of rupees into such villages deep inside India's forested regions and remote corners. Many of them are now celebrated as the faces of India's liberalized, rejuvenated economy, and revered speakers at the World Economic Forum and other global gatherings. They are also important players in Indian politics, both actively and as key financiers. Celebrated in New Delhi and New York, they are the villains of India's rural heartlands, accused of plundering natural resources and playing havoc with the lives of the poor.

The Agarwal community is often spoken of as India's foremost business community – astute, risk-taking, innovative and possessing deep financial acumen. They are today the dominant force in Indian business.

When the British Empire was flourishing in the Indian subcontinent, a large number of Agarwals migrated from their homes in north India to Calcutta, then India's capital and a key port city. A smaller group made their way deep into the heart of central India and settled in various parts of what was then Central Province, with its picturesque mountains, thick jungles populated by tribals, and fertile land. Some of those Agarwals reached a region watered by the Kelo river. After this incredible journey, they settled down as successful farmers and businessmen in those areas. Even today, if you look around in Raigarh – a district town in Chhattisgarh famous for its mines, electricity and steel industries – you can only admire the audacity of the Agarwals. They dropped anchor in a little town, known only for its river and fertile land. The mineral deposits were yet to be mined, and the thick forested region was accessible only via a railway link, or a difficult road journey.

The fertile land watered by natural streams and the once-famous agricultural markets are gone. All that remains of Raigarh, and neighbouring areas like Korba, are mining towns permanently blackened by soot.

The government and the mining companies are digging away in villages, virgin forests, pure rivers, and the very values of equality and constitutionality. So great was their greed that even the locals, generally ignorant of the ways of government and corporates, were galvanized into protests that continue to draw attention to the predatory nature of Indian capitalism. In Raigarh, this struggle has turned into a stand-off between members of the Agarwal community, who have taken up leadership positions on both sides. It is incidental, but fascinating.

Among the earliest Agarwals to reach Raigarh was Seth Kirorimal, who was born in what is now the state of Haryana, in the late nineteenth century, but made his fortune doing business in Calcutta. In his late forties, Kirorimal shifted to Raigarh along with his wife and daughter. All his fortune was put into a charitable trust that would work to expand education and health facilities in the region. Evidence of his philanthropy was everywhere in Raigarh – hospitals and educational institutions among them. And not just there either – one of Delhi University's most respected colleges and several educational institutions in Haryana and elsewhere are products of Kirorimal's philanthropy several decades ago, long before it became fashionable among the Indian elite. By the time he died in the early 1960s, Kirorimal had scripted one of the least celebrated but most glorious stories of philanthropy in a country where such selflessness is rare. His grandson, Rajesh Moda, says the family trust does not accept any donations from outside the family even today.

Around the time Kirorimal was beginning to think of philanthropy, Ramkumar Agarwal was born to another migrant family in Raigarh. It was 1 January 1924. The young boy soon became active in the Indian freedom movement and after Independence, was an active politician in the state assembly for years. In the twilight of his life – as the region began to metamorphose into a mining township – he became one of the most vocal advocates of the region's ecology, environment and people's rights.

A few years after India became independent, Jainarayandas Agrawal and his wife too left their home in what is now the state of Haryana in search of better opportunities and reached another part of the parent state of Punjab, but it was a fruitless trip. Having heard of the great potential of Raigarh, the family moved there. In 1954, their fifth child was born in this town. He was named Ramesh Agrawal.

Some years later, yet another Agarwal arrived in Raigarh. But this one was not a migrant to this forested region. He was a canny businessman looking for new opportunities. Om Prakash Jindal was a small-time businessman from Hisar, now in Haryana, who went on to establish a flourishing business in power and steel, become a politician, a member of the Haryana state assembly, a minister in the state, and then a member of the Indian parliament. Jindal set up a small sponge iron plant sometime in the late 1980s in Raigarh. From then on, there was no looking back. Today, the O.P. Jindal group, run as independent units by his four sons, is a collective valued at over Rs 1,20,000 crore.

As Jindal senior, and later his son Naveen Jindal, took their businesses in mining, power production and steel manufacturing to new heights in Raigarh, people such as Ramkumar Agarwal and Ramesh Agrawal ranged themselves against them. The tribal population of the region were on both sides of the divide too. Many of them were employees of the Jindal group, and many others were among the protestors. The two members of the local Agarwal community gave voice to the tribals of the region, petitioning courts against the Jindals' aggressive mining practices. They accused the group of diverting local river water for industrial purposes, and of polluting Raigarh. Both of them, along with other activists, spent many weeks in jails, and did the rounds of courts to face cases slapped on them by the Jindals. In 2012, when Ramesh Agrawal was shot at and injured, activists claimed that it was a Jindal conspiracy. The stand-off intensified after 1998, when the Jindal group got its first coal block in Harihar Patel's Gare village.

In Gare and nearby villages, JSPL's frenzied growth has covered the lives of the locals in fly-ash and coal dust. Their footprint is more lasting than that of Kirorimal today. Many even refer to Raigarh as 'Jindalgarh'.

On one of the highways that lead to Raigarh, there is the O.P. Jindal Airport, then the Fortis-O.P. Jindal Hospital, followed by the O.P. Jindal School. India's first private sector mega power project is now running just outside Gare village, and it is inching towards the capacity to produce 3,400 MW of electricity. In another part of Raigarh, one of the world's largest sponge iron plants, capable of churning out three million tonnes of steel annually, is operational.

Raigarh is flooded with hoardings advertising Jindal Panther Cement. Outside Jindal establishments, photographs of Jindal junior, Naveen, who now runs JSPL, are a permanent fixture. In some photos there is a faint smirk, in others, the young business tycoon struggles to smile, and sometimes he appears to gaze deep into the viewer's eyes. Next to the photographs are pronouncements about JSPL's corporate ideals and values. Environmental sensitivities and responsible development are among those slogans.

Naveen Jindal first reached Raigarh as a young understudy to his father in the early 1990s. He was preparing to leave for the University of Texas in Dallas to study for his MBA. There, he went on to become president of the student government and receive the Student Leader of the Year award.

Jindal adopted the American practice of flying the national flag and hoisted an Indian tricolour at his factory premises in Raigarh on his return from the US. But the flag code of India, as it existed then, permitted private citizens to hoist the national flag only on two days in a year – Independence Day and Republic Day. He was told to pull down the flag. Jindal approached the Delhi High Court, challenging the rule. Thanks to his fight, in 2002, the Union government announced that Indian citizens were free to fly the national flag on all days of the year. A new flag code was issued, and by 2004, the Supreme Court decided in favour of Jindal. He set up the Flag Foundation of India, which has since been hoisting huge flags around the country. 'The tricolour is a common factor of inspiration for every Indian; it is indeed a true expression of pride for our motherland,' the foundation declares on its website. It claims to have launched a 'revolutionary movement' to 'bring together the vibrant youth that aims to be the instrument of change in our country to make India and its people proud, happy and prosperous'.

Within months of grabbing national attention through his flag fight, Jindal was nominated by the Congress in 2004 as its candidate from the Kurukshetra Lok Sabha constituency. According to legend, this is where the epic battle of the Mahabharata took place. Perhaps Jindal's was the new righteous clan – at least in the eyes of the voters who sent him to parliament with a massive victory.

Jindal was now a member of parliament and his company grew rapidly. By 2010, JSPL had been allocated several coal blocks, which together held 2,580 million tonnes of coal. Boston Consulting Group said he was the second-highest value creator in the world. In 2011, he was among India's most powerful CEOs according to a survey conducted by *The Economic Times*. *Forbes Asia* placed JSPL in its 'Fabulous 50' list. *Business Today* magazine ranked him the best Indian CEO and *Fortune Asia* said he was among the twenty-five hottest people in business. His alma mater, the University of Texas, renamed its school of management after this famous alumnus whose group was now valued at about Rs 24,000 crore.

However, a detailed report by the federal auditor CAG in 2014 and several criminal investigations by the CBI, showed that his group and other private and public Indian enterprises were beneficiaries of windfall gains to the tune of Rs 186,000 crore in the allocation of coal blocks since India liberalized the sector. The government, Indian investigators alleged, allocated precious resources using arbitrary methods. The Supreme Court struck down the allocations in September 2014.

The CBI filed two criminal cases against Jindal's companies, alleging irregularities in obtaining coal blocks in Gare village and in Jharkhand. Activists alleged that the Jindal group was pocketing cheap coal, producing electricity at low cost and selling them at a very high rate. The business was simple, and profits huge.

In 1990, when Harsh Mander, then part of the Indian Administrative Service (IAS), was posted to Raigarh as district magistrate, the still mostly agrarian township was famous for the Raigarh gharana of the classical dance Kathak.

O.P. Jindal and a young Naveen were there too, running their factory and probably exploring the possibilities of mining. Mander recalls meeting Naveen a couple of times. 'I would advise him, all unsolicited, about setting up an industry that is compatible with environment and local sentiments, and how you don't have to be predatory,' Mander told me one afternoon in the small office of the NGO that he now runs in Delhi.

'What did Naveen Jindal say,' I asked.

'I would rather not say,' he said, smiling.

The young IAS officer soon began to take on the dominant powers of the district. One of them was his schoolmate Dilip Singh Judeo, a member of the erstwhile royal family of Jashpur. Both of them had gone to Mayo College in Ajmer, one of India's oldest public schools. Mander ordered the distribution of over 2,000 acres of land confiscated from Judeo's family under land ceiling provisions to landless tribals. Around the same time, he also initiated action against the Jindals for petty offences. Within months, Mander was abruptly shunted out by the government. But the youth movement he started for spreading literacy nurtured several young men who, years later, have become the leading activists of the region.

For Mander, Raigarh epitomized the new trajectory that governance has taken in India since the economic liberalization of the 1990s.

'I revisited Raigarh exactly twenty years later,' he said. 'I was amazed at the devastation I saw, the extent to which it has been exploited. It symbolizes the whole question of what constitutes development and who benefits. There was one imagination of government when I joined the civil services in 1980; there was no doubt that the theory of government was that its primary duty was towards the poor and the disadvantaged. There were lots of deviations from that ideal, but then they were perceived and recognized as deviations from that ideal.'

The new theory is that a government that facilitates the market will benefit everyone, get people jobs, create wealth and educate people. 'Raigarh is a laboratory that shows where government will go if it follows the first model and where, in an extremely opposite direction, the government will go if it follows the second model. Even assuming that there is no cronyism happening, assuming that everyone is doing bona fide duty from the government's side, I would see a young officer posted in my position, a generation later, genuinely confused about what his or her duty is. Because twenty years ago, I think generally there would have been a basic agreement that your duty was to defend the poor people, the tribals, their rights; and that industry is not a bad thing but it needs to respect the laws of the land, it needs to be sensitive especially to vulnerable communities, it needs to be sensitive to the future generations.'

He argued that the Indian administration was being retrained to meet the expectations of this new liberalized India. The duty of the new officers was to push aside all kinds of obstacles and facilitate industries, and if there were laws for protecting the tribals and the forest, and for land acquisition, their duty was to help the entrepreneurs overcome them, because India wanted all those thousands of megawatts of electricity and ores. 'Defending the interests of the people who are opposing those projects can be seen as being against nation building. It is profoundly different from the values of human struggle, our Constitution, etc.,' Mander argued.

The big-time businessmen are probably the biggest beneficiaries of this new orientation in governance. Those ranged against them have been losing the battle from the very beginning.

One day in 1998, about a couple of hundred residents of Raigarh crowded into a train compartment, raising occasional slogans. They were accompanied by policemen. Ramkumar Agarwal, now a senior leader even though he was no longer part of electoral politics, was at the head of the group that was going to a court in Haryana, where O.P. Jindal had filed a defamation case against Agarwal and his associates. The lower courts of

Haryana had started issuing notices to the residents of Raigarh. Neither the protests nor the affected businesses were in Haryana. They had no connection with the state at all. It was just that O.P. Jindal was a politician with immense clout in that state. Filing cases against people in faraway courts is the standard harassment practice in India.

Agarwal had had much experience of these tactics in his long life. As a career politician, he had led an aggressive expansion of education facilities in the region, and sent school pass-outs into villages to teach the locals. According to Anil Agarwal, his grandson and now a Congress leader, almost 12,000 people got employment thanks to Ramkumar's efforts in education and helping form cooperative societies in the region. As the Jindals began to furiously expand their businesses, Ramkumar Agarwal became a key rallying point for the locals.

He and his associates were regularly harassed. Their businesses began to suffer, they would suddenly get high electricity bills, petty cases would be lodged against them, and even Ramkumar's status as a freedom fighter was questioned. His relatives in other parts of the country, even as far away as Mumbai, began to face unexplained harassment. Hidden forces were at work, and it seemed like even the government was working against him. But the old man would not give up.

Sometime around the middle of the 1990s, the Jindal group began construction of a dam within the city limits for their industrial consumption. Ramkumar was enraged; he had for years struggled to get sanction for a dam to irrigate the farming lands of the region. Ramkumar led a hunger strike against it for several days in 1997. Satyabhama, a tribal woman, was among those who participated. At the protest site, she fell sick and died in a hospital on the afternoon of 26 January, Republic Day. 'There was conspiracy and confusion,' Anil Agarwal said, but documents were inconclusive. Ramkumar and several others were booked for abetment to murder and jailed. Ramkumar ended up selling most of his ancestral properties, his health began to deteriorate and he died soon after.

On 29 January 2005, almost eight years after Satyabhama died, a public hearing on the Jindal group's plans for a steel plant was to take place. Thousands of people – traders, tribals and activists – flowed into a mini stadium in a show of resistance. The law mandates that, in the case of polluting industries that affect local people, such a public hearing must be held. Without adequate security arrangements, the public hearing deteriorated into chaos and had to be abandoned. It was the beginning of a new round of protests against the Jindals. In the front line this time was Ramesh Agrawal.

'As more and more industries started coming up, we realized we needed to educate our people,' Agrawal told me one afternoon. We were sitting in his first-floor residence, the entry to which is secured through an electronically controlled door on the ground floor. All of these security arrangements and the coming and going of strangers cause disquiet in this household.

As the second wave of agitations began, the activists faced troubles very similar to what their predecessors had gone through. O.P. Jindal had died in a helicopter crash in the summer of 2005 and Naveen Jindal was in charge of JSPL. Activists were booked under various sections and jailed. One early morning in 2011, police surrounded the residences of Ramesh Agrawal and two of his associates, including Harihar Patel, in a dramatic raid. Agrawal spent seventy-three days in jail. While still in jail, he was abruptly taken to Raipur on the pretext of ill health and kept at a government hospital until late evening. Then doctors ruled that he was fit to go back to jail. 'I was probably lucky to emerge alive from jail,' he said.

Ramesh Agrawal and his associates moved the Supreme Court, the state high court, the National Green Tribunal, and other available avenues for a case against Jindal and other polluting industries. Given the Jindal group's extensive interests in the region, most of the cases were against it. 'People in the cities of India like these industries. They may talk about pollution, but money and facilities such as electricity are able to suppress their concerns. Maybe ten or fifteen years down the line, they will wake up to what has been done to our countryside,' Agrawal said.

When Agrawal was a child, Raigarh was a land of thick jungles and wild animals. Today, his house needs to be cleaned three times a day. Otherwise the family would need to wade through dust and other pollutants from the nearby factories.

In early 2012, Ramesh Agrawal won a court case to block JSPL from opening a second coal mine near Gare. For Naveen Jindal, by then an MP of the ruling Congress party, it was a huge setback.

On 7 July 2012, Agrawal was at his shop, Satyam Cyber and Computers, as usual. He had opened it at around 10 a.m., and at about 11.30, two young men came on a motorcycle and started asking him about the cost of computers. He said he didn't deal in them and would call his sons. 'Please sit down,' he told them. That's when one of them pulled out a gun. Agrawal saw the weapon and threw his mobile phone at the man. Three bullets were fired, two of them piercing his left leg. Bleeding, Agrawal slumped on a chair but managed to dial his residence number, even as the shooters escaped.

Police filed a charge sheet in the local court accusing seven people – including an employee of Jindal and the owner of a private security agency that worked for the group – of conspiring to kill Agrawal. While JSPL has repeatedly denied all allegations of involvement in the firing, activists continue to say the group was behind it.

The shop where Agrawal was shot at is a few metres from Subhash Chandra Bose junction. Under his statue, on cheap tiles, Bose's famous war cry is etched in Hindi: 'Give me blood, I will give you freedom.' Agrawal gave blood, but there was no freedom in sight.

Agrawal sat on a chair, his left leg on a stool, wrapped in plaster. The local doctors had botched up the treatment, forcing him to undergo over a dozen surgeries in Mumbai. Every two months, he took a train there to visit doctors. By early 2015, doctors pronounced that his bone was fine and that he would regain full mobility.

What have all these struggles achieved, I asked the man who was honoured with the Goldman Environmental Prize in 2014. 'The industries have become more conscious now. We work at least as a speed breaker against their reckless drive,' he replied.

Are you not staging a losing battle, like Ramkumar Agarwal and his associates before you?

'I don't know. But at least people are aware now. They are ready to fight.' He paused and added, 'They will not give up easily now.'

━━⌒⌐

Over a hundred kilometres from Raigarh, the tribal belt of Korba too is bathed in fly-ash and coal dust. Korba's roads are permanently lined thick with pollutants that fall off trucks.

Spend a few days in Korba and you will see an unusually large number of vehicle accidents; trucks that carry coal without adhering to fundamental safety and environmental norms; trees and buildings painted in coal soot; and, of course, the acidic smell typical of mining areas. Korba is one of India's biggest coal deposits, a place where generations have grown up breathing in coal dust. The area has been mined since before independence.

Large fly-ash ponds lie exposed and unprotected. From the bottom of Bharat Aluminium Company's (Balco) largest fly-ash pond, I saw a thick mixture of water and fly-ash dripping into the Hasdeo river. Under the main bridge of Korba town, the river water turned white.

I drove into Korba with Sudiep Shrivastava, a lawyer friend from the nearby city of Bilaspur. He is among the leading anti-mining and environmental rights activists, petitioning every available legal forum – from local courts to the Supreme Court – against irresponsible mining companies and against the corrupt government machinery.

At Korba, we met Laxmi Chauhan, who runs the NGO Sarthak. He and others like him have been fighting the many unbridled industrial projects in the region, and this too was part of the story of Korba. Chauhan took us on a drive around the fly-ash ponds. These were large open tanks that grew year after year, as plants dumped more fly-ash on them. A group of young girls were taking an evening stroll on the soft ash of one of these ponds. It was a deeply worrying sight. Further down, the water sources were every bit as polluted as this land. I thought of my own daughter back in polluted Delhi. Her generation, be it in mining towns or glittering metros, are denied what ought to be a basic right: a clean future.

At another location just a few kilometers from Balco, we drove steeply up a pond and came on top of it. It was an impressive sight; like a huge open lake, the fly-ash pond stretched into the distance. From up there, Korba looked as if it hung from a mesh of wires. High-tension lines from power plants criss-crossed the region. These lines carried electricity to the power grids, and then on to the rest of the country. The place looked eerie, abnormal.

In his career as an activist, Chauhan had taken on Lanco, promoted by the politician L. Rajagopal, the government-owned National Thermal Power Corporation (NTPC) and other giants. His biggest worry, though, is Balco – an integrated aluminium plant that the government divested in 2001 to hand over management control and 51 per cent stake to Anil Agarwal's Vedanta group. Chauhan and Shrivastava pointed out that Balco had shut down parts of its aluminium operations and was building new power plants. Perhaps it was more profitable to produce cheap electricity and feed industrializing India's unbridled appetite than to produce aluminium. But no one from the government, which still held a 49 per cent stake in Balco, seemed to be asking why one of the core industries of India – divested with the express purpose of making aluminium production more efficient and profitable – was shifting to power generation.

There is a grand conspiracy of silence in the townships where these industrial houses are the biggest employers. 'Do you think employees of Balco will risk losing their jobs,' Chauhan asked.

On 23 September 2009, when a chimney under construction at Balco collapsed on more than a hundred workers who had taken shelter under it from a thunderstorm, killing at least twenty-five of them, there was much (albeit short-lived) media attention. Reports spoke about problems with the chimney construction. But in early 2015, when I visited Korba, nobody seemed to know what had become of the families of the people who had died in the tragedy. Each family was paid a paltry sum of

Rs 5 lakh as compensation, some media reports had said. The fact that the chimney was probably being built on classified forest land, or that the local municipal authorities had ordered that chimney construction be stopped only a few days earlier, had little impact locally. People have moved on, and the case has been buried in the famously slow-moving lower courts.

∽

Headquartered in London, Vedanta Resources Plc is run by Anil Agarwal, a college dropout from Bihar. He started his business in Bombay in 1976 and it has since shown an impressive and often controversial growth. Today, Agarwal runs businesses around the world, mostly in extraction industries. Vedanta has interests in aluminium, copper, zinc, lead, iron ore, petroleum and power. Agarwal's meteoric rise to the opulent life he now lives in London is legend.

One December day in 2014, I visited Patna, where Anil Agarwal was born and lived until the age of eighteen, when he left for Bombay. In the city's Miller School, Agarwal's alma mater, almost everyone I met had a story to tell me about the tycoon's visit in the summer of 2011.

Rampravesh Ram, almost fifty and an attendant at Miller School, spoke about the expensive gift he received, a smile shining through his beard, moustache and stained teeth. That visit led to the gift of a watch – his first. It was golden, with Vedanta written in bold letters on the dial. His daughter, who was studying in the same school, got a watch and a school bag. 'It was a day of great happiness,' he told me.

Miller School is a landmark in Patna, and not just for its students. Its playground is among the biggest in the city and the century-old school has produced hundreds of civil servants, political leaders, lawyers and other eminences. It is now officially called Martyr Debipada Chowdhury Memorial School, named after a class nine student of the school who was one of the seven people shot dead by British forces on 11 August 1942 during India's agitation for freedom. In the courtyard, an amateurishly crafted bust of the martyr is surrounded by many potted plants and flowers. The building's yellow walls have turned green with moss.

Rampravesh remembered the man who gifted him the watch. 'He was a very rich man, a student of our school. I haven't seen or heard of anyone so rich,' he said.

Raja Ram, principal of the school in 2011, remembered how the visit unfolded. His mobile rang one summer morning. At the other end was a CEO of the Vedanta group, calling from Mumbai. In the three decades that Ram had been a teacher there, he had never received such an eventful phone call. The CEO said their group's chairman, Anil Agarwal, was a former student of the school and wanted to visit his alma mater.

'He is most welcome. All our alumni are welcome any time,' Raja Ram said.

Next morning, Agarwal, his wife and son reached Patna, probably in a chartered aircraft, and drove down to the school, accompanied by several Vedanta executives. 'I was the principal and he was an ex-student. So I didn't go out to receive him,' Raja Ram recalled. The visitors were ushered into his small office around 10 a.m.

Raja Ram offered the visitors tea, but Agarwal said he did not drink tea.

'What else can I serve you,' Ram asked him.

'Okay, I will have your tea,' Agarwal replied, accepting the government school principal's modest hospitality. He was served tea in a small glass tumbler.

Agarwal had graduated from the school in the 1960s, and recalled that its playground did not have boundary walls then. He mentioned one of his seniors from school, Lalu Prasad Yadav, a key figure in Indian politics. Lalu is among a handful of chief ministers in India who have been sent to jail for corruption. Even during his school days, Lalu was a leader, Agarwal recalled. He said the school building remained the same.

Agarwal was dressed in a simple half-sleeved shirt and trousers. The principal recalled that the tycoon wore a pair of traditional mojari shoes. 'His wife and son were also dressed simply. I could have never imagined that they were so rich,' he said.

The principal walked around the campus with the Agarwal family and a TV crew recorded the entire visit. After sometime, Agarwal sat on the stairs of the school and children gathered around for an impromptu question–answer session. He told them that, after school, he had joined the city's Commerce College but discontinued studies and left for Bombay.

'You are such a sharp, intelligent man, why did you not study further,' one student asked.

'I was never really interested in studies, I wanted to do business. I wanted to make money; it is my hobby,' Agarwal replied.

One of the teachers at the meeting told me that Agarwal was asked about his family roots in Patna. He said vaguely that he was from Pataliputra, a Patna neighbourhood where archaeologists have discovered the remains of a historic city.

Raja Ram, now retired, could not recall anything that Agarwal told him about his family or childhood. 'Later, somebody told me that his family was into scrap,' he said.

Wrapping up his nearly two-hour-long visit, Agarwal told the principal to work on a new building to add to the school compound. Get necessary permissions, he said grandly, assuring the principal that the entire cost would be taken care of. By noon, the Agarwal family had left.

The principal got down to preparing a project to construct a new block of about fifteen big rooms, with an auditorium, several laboratories, a library and other amenities. It was estimated to cost about Rs 10 crore. He sent the project report to the government. He has not heard from anyone since, least of all Agarwal.

A few months after that visit, some executives from Vedanta landed at the school with about 1,300 watches and bags, inscribed with the group's name. The bags were distributed to the children, while the watches were given to the children and staff. That was the winter morning that the school attendant was given his life's first watch.

'There was one more occasion when the Vedanta people came here. They came from Kolkata probably, with two trucks, and did some extensive shooting,' Sushil Kumar Sinha, a senior teacher of the school, recalled. 'There were about fifty people and they shot as if they were shooting a Bollywood movie. They interviewed the new principal and students,' he said. 'We haven't seen the film. But it must be a beautiful film.'

As Vedanta mounts an aggressive international campaign against allegations of irresponsible mining practices around the globe, its slick videos are being promoted on Internet and as sponsored features on TV channels. Some of those videos have visuals of Miller School with a voice-over in a foreign accent about Agarwal's humble origins.

Miller School is not alone in its wait for the Vedanta group promoter's largesse. Over 600 kilometres away, in the new capital city of Chhattisgarh, Naya Raipur (New Raipur), a large hospital complex lies unfinished.

The steel frames and bare concrete walls in Sector 36 were protected by a few securitymen, who stopped me at the gate when I visited in early 2015. One of them carried my identity card to his senior. A few minutes later, he returned to deny me permission to meet the officials or tour the premises. The Vedanta Cancer Hospital is part of Agarwal's corporate social responsibility programme. There has been no work on the site for the past two years.

When I was leaving, one of the guards said, 'We heard that Anil Agarwal is giving away most of his fortune to the poor.' Marking a decade of his flagship Vedanta group's listing on the London Stock Exchange, in September 2014, Agarwal had pledged 75 per cent of his over Rs 22,000 crore fortune to philanthropy.

'Do you think we will get something out of it,' the guard asked.

What was his salary?

Rs 6,000 a month, he said.

Before I left, I told him I would pray that he too figured in Agarwal's list of beneficiaries.

〜〜

Another afternoon in early 2015, I was in Gevra, one of those Indian villages where development is marked by a huge opencast mine and not by its people. My two companions and I walked briskly down a steep drain, jumped across the dry water passage and scrambled up a narrow ridge. Before us, as far as the eye could see, was one of Asia's biggest opencast coal mines. Smoke from that afternoon's dynamite explosions was still rising, and dozens of trucks rode up from the mine's dark belly. Temporary roads snaked around the mine, lit up by lamp posts even in the afternoon. It was that dark inside. An excavator stood at the edge of a road, scooping the overlying sandstone and revealing another layer of coal.

By the time we got back to our car, I was somewhat bruised and we were all fairly dusty. That's when Gandhi Giri Goswami came rushing on a bicycle. From the right handle of his bike hung a bucket with a piece of soap, a towel and fresh clothes. His brother, Subhash Chandra Bose, and friends were playing cricket. Their father, a low-grade staff at a local court, had named his children after the two giants of India's freedom struggle.

The nineteen-year-old Gandhi Goswami and his family moved into their present house, about 50 metres from where we stood, about a decade ago. 'When we came here, it was all thick jungle, and there were some houses there,' he said, pointing to the expanse of the opencast mine.

Two sides of his house open on to the ground where they play. A few metres from their playfield stand concrete slabs that declare the out-of-bounds areas, which the three of us had crossed illegally a few minutes ago. If you ignore those warnings and take a few careful steps, you can see the enormous pit of coal that we just saw.

Dark smoke was floating up from the mine run by Coal India, the public sector behemoth that controls the major part of coal mining in the country. 'It's from the blasts,' one child said casually. They are used to it. 'Every day at two in the afternoon, the blasts take place,' he added.

Goswami's family and neighbours were told in 2014 that they would have to shift out in a few months, as the mine was set to expand further. The two brothers did not protest. It was fate, and who were they to raise questions about the decisions of the visible and invisible masters of the new economy? As I finished the final review of the book in early 2016, I wondered if the opencast mine had devoured their playfield and house, if the two boys were in search of a new home.

'Our cities are lit up with their tears,' said Sudiep Shrivastava, my lawyer friend. Angered by the ruthless plunder of India's tribal areas, Sudiep has been studying and documenting the goings-on in the mining belt of India. In September 2014, when the Supreme Court struck down the allocation of 214 coal blocks – including those belonging to the Jindal group and Vedanta – as illegal, it quoted extensively from Sudiep's submissions.

Sudiep's life as an activist began when the people of Bilaspur held protests, often violent, demanding the headquarters of a railway zone in their city. A railway zone would bring more jobs, more traffic and economic prosperity, they argued. He went on to become a lawyer and is now active in various forums in New Delhi and Chhattisgarh. You cannot hold a conversation with him without talking about how the mindless mining of India's heartland is leading to a major environmental crisis.

All through our trip, Sudiep pointed out to me the many hills and hillocks that had cropped up across the landscape. They were formed of sandstone and other extracts from the coal mines, and now small trees and undulated grass stretches had grown on them. At many of the power plants, he drew my attention to the thick white plumes of smoke emerging from the chimneys. The plants have switched off their pollution control devices to save on electricity. 'They push out pollution into our skies,' he lamented. Monitoring how industries adhere to pollution control standards, he said, is the biggest challenge.

A large amount of India's mineral deposits lies in a stretch across the ecologically sensitive and biodiversity-rich central region of the country. Two broad kinds of violence and protests are playing out here. On the one hand the residents and activists of these areas are protesting against the reckless industries that are making their fortunes at the cost of public health and environmental damage and on the other is the violence between armed left-wing extremists and government forces.

Both movements are reflective of the desperation among some of India's poorest people. Governments and political establishments have termed the civilian protests as anti-national efforts by foreign-funded non-governmental organizations (NGOs) and the armed rebellion as terrorism. When governments are confronted by big challenges, they react by breaking them down into several small issues that can be given easy labels. Meanwhile, people die of illnesses caused by pollution, and the forests and natural resources of the land are shrinking at alarming rates.

According to estimates presented by scientists from across the globe at the American Association for the Advancement of Science in 2016, of the fifty-five lakh deaths caused by air pollution in 2013, over half were in India and China. India alone accounted for fourteen lakh of those deaths. Air pollution, scientists say, is the fourth-highest risk factor for death globally, after high blood pressure, poor diet and cigarettes. We can only hope that the dying poor of the tribal regions are at least counted in these statistics.

Although the Indian government claims that the country's forest cover has increased by 5,081 square kilometres between 2013 and 2015, beyond the statistics is the stark reality: around 2,510 square kilometres of very dense and moderately dense forests have been wiped out during that very period. And 2,254 square kilometres of moderately dense forest have now turned into non-forest lands.

Back in New Delhi, I drive to Connaught Place every other day to meet contacts and acquaintances at the many new restaurants that are bringing a new generation of youngsters to the old marketplace. CP, as it is called, has had a rebirth after the metro connected it to the rest of the city and the obsolete Rent Control Act eased up to facilitate businesses.

A gigantic national flag was hoisted in its central park in March 2014 and flutters there to this day. The flag is 60 feet wide and 90 long wide and is hoisted on a high mast. Eight 2,000-watt bulbs illuminate it at night; it looks stunning against the city's polluted night sky. This well-protected flag was installed by Naveen Jindal's Flag Foundation of India and is among the biggest in the country. I often wonder if the poor of Raigarh know that their nation's biggest flags are now hoisted and looked after by Jindal.

10

A House for Mr Ambani

Across the road is a camel-coloured wall several metres high, with two massive iron-grille doors, intricate and wood-framed. When the doors slide open, you catch a glimpse of giant pots and green gardens inside. Outside are several private security guards in ash-coloured safari suits, and a dog on a leash. Flanking the doors, at sentry posts, are two paramilitary commandos holding automatic guns. In front of the security posse, to my left, is a police patrol vehicle with men in civvies. A couple of metres ahead are more armed men in uniform. A narrow pathway runs along the compound wall, down to a small door, which too opens into the compound. To my right, where the wall ends, a few youngsters stand smoking. It is a pleasant February afternoon in Mumbai.

I look up. Several floors of the tower are covered in green creepers. The architect is known to build energy-efficient buildings, even if they are glass and concrete. What looks like real plants hang out of the balconies above. Some bougainvillea flowers are visible too. There are many large balconies, and slanting beams and a lot of glass. Not a human being in sight. I can't see the top end of the building. My friend Zakir, who is not particularly tall, gave up even earlier. The 170-metre-tall Antilia, the residence of India's richest man, Mukesh Ambani, is too huge for us to fully take in. He is publicly estimated to be worth over Rs 1,50,000 crore. The building has only twenty-seven floors because of the extra-high ceilings; in a standard construction, it would have had sixty floors.

We are the only tourists outside Antilia that afternoon, but shop owners in the vicinity tell us that people visit from all parts of the world to see what is perhaps the costliest house built in recent memory. The Ambanis are reported to have spent almost Rs 10,000 crore to create a home that soars into the Mumbai sky in the southern part of the city.

The 4,00,000-square-foot house has been featured in many global publications as one of the world's most stunning residences. The author Shobhaa De, who was among the specially chosen eighty guests at the house-warming party in November 2010, gushed that it was the Taj Mahal of the twenty-first century. Film-maker Shekhar Kapur was quoted by De as saying, 'It's great to breathe fresh air at this height and leave Mumbai's pollution down below.' Given his cinematic sensibilities, Kapur's statement may have been pregnant with meaning. De said the Versailles Palace's ballroom would be a poor cousin to Antilia's glitzy counterpart. 'It was possible to believe for one mad moment that we were all at Cinderella's Ball,' she gushed.

Not everyone is as impressed. Author Arundhati Roy, in an article written in 2012, wondered why the Ambanis chose to call their building Antilia. She wrote: 'Antilla is the name of a set of mythical islands whose story dates back to an eighth-century Iberian legend. When the Muslims conquered Hispania, six Christian Visigothic bishops and their parishioners boarded ships and fled. After days, or maybe weeks at sea, they arrived at the isles of Antilla where they decided to settle and raise a new civilization ... By calling their tower Antilla, do the Ambanis hope to sever their links to the poverty and squalor of their homeland and raise a new civilisation? Is this the final act of the most successful secessionist movement in India? The secession of the middle and upper classes into outer space?'

It's not just the liberal intellectuals who are uncomfortable. 'It makes me wonder why someone would do that. That's what revolutions are made of,' fellow billionaire Ratan Tata said in an interview to *The Times* of London in May 2011. 'The person who lives in there should be concerned about what he sees around him ... If he is not, then it's sad because this country needs people to allocate some of their enormous wealth to finding ways of mitigating the hardship that people have.'

As the Indian media buzzed with his comments about Antilia, the Tata group issued a clarification: 'We would also like to clarify on stories in Indian media regarding Mr Ambani's home. The report is out of context and factually incorrect. Mr Tata's comments on wealth are in the larger context of the growing disparity in the society. The comments seem to have been deliberately sensationalized.'

Across the road from Antilia is a row of small shops, each just over a hundred square feet. One sells vegetables, the other daily-need items, such as bread and sugar, a third one has combined two shops to open a designer store, and there is an ATM. The last shop after the ATM is closed, its shutter freshly painted.

The talk in the market is that Ambani's people have been approaching the shop owners to buy them off, so that this eyesore of a market can be permanently shut down. The owner of the last shop accepted Rs 4 crore and left. According to the market legend, a man who sat outside the shop, selling vegetables on a small wooden stand, got Rs 1 crore to vacate the place. The vegetable seller has now bought a big house somewhere far away from this locality, and has gone back to selling vegetables elsewhere – at least, that is what they say.

Those tiny shops may have set a new record in property prices even on a stretch of road where billionaires such as Ambani and Kumar Mangalam Birla have their homes.

One of the merchants there tells us he was offered Rs 3 crore, 'but I have placed Rs 5 crore as my demand'. The shop owners are obviously enjoying their new-found fame and the possibility of unanticipated riches.

Antilia, where some 500 people work, has a large canteen for employees in its premises. None of this has resulted in any direct business for the shop owners. I ask one of them if he has ever had a situation where someone from the Ambanis' staff has been sent down for an emergency packet of bread or some sugar.

'You think they eat these things,' he says, gesturing contemptuously at the stuff in his shop. 'Very rarely, someone from their canteen buys bread.'

Another one says that Antilia has definitely resulted in additional sales. Tourists like me drop in for a bottle of water, or an aerated drink. The exercise of stretching to look up and down the skyscraper can be strenuous in Mumbai's balmy weather. And outside Antilia, there is no vantage position from which you can take in the entire building at close quarters.

Ever since construction of the building started sometime in 2002, this little market has evolved into a world of stories, fables and rumours. One shop attendant says there are 150 dogs inside the building, and twenty people to take care of them. An older man says, 'That is an exaggeration, there are probably about forty dogs in there.' I can definitely see one dog on a leash outside the building.

Another says there are gardens, a swimming pool, a cinema hall and such amenities inside. But there is no way they can confirm anything, because neither the residents of Antilia nor their guards or staff hang around in the market. The only member of the Ambani family who steps out occasionally is Anant, the youngest of Mukesh and Nita Ambani's three children. The young man, who struggled with his weight – until 2016, when he appeared in public after a dramatic reduction in body mass – occasionally takes a stroll along the road, accompanied by bodyguards. His siblings, the twins Isha and Akash, have never been spotted outside. Sometimes, their uncle Anil Ambani, who stays a few kilometres away in their ancestral home, comes running around the area, locals said.

When the Ambani kids step out, it is news. On 7 December 2013, when a black Aston Martin Rapide belonging to the Reliance group rammed into two cars late in the night, not very far from Antilia, the media reported that Akash Ambani was driving it. The reports naming him disappeared from websites soon and television channels stopped talking about it. A day after the accident, an old-time driver of Reliance, fifty-five-year-old Bansilal Joshi, presented himself before the police and claimed he was behind the wheel. He said he got away from the accident site by getting into one of the two SUVs that was accompanying his car. The records of the accident no longer point to the young Mr Ambani. Yet, like many things about the group, questions still swirl around.

One of the workers at the market tells me that a priest has been visiting Antilia regularly to conduct special prayers to free the building of bad spirits. The priest apparently dug ten to twelve feet below the building's basement, which is anyway some six storeys below ground level. 'The prayers are having only 10 per cent effect,' he adds.

One of the oldest members of the market says that, while he doesn't know much about the special prayers and rumours about spiritual trouble within, he knows that an orphanage stood on that plot until about fifteen years ago. About sixty-odd Muslim children lived in an old building there, and it was a wakf property. Every morning, they travelled to a nearby school in a bus, and returned in the evening, the old man says.

As per Islamic traditions, land, cash or other assets donated for religious or charitable purposes is held permanently under the wakf laws. India has a long tradition of wakf and has a central law, the Wakf Act of 1954, under which thousands of acres of land and hundreds of buildings are administered by Wakf Boards in each state.

'There was a graveyard here before the orphanage came up,' the old man says, jogging his memory. Just how did the graveyard and waqf land on which an orphanage stood become the home of India's richest family? The details are available to those who seek them – in government records, court cases and some recent complaints.

There is another story behind the plot of 4,532 square metres on Altamount Road where Antilia stands – one that is emblematic of Mumbai's transition from a British port city of textile mills and opium exports to the financial capital of the country.

Over a century ago, the plot belonged to another of Mumbai's richest residents, his influence probably as large as that of Mukesh Ambani now. Sir Currimbhoy Ebrahim was an Ismaili Dawoodi Bohra Muslim, born in 1840 into a family that was already making its fortune in trade between Bombay and Africa's eastern coast. Family history credits him with aggressively expanding its business, first into opium and silk exports to Hong Kong and Shanghai, and later acquiring textile mills in Bombay. At the height of its glory, Ebrahim's empire had offices in Bombay, Calcutta, Hong Kong, Shanghai, Kobe and parts of Africa.

The British Empire awarded Ebrahim a baronetcy in 1910 and the founder of modern Pakistan, Muhammad Ali Jinnah, was among those who sang paeans of him. According to available records, in 1894, Ebrahim started the Currimbhoy Ebrahim Khoja Orphanage for the welfare of orphans from his community. The plot on Altamount Road, according to some records, was actually given to him by the maharaja of Gwalior for purposes of charity.

From that point on, there have been disputes over the facts regarding the plot, which is what helped Antilia Commercial Private Limited to acquire it in 2002. Official records show that the property was owned by Currimbhoy Ebrahim Khoja Orphanage Trust. It is important to note that it was a trust that owned the property.

Here is the first of the many issues: if this was a plot committed by a Muslim for welfare activities of his community, it must be under the Wakf Board of the state, and not a private trust.

What complicated matters was that this particular trust and over thirty others, all of them donations from the Ismaili Dawoodi Bohra community, had moved court several years ago saying they did not want to be counted as wakf properties. When the court case came up, the Maharashtra state government ordered an examination of their demand. The Wakf Board came up with a modified list of properties that excluded the Bohra community trusts in the list of wakf properties. However, a new CEO was appointed to the Maharashtra State Board of Wakfs and he withdrew the list, saying that they were not empowered to amend the list of properties.

Even as the issue dragged on, Antilia Commercial Private Limited bought the plot for Rs 21 crore from the trust. The price of land along that road at that point of time would have been at least twenty-five times the paid amount, one of the senior-most officials appointed to look into the issue told me. The official said that, sometime later, the Ambani company paid Rs 16 lakh to the Wakf Board as a donation, as part of a so-called settlement. The case regarding this property has been shuttling between the Wakf Board and the Bombay High Court, even travelling to the Supreme Court of India. In an Action Taken Report submitted to the Maharashtra state assembly in September 2015, the Wakf Board said that the deal was void. Retired judge A.T.A.K. Sheikh, who was asked to look into the deal in the wake of protests in 2007, said, 'The land was sold to Ambani without the permission of the Wakf Board. As per the Wakf Board rule 32 (2) J, while selling any land, the board has to take 2/3 members prior approval and such resolution needs to be passed in the meeting as well. Therefore, the decision of giving land is void.' There is no final closure even today, the official says.

In New Delhi, when a complaint regarding the transaction landed at the Union Ministry of Minority Affairs, a group of senior officers took a firm stand. The secretary wrote to the Maharashtra government on 1 December 2010: 'Prima facie it appears that the laws and rules under the Wakf Act 1995 were not correctly applied when the sale of the wakf property of 4532 square metres, at Altamount Road was made to Antilia Commercial Pvt Ltd. In the process, the destitute in the community were deprived of an orphanage which was being run there and it has also caused substantial financial loss to a wakf property. The government of Maharashtra may, therefore, consider referring this matter to the Central Bureau of Investigation for an investigation.' The implication was that there was a criminal conspiracy behind the transaction.

'This case shows how some powerful and rich in the country in connivance with corrupt public servants are able to make a mockery of law and constitutional system,' Ashish Joshi, a director in the ministry, wrote to the Central Vigilance Commission on 25 October 2010.

But none of those recommendations had much of an impact on the case. Joshi said he was victimized for taking a stand, and shunted out to an obscure posting in Haryana. When I checked on him in early 2015, he was working with a department responsible for providing night shelters to the homeless in Delhi.

Joshi now had little time to think about his brush with Mukesh Ambani's Reliance group. But it is all-pervasive in India, there is no escaping Reliance – pillows, electricity, mobile network or petrochemicals, you are bound to encounter it at every turn. Rumours abound about their immense influence on Indian politics. A few of their employees and close associates have been members of parliament. However, there is no evidence of the Reliance group making substantial official donations to any political party.

The meteoric rise of the Reliance group, of which the two Ambani brothers own different parts, is a case study of the possibilities India offers to those who know the right people and can influence decisions.

Mukesh and Anil Ambani were at the vanguard of the industrialists and other luminaries who helped Narendra Modi sanitize his image of the stigma of the Gujarat pogrom of 2002. However, the Ambani family is not exactly a Hindu right-wing camp loyalist. Modi's political arch-rival Sonia Gandhi was famously photographed in 2005 in Moscow in a Reliance private jet.

The Ambanis' shifting political loyalties is representative of the challenges faced by the modern Indian businessman. Even if a company wants to do business fair and square, politics won't let them.

The construction of Antilia began in true earnest sometime in 2008. Perkins+Will, an architecture firm that has designed several universities and high-rises around the world, drew up the plan. Leighton Holdings of

Australia was the main contractor, and a number of other companies were roped in to erect the tower.

The year 2008 is an important one in contemporary political history. This is when the Union government began to be besieged by allegations of large-scale corruption, nepotism and malpractice, and many Indian billionaires were exposed as crony capitalists. The image of the economist prime minister, once celebrated as the father of India's liberalization, was being reduced to that of an inept politician who condoned corruption, even if he was personally clean. The 122 new-generation unified access service licences given to telecom companies early that year clearly manipulated norms and massive bribes were paid to various people for procuring those 2G licences.

By 2010, around the time that Antilia was getting ready for occupation, a CAG report said that the loss to the public in the 2G radio spectrum scandal could be as much as Rs 1,76,000 crore – an amount that was beyond the comprehension of most Indians. Soon, various agencies began investigations and a bench of the Supreme Court regularly monitored the case. Among the key accused were the companies of Anil Ambani, Mukesh Ambani's estranged younger brother who continues to live in the eighteen-storey family home named Sea Wind, from which the older brother and his family moved to Antilia.

Under the family agreement, when the two brothers parted ways acrimoniously in June 2005, Anil was given the telecom business and Mukesh agreed to stay away from it. Now that he had a free hand, the younger brother worked aggressively to expand the business by providing mobile telephony through the more popular GSM (Global System for Mobile Communications) rather than his group's CDMA (Code Division Multiple Access) technology. The investigation agencies said Anil's group had propped up proxies to bypass restrictions against monopoly and cross ownerships and was an active participant in the 2G scandal.

In 2010, when the specifics of the 2G telecom scam were filling up news pages and prime-time television minutes, and public anger against high-level corruption was beginning to spill over on to the streets, there was a genuine expectation that India would take a decisive turn against corruption. But there were also realities of business at work, most of which neither the public nor the media had access to.

On 23 May 2010, the Ambani brothers announced that they were scrapping the non-competing agreement, allowing both to operate freely wherever they wanted. This meant Mukesh could enter telecom, finance and power, while Anil could enter petrochemicals. Soon it emerged that Mukesh Ambani's Reliance Industries Limited had been quietly working towards re-entry into the telecom sector all along.

On 24 May 2010, when the Department of Telecommunications opened its auction site for allotting 4G spectrum, meant primarily for Internet broadband services, India's telecom giants focused their energies and resources on financially lucrative sectors such as Mumbai and Delhi.

There was one exception: a little-known Internet service provider, Infotel Broadband Services Pvt. Ltd, with an annual turnover of just Rs 18,00,000 and one subscriber.

Infotel was aggressively bidding across India. Its promoter Mahendra Nahata had in the past once defaulted on government licence fee in the telecom sector after making similarly high bids. But the officials seemed unconcerned. When the bidding ended, Infotel had agreed to pay a whopping Rs 12,847.77 crore for a national licence. That was 71,000 times the company's annual turnover. Nobody questioned it – it was as if the government didn't want to know how he would pay the mind-boggling amount.

Within hours of the close of bidding, on 11 June 2010, Infotel was taken over by Mukesh Ambani's RIL group. As RIL made its entry into the broadband sector, there were whispers about how his group had manipulated the auction to ensure a back-door entry for itself. A central audit found several anomalies in the entire tender process, including a case of possible forgery of bank guarantee documents submitted for the bid. When I was probing 4G allocations, Mahendra Nahata lectured me about how the CAG, CVC and other investigation agencies had been holding back the nation from realizing its full financial potential. He urged me to write about the negative role they played.

Around this time, RIL was also battling the CAG over the latter's demand that all records regarding oil and gas extraction from the Krishna and Godavari basins in the eastern region be made available. RIL had been granted permission to extract in the region after India's biggest reserve of natural gas was found there a decade ago. It was to share profits with the government, and there was an allegation that the Mukesh Ambani firm was inflating expenses while suppressing output figures. At the end of a long stand-off, on 8 September 2011, the CAG tabled a report in parliament questioning the motives of both RIL and the government. It said the public exchequer had lost hundreds of crores of rupees in the bargain. These controversies are not unusual in the running of big businesses in India.

The Ambanis were not overly worried. Mukesh Ambani's family was, in fact, busy putting the finishing touches on their new house at the time. They had planned a year-end house-warming party. Two high-tension power lines were drawn into Antilia, at least one of them from the US consulate nearby. Besides these lines, each intended as backup to the other, global engineering giant Caterpillar installed two FG Wilson diesel generators to provide two more layers of electricity backup. This four-layered power supply backup system is one that no other Indian building is likely to have.

Media reports said Nita Ambani flew to Sri Lanka to buy 25,000 pieces of chinaware crockery of the Japanese brand Noritake worth over Rs 6 crore. The house-warming party was held on 25 November 2010. In De's piece, there was the declaration: 'From that impressive height and with those panoramic vistas, Mukesh and Nita are clearly the undisputed masters of all they survey – east, west, north, south.' That was no exaggeration.

Since that day, Antilia has hosted the who's who of India. When India's cricketing icon Sachin Tendulkar scored his hundredth century in international matches, the Ambanis put on a grand event. In attendance were the biggest stars of Bollywood and Indian sports, politicians and others. Another day, the family had a do for the designer duo Abu Jani and Sandeep Khosla as they completed twenty-five years in the fashion industry, and among those who took to the ramp were Nita Ambani and the actor Amitabh Bachchan.

~

Prime Minister Narendra Modi mocks this oligarchy; in fact, he fashioned an effective political platform out of his outsider status. Modi's career is a great template for those who are not interested in minting money for future generations – the Indian prime minister has never had anything to do with the wife he abandoned, and he has no children. His mother still stays in her old home in Gujarat, even as Modi moved into the prime minister's official mansion in Delhi.

On 16 May 2014, the verdict of an election in which fifty-five crore people voted was a clear rejection of the indecisive and mostly corrupt Congress government that had ruled for a decade. It handed the baton to the BJP, led by its divisive prime ministerial candidate. That the Supreme Court had twice indicted Modi's Gujarat government – once as modern Neros in the context of the 2002 anti-Muslim pogrom in Gujarat, and a second time for 'non-application of mind' when ruling on the 2002 Akshardham terrorist attack – did not matter to India's electorate then. Many believe the government was complicit in the violence against Muslims during the Gujarat riots. In the Akshardham attack, the state police had framed innocent Muslims against whom there was no credible evidence, and the state's home minister, Modi himself, did not apply his mind, the apex court said on the very same day the results of the 2014 general elections were declared.

Yet, the Gujarat chief minister secured a majority for his party, a first in over three decades for an Indian political party. As India and most of the world took in Modi's massive victory, the day also marked a milestone for one of his close associates.

Some 1,400 kilometres from New Delhi, in Mumbai, the big business news was the signing of an agreement by Adani Ports and Special Economic Zone Ltd to buy Dhamra Port in Orissa on the east coast of India for Rs 5,500 crore. Two of India's most venerable business houses, the Tatas and Larsen & Toubro, who were equal partners in the port, were the sellers in the largest port sector deal in a decade. For the Gujarat-based Adani group, led by Gautam Adani, it was yet another strategic success in a dizzying growth that paralleled Modi's decade-long rule in Gujarat. It was on a chartered aircraft belonging to the Adani group that Modi whizzed around India in his high-decibel, expensive and aggressive electoral campaign in 2014. As Modi campaigned, Adani's fortunes soared. In the three months leading to the elections, the three publicly listed companies of the Adani group gained over 100 per cent in share value, even though Indian stock exchange gains were marginal on the whole.

As the Modi campaign was picking up pace, Indian investigative agencies stumbled upon a massive illegality perpetrated by the Adani group, of funnelling some Rs 5,468 crore out of India using inflated power equipment bills. The Directorate of Revenue Intelligence (DRI) found that the Adani group had paid Rs 9,048.8 crore for import of power and transmission equipment, though the actual value of the equipment from China and South Korea was only Rs 3,580.8 crore. The difference of Rs 5,468 crore was siphoned off by the Adani group via Dubai to Electrogen Infra Holdings, controlled by Shantilal Adani, the eldest of the Adani brothers, in the tax haven of Mauritius, the investigation agency found. DRI claimed possession of foolproof documentation, but the Adani group claimed that this was the Congress's political vendetta against it for the group's proximity to Modi.

According to my contacts in the SIT on black money – incidentally, this was one of the first major policy initiatives Modi announced as prime minister – the Adani case is the biggest one they handle. Potentially, the group may have to pay a fine of up to three times the amount siphoned off: almost Rs 15,000 crore. None of this has affected Adani's camaraderie with Modi. In fact, he has even been accompanying the prime minister on most of his foreign trips.

However, Adani does not have a monopoly on his attention. Modi's snapshots are displayed outside Antilia too. According to the local shop owners' lore, though, he has not yet graced the house with a visit. Not that he has shied away from Ambani functions. He flew in to Mumbai on 25 October 2014 to inaugurate the HN Reliance Foundation Hospital in Mumbai. At the function, Modi claimed that plastic surgery and other advanced medical capabilities were available thousands of years ago in ancient India – a familiar rhetoric of the Hindu right wing, peddling mythology as history. The speech was telecast live, as Mukesh Ambani, his wife Nita and others shared the stage with him.

The growing cry against corruption – which was instrumental in Modi's election – began sometime during former prime minister Manmohan Singh's second tenure. By the end of 2010, several Indian agencies had started probing the 2G scandal. Singh downwards, several officials were accused of acts of omission and commission, many major Indian business houses were indicted.

In the summer of 2011, when Gandhian leader Anna Hazare and his supporters started a hunger strike against corruption in New Delhi, millions joined the protest on the streets of India. Many believed that this would be a turning point in tackling government corruption, that the dawn of more transparent governance was just around the corner.

The CBI filed its first charge sheet on the 2G spectrum scandal on 2 April 2011 before a special court set up by the Supreme Court, in a dingy complex next to India Gate. The many national celebrities accused in the case and dozens of journalists crowded into the courtroom every day. Some of India's finest lawyers also dropped in to seek bail and defend their clients, no doubt for astronomical fees. You couldn't stand in the courtroom for a few minutes without rubbing shoulders with a national-level politician, a celebrated film producer or a billionaire. Expensive perfumes and designer clothes were everywhere. The names of many important members of the ruling UPA and of the civil service came up repeatedly. The CBI, the Enforcement Directorate and the Income Tax Department were all looking at various aspects of the kickbacks, siphoning of money to tax havens and other dubious goings-on around the 2G scandal.

Months rolled by, the UPA government proved rudderless, and the nation expressed its anger about corruption as never before. The CBI was opening investigations into several cases of alleged corruption and malpractice in high places. In Mumbai, its officers were probing the Adarsh Apartments scam, which was constructed in the name of war widows and distributed to politicians, civil servants and military generals. It was investigating several alleged irregularities in the conduct of the Commonwealth Games held in 2010 in New Delhi. Irregular allocation of coal mines to private companies across the mining belt was also under probe – a CAG report said alleged losses in the allocation were on the scale of the 2G scandal and pegged it at Rs 1,86,000 crore.

Then, on 3 December 2012, senior police officer Ranjit Sinha took over as CBI chief, assuring the nation that 'the motto of the organization – "Industry, Integrity, Impartiality" – will be upheld in full earnestness. The officers and staff of the bureau will conduct investigations entrusted to them, in a fair and free manner, without any kind of fear or favour.' Sinha quoted Isaac Newton, saying he could see farther only because he stood on the shoulders of giants. He also got down to work immediately. Sinha was easily accessible to reporters and gave fiery quotes. For months, his brave pronouncements about taking on the corrupt were celebrated in the media and he seemed to emerge as a middle-class hero. Indeed, a few media houses proclaimed him as one.

Meanwhile, Sinha himself was busy meeting with many of the accused under investigation by his agency. His official residence in the heart of New Delhi became the favourite port of call for scoundrels. There was no official recording of any of those visits and senior CBI officials were not present during the meetings. However, the trusty security guards at the entrance to Sinha's colonial mansion were doing their job well. They maintained a logbook on his visitors, and those logs emerged in public in 2014. I also gathered official files of the CBI on the Adarsh scandal that showed he was probably trying to scuttle the very cases that he was supposed to be investigating. In November 2014, the Supreme Court asked Sinha to keep off the 2G scandal investigations, calling his conduct 'grave and serious', and twelve days later, on 2 December, he retired.

The Narendra Modi government, for all its anti-corruption rhetoric, has been conspicuously silent about the CBI chief's diabolic games. Was it because Sinha was also overseeing investigations into the many extrajudicial killings in Gujarat when Modi was the chief minister? Among those under investigation was Amit Shah, Modi's trusted aide and now among India's most powerful politicians. Although he is a murder accused, Shah was appointed national president of the BJP after its electoral victory of 2014. We will never know the real reasons for Modi's silence. As for Sinha, he now leads a peaceful retired life.

In India, meanwhile, nothing has changed. According to several sources in the intelligence agencies, market estimates and even formal studies, the scale of black money involved in politics has only gone up, as also the scale of corruption. Then again, it's only business as usual; the BJP will do nothing that the Congress has not already done. All political parties are hugely dependent on black money to run their operations.

A report by the Centre for Media Studies in March 2014 had estimated that political parties, the government and candidates would spend about Rs 30,000 crore in the general elections of 2014. In reality, by the end of campaigning, the political parties declared a total spend of less than Rs 2,000 crore, all combined. The BJP and its candidates visibly outspent every other party. A few months after the elections, political parties submitted their official expenditure details to the Election Commission.

What did those figures look like? The BJP said it had spent a paltry Rs 714 crore and the Congress just Rs 516 crore. Only a few activists were outraged. Neither political leaders nor the Election Commission of India commented on the patently duplicitous figures.

Many members of parliament have confessed to me in private that they usually end up spending up to Rs 50 crore for their campaigns – as against the limit of Rs 70 lakh they are officially allowed to spend in large states. Some also had to pay money to buy their tickets. In many states, almost every voter is showered with cash, liquor and other freebies. Advertising agencies and media houses are usually flooded with political advertisements; economic activity in several sectors such as construction dips as money moves into the electoral arena; and there is a sudden surge in cash flow in the market. None of this is reflected in the official declarations of the political parties. The only logical conclusion, therefore, is that Indian political parties exist more in the black market than in the open.

⌒

Let's return to the day of our visit to Antilia. It is almost 5 p.m. Employees are emerging from the small metal door to the left of the building. They hop into private SUVs or shuttles that will carry them to nearby bus stops and railway stations. Security guards are keeping a close watch on the proceedings.

My friend Zakir has drifted away to smoke a cigarette. Mumbai's evening sun is bright, but I cannot not figure out which way the shadow of Antilia falls. It must cast a giant shadow that stretches across buildings and roads. Could it be providing temporary shelter to Mumbaikars?

Four youngsters in ill-fitting clothes, two of them with worn-out backpacks, walk along the side of the road. They are probably new migrants to the city, or returning from their jobs to congested accommodation somewhere in Mumbai. Or they could be, like me, sightseers. As the group reach the compound wall, they fall into a single line and look up, forming something like a saluting military column.

When they are in the middle of the pavement outside the building, they slow down a bit. As they reach the end of the compound wall, one of them says in Hindi: '*Kya c—hai, poora dikhta bhi nahin.*' What (expletive), you can't even see the whole thing.

Epilogue

Tihar Jail is Asia's largest prison, housing over 13,000 inmates at any point of time. It was built to house 6,250 prisoners. Over 10,000, or about 75 per cent, of its population on an average are undertrials – victims of India's slow-moving judicial system – and at least some of them are likely to be innocent. From murderers to women and men accused of dowry harassment, to militants linked with armed movements, Tihar Jail is a microcosm of India itself. It is also a barometer of the country's struggle to emerge as a liberal democracy.

Some of India's richest and most powerful families are regular visitors to Tihar Jail, as Indian law enforcement occasionally catches up with the modern-day oligarchs. There are no dependable studies or comparative figures, but everyone acknowledges that Tihar has not seen quite as many eminences as it has in the recent past.

Subrata Roy, chairman of the Sahara India group, was among Tihar Jail's inmates in February 2016. Roy's total assets are not known, but he is counted as among the country's richest and most influential people. Like many of his peers, the Sahara chairman too had a meteoric rise from his humble origins in Uttar Pradesh three decades ago. Roy has been in jail since 28 February 2014 for having failed to comply with a Supreme

Court order to deposit the Rs 24,000 crore that his group claims to have collected from retail investors.

Without going into the quality of criminal investigations, it is safe to conclude that those at the top are increasingly under scrutiny. Many lower courts are punishing even the most powerful without mercy; and the higher courts are mostly uncompromising too. This democratization of the legal process is what Tihar's prisoner demographics represent: the son of a senior political leader who owns a sprawling business empire, a senior police officer who once worked in the office of the prime minister, a former chief minister of Haryana, a couple of god men with millions of followers, among others.

The all-powerful chief minister of Tamil Nadu, Jayalalithaa, was summoned to a trial court in neighbouring Karnataka in a disproportionate assets case and sentenced to jail on 27 September 2014. She became the first sitting chief minister of an Indian state to be disqualified from holding office due to conviction in a criminal case. In May 2015, the Karnataka High Court acquitted her of the charges, and later that month, she assumed office as chief minister again.

A few months before her humiliation, another senior politician, Lalu Prasad Yadav, who has been a Union minister and a chief minister of Bihar, was convicted for corruption and spent months in Birsa Munda Central Jail in Ranchi. He was disqualified from the Lok Sabha. In Maharashtra, Chief Minister Ashok Chavan was forced to resign in November 2010 after it turned out that his family members were among the apartments owners in the Adarsh scam.

Several senior members of Dr Manmohan Singh's government and his party have been arrested and sent to jail in recent years, even though the Congress party was in power. In a court complex near India Gate in New Delhi, many of India's rich and powerful are on trial for their alleged involvement in the 2G scam.

For many years after India emerged as a democracy, its law and justice administration suffered from a colonial hangover. Very rarely was an influential person put on trial. When Prime Minister Indira Gandhi faced the courts in the 1970s, it was an exceptional moment. If an honest officer took on a powerful corrupt person, it was almost certain that the officer's career would be ruined.

Gradually, India is transforming, its democracy maturing. Several progressive legislations are opening up access to governance processes, chief among them the Right to Information Act, 2005. Dozens of activists are using the Act across the country, even if some others paid for it with their lives. Laws governing prevention of corruption and protection of whistle-blowers are being modernized. Voluntary groups of gritty activists are taking on the state. Dissent is deepening and maturing.

An anti-corruption movement in 2011 brought thousands of people out on to the streets and forced the political establishment to accept many of their demands. It produced a new political party, which promises transparency in political funding and a new concept of governance that will consider the realities of the staggering number of poor in India. It is still early days for the party, of course.

Analysts say that the roots of large-scale corruption in contemporary India lie in the opaque funding of political parties. Almost all mainstream parties are heavily dependent on black money from the corporate world, which, in the end, extracts its pound of flesh. There is gathering resentment against this practice and its implications for the ordinary citizen, who is way down the food chain.

Beyond long-term trends and academic analyses, though, are the here-and-now realities of India, and they are disconcerting. Every time a scandal breaks out, people are hopeful that it will usher in a more transparent phase of public life. But each time, middlemen, politicians, civil servants and other players find new ways to manage their careers in the post-scandal phase. Then new middlemen emerge, as do more bribes, and smarter ways to hide misdeeds. If anything, these scandals appear to create a new momentum for the corrupt system to reassert itself.

From the shadow that fell on the young Rajiv Gandhi's integrity to the collapse of the coalitions and politicians who came after, from the Hindu right's attack on Babri Masjid to the anti-Muslim pogrom in Gujarat in 2002, from the vigilante groups that murder citizens for possessing meat to the banning of books of great academic value, from misogynistic religious beliefs that deprive women of their fundamental rights to religious movements that fish in India's troubled waters – India's billion-plus people carry the cross of its illiberal democracy. Yes, there is change coming. In the long term, we might just be working to build a nation that works for its people.

The long term is, however, too far away. In the long term, we would all be dead.

In the short term, too many Indians live without hope in a crony capitalist state. This monopoly of the few over the resources and will of the state must end.

Acknowledgements

The duplicity of our times flows through these acknowledgments too. I am unable to name most of the people who, over the years, played a critical role in making this book possible even though it is to them I owe my greatest gratitude. Most of them want to remain anonymous, and some are concerned about possible repercussions. This book was made possible by their brave commitment to causes greater than monthly salaries and job safety. My Deep Throats have handed me crucial documents from the Indian establishment that helped me understand the nuances and undercurrents of the issues I have tackled here. I wish I could publicly thank all of them.

Innumerable strangers helped me every step of the way. Auto-rickshaw drivers, parking attendants, groundnut sellers, vagabonds, MNC executives, politicians, civil servants, foreigners, dreamy-eyed idealists – they all had something to say. Everyone here lives with a little bit of guilt and a lot of contradictions. Most regret paying bribes, many are angry at themselves for accepting bribes, everyone is irritated with the way people use influence to scuttle the rightful claims of others and almost all of us find a way to influence someone to jump the queue. I hope they will find themselves somewhere in the book, even if they don't recall meeting me ever.

However, the people who told me some of the greatest truths about modern India will never even know about this book, because they cannot read.

It was almost a decade ago, when I was completing my masters at the Fletcher School of Law and Diplomacy (in Medford, Massachusetts, USA) that I began to seriously think about writing a book on contemporary India. The outstanding graduate programme, with its 360-degree perspective of the world and many outstanding teachers and classmates, gave me new frameworks to look at my own country. I am especially grateful to Professor Deborah Winslow Nutter, a warm-hearted and determined professor of leadership, who ensured that I join Fletcher. Dean Nutter has been nurturing leaders in every continent, in every other country.

Saroj Rath, a history teacher and researcher in Delhi, worked with me in libraries and archives, and we gathered hundreds of pages of photocopies and notes on various institutions of Indian democracy. I have hardly used any of that material in this book. What I started to do – an academic assessment of Indian institutions – is not what I ended up writing. But the material has been of immense help, and Saroj remains a close associate.

Several people assisted me as I travelled across India. In Chhattisgarh, advocate Sudiep Shrivastava gave me a conducted tour into the underbelly of Indian democracy; in Raigarh, Anil Agarwal wouldn't let me pay the hotel bill; and in Korba, Laxmi Chauhan took me on an unusual hike to the many ash ponds where India stores away its dirty secrets.

Every time I landed in Mumbai, Zakir Ahmed would be at the airport to pick me up, and the two of us, along with Prem Shukla, would wind up our day with long conversations. Though they are on two extremes of the Indian political spectrum, both put aside their differences to help me understand the criminal underworld. Many others in the commercial capital, including Rakesh Maria and Mahesh Nair, have been of great assistance. I received selfless assistance from numerous people in places such as Kerala and Delhi. It is a long list, and I can't mention everyone by name here, but I remember all of them with gratitude.

This book is also, in many ways, a narrative of my life as a journalist. My first editor, John Dayal, taught a generation of reporters to go out and seek inconvenient truths. I have been fortunate to work with many other outstanding editors of our generation – M.J. Akbar, Nikhil Lakshman, Gautam Adhikari, R. Jagannathan, Ayaz Memon, Vinay Kamat, Arati R. Jerath, Seema Mustafa, Shekhar Bhatia and others.

At *The Times of India*, Jaideep Bose was an indulgent boss. The late Arindam Sengupta, Diwakar and colleagues in the national bureau and other departments of *The Times of India* and *The Economic Times* have been of immense help in sharpening my arguments. At *The Hindu*, which I joined in September 2015, N. Ram, Mukund Padmanabhan, Malini Parthasarathy, N. Ravi and other colleagues run a unique institution that allows me the latitude to look for truths that are hard to publish. In both the newspapers, dozens of colleagues and friends helped me through the writing of this book. A big thank you to everyone on that long, long list.

Basharat Peer gave me several suggestions very early on about improving the book structure, Jonathan Shainin gave valuable inputs on narration and other aspects of the book, and Vinod K. Jose has been a positive influence all through. My classmate and senior journalist Geri Smith in Washington DC, and the team at Style Matters – Robert Murray, Suzanne Murray and Christophe Leroy – helped me pin down the final structure.

There are a large number of childhood friends who continue to be my debating companions and intellectual partners. They are far too many to list, but I must mention Byju Sukumaran, Soni Somarajan, Ceejo Thomas, Syam Kumar, Robin P.R., Ullekh N.P., Arun S., Rajesh Unni, and Lijo Stephen Chacko, who have all been part of this book's journey. Beyond them, the larger fraternity of my alma mater, Sainik School Kazhakootam, one of the many public schools produced by India's socialist past, has had a significant impact on my writings.

Journalist friends Aniruddha Bahal, Paranjoy Guha Thakurta, K.N. Ashok, Jayanth Jacob, Jigeesh A.M., D. Dhanasumodh, Sudhi Ranjan Sen, Gautam Datt, Ajmer Singh and Dalip Singh; and friends from other walks of life including Anisa Draboo, Rajiv Jain, Riyas Komu and many others have selflessly assisted me with their time. I have greatly benefited from their suggestions, expert reports and many comments.

P.N. Shanavas, my schoolmate, a successful entrepreneur and gifted photographer, is someone I repeatedly turn to without any hesitation for all kinds of help and troubleshooting.

From the moment the concept note reached them, my agents Gillon Aitken and Shruti Debi have been enthusiastically encouraging me at every stage of the book. They helped me stay focused and on course.

I owe a great deal to HarperCollins *Publishers* India, its publisher and chief editor Karthika V.K., who has been supportive of my efforts from the time she saw the first proposal, and to Ajitha G.S., who suggested the final structure of the book and edited it. Thanks also to Shamya Dasgupta for reading a version of the manuscript.

Finally, this book would not have been possible without my unique childhood, an intense monsoon of experiences. My parents, K.M. Joseph and Annamma, audaciously sent me to a boarding school despite the family's financial struggles; my siblings – Joy, Siby and Soji – gave up many childhood indulgences so that I could have the best education and a better life. Many of my observations here were sharpened over the years through my conversations with them.

Our sensibilities and values evolve as we grow older, and I couldn't have asked for a better companion than Priya to start a family and grow older with. Our daughter, Supriya, is the greatest gift we have ever received.

This book is in part my little effort to help make India a better place for Supriya, her numerous cousins and friends. Priya and Supriya have put up with my struggles against mediocrity and erratic behaviour, and have always given in to my demands and indulged me. My mother-in-law, Dolly Solomon, remains a strong pillar of support at every step.

If you have been a reporter in a country like India for two decades, you will have to publish the census roster to thank everyone who has been of assistance to you. In the chaos of this country, some of the warmest hearts glow. I will remain eternally surprised by the idea of India, and remain optimistic that a day will come when no one in this land goes to bed hungry or afraid. This book, ultimately, is an expression of the angst and frustration of my fellow countrymen, who give up often because India failed them.

About the author

Josy Joseph is an award-winning investigative journalist based in New Delhi. His stories have repeatedly fostered public debate, and continue to contribute to significant policy and systemic changes in India. His investigative stories include the Adarsh Apartment scam, Naval War Room Leak case, several aspects of recent scandals such as the conduct of the Commonwealth Games, the 2G Spectrum Allocation scam, and other government decisions that have highlighted nepotism and corruption in governance at all levels.

The Prem Bhatia Trust elected him India's best political reporter of 2010 'for his scoops and revelations, which include a list of scams that have become familiar names in the political lexicon'. In July 2013, the Ramnath Goenka Foundation run by the Indian Express group awarded him the Journalist of the Year in print media.

Joseph has been with *Delhi Mid Day, The Asian Age, The Blitz, Rediff. com, India Abroad* and was editor, special projects, with *The Times of India* until August 2015. He is presently the national security editor of *The Hindu*.

Joseph holds a master's in international relations from the Fletcher School of Law and Diplomacy, Tufts University, and Bachelor of Science in mathematics from Kerala University.

He lives in New Delhi with his wife Priya and daughter Supriya and available at www.josyjoseph.in

231